IN PURSUIT OF THE SPECKLED GUM BALL

Cover

Illustrations

by

Thelma Dodd

IN PURSUIT OF THE SPECKLED GUM BALL

Hiram K. Myers

Library of Congress Number:		2003095384
ISBN :	Hardcover	1-4134-2367-1
	Softcover	1-4134-2366-3

This book was printed in the United States of America.

To order additional copies of this book, contact:
Xlibris Corporation
1-888-795-4274
www.Xlibris.com
Orders@Xlibris.com
20775

CONTENTS

PART III

Maple City and Leland, Michigan
1945-1949

This memoir is dedicated to Henry Crain,
who saw goodness in me as a child and took the time
to tell me.

ACKNOWLEDGMENTS

With special thanks to the following:

Nancy Jo Myers, my bride of twenty-five years, who offered encouragement and assistance at every opportunity, was always there to listen, meanwhile critiquing and giving the lie to the old saw about not reading your material to anyone called "Honey." Were it not for her, I would still be cursing the first paper jam in the printer, and when it came time to prepare the final draft, she was there, proofing and putting in the finishing touches.

Carolyn Wall, my instructor, mentor and writing guru, who patiently provided answers to all questions, regardless of how elementary; and more importantly provided confidence, inspiration, editing, and advice—the best of which was to stop being so damn verbose.

Members of my writer's workshop: the late Eric Bishop, Shirley Jean Trochta, Shirley Pritchard, Gary Johnson, Glenda Carlile, Judy Gigstad, Harolyn Enis, Bill Ellis, Maria Homic, and our instructor, Carolyn Wall, all of whom listened and gave invaluable insight and support as scenes for this book unfolded.

My children: Michelle, Keith, Lori, Tamara, Dennis, and Bryan, whose love, encouragement, and patience played such a big part in making this work possible.

Shirley Jean Roth, my sister, who, although she remembers our family from a different time perspective, willingly and lovingly provided information about many of the episodes in the early chapters.

The late Miss Mary O'Brien, my English teacher at Leland High School, who not only tolerated my unruly and sometimes obscene behavior, but also taught me to appreciate the beauty of the written word.

Doctor Everette, Ph.D., Central Michigan University, who sparked the flame of creativity and the desire to tell my story on the printed page during freshman composition many years ago.

And last but by no means least: Otto F. Gerkensmeier, USNR, Radarman First Class, called to active duty during the Korean War. He became my Operations Division supervisor, the first male authority figure in my life for whom I had respect and affection. Otto inexplicably took me under his wing and, to his lasting credit, gave caring guidance and provided the basic understanding that ultimately unlocked my demon-filled closet.

Difficulties are meant to rouse, not discourage.
The human spirit is to grow strong by conflict.

William Ellery Channing (b.1780—d.1842)

IN PURSUIT OF THE SPECKLED GUM BALL,

first in a trilogy of autobiographical memoirs on the life and times of Hiram K. Myers.

PREFACE

Like old movies running on an out-of-control camera, many episodes of my youth re-play themselves nightly. They destroy relationships and negatively impact professional, familial, and recreational activities. *The past is dead,* I have told myself over and over. I chant a litany of self-help mantras: *I can. I will. I am. Nothing in the past, let alone events of more than a half-century ago, can hurt me now;* on and on—adding new phrases daily with the hope of gaining relief and insight. Reality, however, is different from the wish. My present is inseparable from past events. No motivation, hope, mood, or relationship in adulthood has escaped their pervasive influence. There are a few happy and pleasant memories associated with my youth, but the negative was so powerful it obliterated the good and continues to exert a significant impact.

This writing is an extension of a lifelong search to discover who I am, and why I'm driven by events so remote as to constitute an embarrassment to admit they still influence. My children are entitled to know where the good and bad characteristics of the man they call Father came from, and how and why their lives were touched by individuals with whom they had little or no contact. Perhaps this writing will compensate in part for my failure to tell them. I was silent about events which manifested weakness, lack of morals, courage, and principles—telling myself that children should see their parents in the best light, when in truth I didn't tell them for fear they would judge me harshly.

For my purpose, this writing must be sufficiently detailed to give insight into those persons and places that played a major role in shaping my personality, requiring disclosure of intimate contact and private thought—much of which has until now remained untold.

Basic insight into the cause of episodic depression was provided by Otto Gerkensmeier, a friend in the Navy. During my sophomore year at Central Michigan University, while enrolled in a psychology course, I put myself through a self-analysis tailored after a treatise on the subject by Karen Horney, Ph.D. This effort at self-help enabled me to partially control the torrents of hostility that for years resulted in antisocial behavior and caused mindless pain and consternation for myself and those with whom I had contact. Vast stores of energy have been burned coping with the simplest day-to-day responsibilities and controlling catastrophic mood swings. Feelings of desolation and abandonment ripped out my self-esteem and called into question every decision. Battles fought with the specter, whether won or lost, subtracted from contribution to family, creative, and societal activities.

This rendering is also for the many adults who deal, day to day, with childhood memories and dreams filled with turmoil, terror, and loneliness; to help them understand that because someone you loved and trusted treats you in a hateful or irresponsible way does not, as the child too often concludes, make you a bad or unworthy person. It is well established that victims of parental alcoholism and abuse rarely fully recover or achieve self-acceptance and must work through those issues day after day for their entire lives. This book is part of that work.

Hiram K. Myers

PART I

Utica, Missouri

1931-1936

CHAPTER 1

The Gold Button

George W. Carpenter washed his hands in a basin of hot water, dried them, and laid a straight razor, forceps, retractors, and other surgical paraphernalia on a small table. He wore no surgical gloves—made no pretenses of creating a sterile field. A pot of water thumped on the stove, sending spirals of steam to the ceiling and fogging the glasses on the end of his nose. A single bulb, dangling from the ceiling, cast a feeble light over the center of an operating table on which lay his patient, Mae Myers. They were alone.

While preparing his instruments, the tall, balding doctor nibbled a saltine cracker balanced between his lips, a habit the locals believed, kept the doctor paper-thin. The surgical procedure was one he had never performed, but this did not ruffle his composure. Nothing could do that after the battlefields of France.

He had returned from the Army Medical Corp in 1919, and resumed the practice of medicine in the small town of Utica, Livingston County, Missouri. The doctor and his wife, Anna, my grandmother, lived in a modest frame house, on a street that had no name. His office consisted of two front rooms in the house next door.

He was not a harsh man, but neither was the doctor given to frivolity nor sentimentality, those senses dulled by the suffering he had attended. He spoke to the point. "Mae, your appendix has ruptured which often causes the bowel to leak into the abdominal cavity causing a condition called sepsis—a generalized infection. If you die—and there's a strong possibility you will—I'll try to save the baby, but there's no way to tell if a seven-month fetus will survive." He patted her shoulder and held a can of ether under her nose. "Now take several deep breaths."

Mae's last thought, before blackness took her, was of a conversation a year earlier while cleaning the doctor's office.

"Come in and have a seat," Doctor Carpenter had said, the ever-present cracker bobbing in the corner of his mouth. "I want to show you something." He fussed about in the top drawer of his desk for several seconds, then laid a small, gold-colored piece of metal on a pad of paper.

Mae leaned forward and squinted. "What's that?"

"The advertisement claims it will prevent pregnancy. It might be something worth trying."

"Phooey," Mae said laughing. "There's only one thing'll prevent that, and I don't see Keith doing it."

The doctor turned the button-sized object over with the point of his pencil. "That's why I think you should try it."

Mae had never dreamed she would end up on Doctor Carpenter's doorstep, but in 1930, Ford Motor Company laid off one hundred thousand workers, and the doctor's stepson, Keith, had been among them. Destitute, the family had little choice: return to Utica and depend on the charity of George and Anna Carpenter, or starve.

In the eleven months since their return, the doctor had never mentioned the burden imposed by his stepson's family, but Mae's mother-in-law, Anna, had suggested she clean the doctor's office as a way to earn grocery money. Nothing wrong with that. What bothered her was Anna's determination that she work, while apparently thinking nothing of her son refusing jobs he regarded as menial.

Mae was also embarrassed that her own father, Will Sherman, whose home was only minutes away, refused to help, and continued to enforce a decade-old ban against her husband coming on his property.

Being dependent on his charity and free medical care, Mae understood perfectly why the bespeckled man across the desk would caution against more children. The birth-control device would have to be implanted for no cost. Her five-year-old daughter, Shirley Jean, would soon start first-grade at Utica Public Schools, and the husband whom she adored took most of the money earned cleaning the doctor's office and bought moonshine and the ingredients to make home-brew, and only God knew what else from that heathen, Greely Bonder. It was plain, she didn't need more kids. She nodded her ascent.

Within ninety-days after the device was implanted, Mae was pregnant. Years later, she told me I must have been special, having been filtered through a gold button.

The old clock on the wall indicated two hours had passed since Mae breathed the ether. She opened her eyes. "Am I still alive?"

Doctor Carpenter peered down over his wire-rimmed glasses. "Indeed, you are," he said. "But, don't get your hopes up. I cleaned the abdominal cavity, but fecal matter was everywhere, so I probably missed some. You're packed with enough sulfur compound to kill a horse, but whether it will kill the infection is anyone's guess."

"The baby?"

"As long as you're alive, the baby will be fine. Your mother, Lillie, is waiting to see you in the other room; says she'll take care of you while you're recovering. I can't keep you here in the office, so Keith can help me get you to your own bed. You won't be moving about much for awhile."

Saturday, August 1, 1931. The sun rose hot in a cloudless sky made gritty by a dust cloud drifting in from the southwest. An outbreak of dysentery in Chillicothe had kept Doctor Carpenter up for forty-eight hours. He gathered a wrinkled coat and medical case from his car and wearily shuffled to the back porch of his house. A rusty hinge squeaked as he pulled the screen open, but something more caught his ear. He cocked his head. It came again, a muffled scream from the house next door where his stepson's family slept.

Within a minute, the medical case was on the floor beside Mae's bed. As he bent over her thrashing body, a drop of sweat formed on the end of his nose, dangled for a moment, and dropped into a gaping hole in her belly. Distended by pregnancy, her abdomen had pulled the appendectomy sutures out of the rotted skin leaving her stomach splayed like a gutted fish. "I'm going to leave it open, Mae," he said. "And it'll have to stay that way until the baby comes."

Twice a day for over a month, the doctor draped a towel over Mae's face, lifted the sheet covering her swollen abdomen and removed the gauze bandages.

"What are you doing down there?" she wanted to know.

"Cleaning you up," he said.

"Why do you have a towel over my face?" The chill of her fever caused her teeth to chatter. It was ninety degrees in her bedroom.

"The smell would make you sick . . . sicker."

"If you can stand it, I guess I could too. I want to see what you're doing."

He grunted and said, "No, you don't."

Her fever raged into early September, soaring at night and easing toward daylight leaving her weaker after each onset. Still wet from the battle of the previous night, she raised her head from the pillow, and asked again to see what he was doing.

By now, the doctor's admiration for this woman had grown to giant proportions. Her refusal to die, the courage to lie in her own body fluids without complaint—her pluck—had changed his mind. If she wanted to see what was killing her, she was entitled.

Doctor Carpenter removed the towel from her eyes, gave her a mirror, and propped her up. She held the mirror over her open abdomen. Towels saturated with greenish-brown liquid and long strands of what appeared to be rotten seaweed were lifted from around her intestines and deposited in a wash basin. Mae fainted. When she awoke, she wanted to know what her chances were. The doctor shrugged. There were still two weeks to full-term, and anything could happen.

Helena Mae Myers was the youngest of five children born to William Sherman and Lillian Osborn Sherman. Her father, tall and wiry, the son of German and Dutch immigrants, was a tireless worker who expected the same of his wife and children, driving them relentlessly to labor on their two-hundred-forty-acre farm. When they balked, he cursed and beat them. Walter and Augustus, the two eldest, left at their earliest opportunities. Their share of the chores then fell to Vern, Mae, and Florence.

The farm prospered under the stewardship of Mae's father, but no amount of success could satisfy him. He flew into wild rages, striking his children with fist and feet, when they failed to "get the rag out," and hit the floor within a minute of being summoned at 4:00 a.m., or for forgetting to latch the grain-bin door, or slop the hogs, or being ten minutes late preparing breakfast, or for lolly-gagging around after school. There was no end to the petty offenses capable of throwing their father into a wild rage.

He kicked Mae in the buttocks so hard and so often, for not moving fast enough or not performing precisely as he ordered, that she lost control of her bladder and frequently wet her pants on the way to or from school. Her school mates, unforgiving, heaped humiliation on her. The constant oppression prompted Mae's mother, Lillian, to say, she'd rather be dead than live another year with the tyrannical head of their house.

That was the mettle of the twenty-seven-year-old Mae Myers who on September 10, 1931, at noon, went into labor, with sulfur soaked towels packed in her open abdomen. At 7:00 p.m., she gave birth to a healthy baby boy, and lay near death, her mouth gaping for breath like a beached carp.

Doctor Carpenter, amazed that his daughter-in-law and her baby were still alive, pulled the swaddling blanket aside. In a casual tone, around the cracker between his lips, he said, "First chance you get, take a look at your baby's hands. Not much to worry about, just a little deformity."

Mae unwrapped the blanket and studied the arms, then the

hands. Doc Carpenter was joking, nothing wrong with the baby's hands. She counted the fingers, recounted, and then recounted again.

"Polydactyl," said the doctor.

"What?" said Mae.

Removal of the excess appendages would be simple. Snip the digits at the place where they joined the hands. Lack of use would atrophy the knuckles, cartilage, and skin. Nothing to it. Within a few years, the abnormality would hardly be noticeable.

While the doctor explained the procedure, a fat woman was pushing a small girl toward the door of Mae's bedroom. Mae's mother-in-law, Anna Carpenter, was born March 24, 1874, in Laclede, Missouri. Formerly she had been married to a railroad worker, H. H. Myers, my grandfather. And Mother told me, although I was sworn to never bring the subject up in the presence of Dad, that Grandmother had also been married to yet another man by the name of Brick McCoy. Her third marriage to Doctor G. W. Carpenter, made her one of the most often married and divorced women in Livingston County, Missouri, and one of the most affluent.

The six-year-old child shoved toward Mae's bedroom door by Anna Carpenter, screamed, "I don't want to see my baby brother. I hate him." Shirley Jean had been left in the care of a cranky grandmother for most of the last three months of her mother's pregnancy, and had long ago concluded that this new baby was the crux of her problem. She had heard, *This is where your new baby brother or sister will sleep,* and, *Won't you have fun with your new baby brother or sister?* and, *The baby will look darling in this or that,* until she could puke. All Grandma Carpenter ever talked about was this new baby that would be delivered by a stork. Ha! She was only in the first grade, but she knew where that baby had come from. She had peeked through the window of Doctor Carpenter's office and watched him examine three different pregnant women. That baby crying on the other side of the bedroom door had come straight out of Mama's pee-hole.

"Shirley Jean!" Grandmother said, puffing from carrying her

ponderous weight up the backstairs in the September heat. "Shush your mouth. Shame on you, talking naughty about your Daddy and Mommy's precious baby boy."

Shirley gave her grandmother a hateful look. *Daddy's precious baby boy,* was the last thing she wanted to hear. She was the only precious thing in Daddy's life, and nobody was ever going to change that. There was no place for another precious child, and besides, she was afraid it would be the same color as Trisa Hartley's, the Negro woman, who cleaned and ironed for Grandmother Carpenter. Trisa's baby had been born two days ago, and Grandmother had drug her off to see it. Yesterday, on the way home from school when she passed McCoy's Blacksmith shop, Dyke McCoy, his noodle-like frame flapping like a scarecrow, with a finger curled through the loop on a jug of Greely Bonder's moonshine, called out, "Hey, Shirley Jean, your mama's gonna have a little nigger baby, blacker than coal, blacker than Trisa's."

Shirley grabbed the doorsill, dug her heels in, and screamed bloody murder. But Anna Carpenter was a big woman, so into the mother's bedroom the little girl went. With raven hair, almond skin, and hazel eyes set above high cheek bones, Shirley looked like an Indian Princess, except for the fists planted firmly in her eye sockets. With her mouth wide open she bellowed, "I don't want to see him!"

Mae held out her hand, and gestured toward the little girl. "Come give Mother a kiss."

Shirley, her lower lip extended, edged blindly toward the bed. Her mother pulled her close and lifted one of the hands away from her face. The sister opened an eye for a peek. The toe-headed thing sucking her mother's breast didn't look a bit like her. But at least it wasn't a pickaninny. The baby whimpered. Shirley took the other hand away from her eye. "How come his hands are bandaged?" she whispered.

"Doctor Carpenter cut some growths off, but it's nothing for you to worry about," her mother said.

"The poor little thing. Can I hold him, Momma?"

Exit of the fetus acted as a purgative. Within two weeks, the infection was gone, and May was cleaning the doctor's office, preparing meals, keeping house, catering to her mother-in-law, and chasing her husband, Hiram Keith Myers, Sr., or Speck, as he was known locally.

Submerged in poverty, alcohol, and the humility of total dependence, the parents had little time or inclination to help Shirley Jean take care of her brother. Dad, absorbed in the ministry of his sickness, and Mom in her role of martyr, allowed the six-year old sister to take charge of her new-born sibling. For six years, one month and ten days, Shirley Jean had believed she was the center of her parent's lives. This scrawny little intruder she had been told to call "Brother" was not only competition, he was a millstone about her neck—he had ruined everything.

She would come to resent every positive characteristic in him, and belittle, blame, ridicule, and chastise him. Every effort on his part was stupid. He was ugly, spoiled, selfish, and demented. Her special place had vanished, and the cause was the baby brother with the oddly shaped hands.

But the call of maternity was compelling. To her astonishment, she became the newborn's mother, father, protector, teacher, and entertainer. By the time he was three years old, she had addicted him to the merry-go-round game, swinging him by the hands in circles, until they staggered and fell to the ground laughing, the world spinning dizzily around them. With a pillow on her feet she lifted him into the clouds on an up and down airplane ride, which ended in a jumbled crash landing on their bed. She wagged him around town in his wagon, bought him candy, played house and doctor, read him fairy tales and comic books, protected him from all harm—except that administered herself—and taught him to lie, swear, and smoke. She became his universe.

CHAPTER 2

Four and Twenty Black Birds

Sis pulled the Red Flyer across the sidewalk leading up to Doctor Carpenter's office and stopped. I was soon to be four years old, and, not ready for the ride to end, gripped the sides of the wagon and yelled, "Pull Sister, pull. Make it go again, pleeeese." Our dog, Rags, jumped to the ground and barked furiously at a nigra man carrying a table from the doctor's office toward a dilapidated old truck.

"What're you doing?" My sister asked, her feet planted directly in the workman's path. He stepped around her, keeping his eyes averted as he headed for the truck.

It was the summer of 1935, and resentment over the outcome of a war that ended seventy years ago continued to pollute the town like a typhoid infested sewer. A Negro could get in a lot of trouble for speaking to—even looking at—a ten year old white girl in Utica, Missouri.

In June, less than a month previous, Lester Parsons, known as one of them "uppity coloreds," had offered to carry Missus Catherine Bailey's groceries to her wagon. Rumor got around that when she handed him the last sack, he took hold of her delicate hand underneath and held it a mite too long, while staring with what was described as unabashed yearning. They found his body two weeks later in the Grand River over by Mooresville.

Sis glared at the man for not answering, then pulled me out of the wagon, dragged me around to the back of the house, up the steps, and into Momma's kitchen. "Why's that nigger carrying stuff out of Doctor Carpenter's office?" she asked.

Mae Myers, bloody to the elbows, pulled at the skin of a catfish with a pair of rusty pliers. Without turning, she said, "Looks like you kids are going to get a room of your own. The doctor's moving his office to Chillicothe." She didn't tell us that the doctor and Grandmother Carpenter had agreed to a separation agreement.

Sis jumped two-feet straight up, clapped, and yelled, "Yippee!"

Mom, thinking Sis was cheering for her own room said, "It *will* be nice to have a little more space." But that had nothing to do with Sis's elation. She was celebrating the prospect of Doctor Carpenter not being around to make her do what she was told.

Soon after Dad, Mom, and Sis moved back from Detroit and then into the rooms behind Doctor Carpenter's office, Sis discovered that the sidewalk leading to the front of the house was littered with wads of discarded chewing gum. To her delight, she found some still containing traces of mint or juicy-fruit favor. On several occasions, as she sampled a used glob, the doctor left his patient, ran out the door, down the steps, and shook her until she spit it out, unless she had already swallowed it—which early on she had learned to do with haste.

The doctor told mom about Sis scavenging for used gum. They lectured her about the pox, whooping cough, and bleeding sores. Sis looked at her feet, dragged a toe across the cement, and paid not the least bit of attention. Even Mom's threat to spank failed. The lure of free gum was too strong.

The day following one of the doctor's severest lectures, Sis hunkered down behind Grandmother's peony bed and watched as Silvia Petersen lifted her three-year old out of a Model T Ford and carried her up the sidewalk toward the doctor's office. At the bottom of the steps, Missus Petersen stopped and held out her hand to the child. Something was spat into it and discarded into the grass, after which the pair entered the office through the screen door.

Sis bolted to where the woman had stopped. Today was her lucky day. She reached down and popped a barely-chewed, still warm wad of bubble-gum into her mouth. The screen door slammed. Doctor Carpenter charged down the steps and grabbed her by the arm. In his free hand something glinted. "How many times have you been told not to pick up used gum?" Before Sis could reply, he pushed the sleeve of her blouse up, and said, "And don't think I haven't seen you peeking in my office window, young lady 'cause I have." He stuck a hypodermic needle in her arm and pushed the syringe home. "There. Now maybe you won't catch the crud, and just maybe from now on you'll do as you're told."

Chewing used-gum might have been a nasty habit, and maybe she shouldn't have been peeking through the doctor's window at naked patients, but a shot in the arm with a real needle! You'd have thought she drank some of Daddy's home-brew. For a year after the hypodermic needle episode, Shirley Jean bawled every time the doctor came near her. So if the man carrying furniture was helping him move seven miles down the highway to Chillicothe, good riddance.

When the Doctor and Grandmother separated, and his office was relocated in Chillicothe, Mother's cleaning job ended. Grandmother Carpenter still gave Dad money, but he used it to drink and gamble, so little of it made it home. Mom couldn't bring herself to talk to Grandmother about it, not with everything else she and the doctor had been doing for the family.

In the fall, Dad got a job picking apples at a local orchard. Pay was a penny a bushel. The trees were prime, the yield average or better, so a person willing to work ten hours a day could pick 150 bushels.

Mom was all cheery the morning Dad left for his first day in the orchard. If he could earn a dollar and a half every day, that would be nine dollars for six days of work, which would buy at least a dozen sacks of groceries.

Before noon, Dad walked back into the kitchen, and pitched the sack-lunch Mom had packed that morning onto the table. He didn't give a damn what Doctor Carpenter thought about him, he wasn't going back to that orchard. Way too hot, he said, and the no-see'ems were swarming the pickers, and the orchard boss was a sorry son-of-a-bitch.

We sat at the kitchen table and ate the sandwiches Mom had packed, listening to Dad tell how bad it was in the orchard. Mom took the twenty-eight cents he had earned and bought potatoes, beans, turnips, cabbage, corn meal, and salt pork. She had two pennies left, and food for two days. At that time, two incidents occurred which started me thinking about how bizarre the decision making process was in our family.

Mom's brother, Vern Sherman, bought the family farm from his father when the elder Sherman retired. In early spring each year, Vern turned his kitchen into a brood hatchery. Mom and Dad would take Sis and me to the farm so we could peer into the lighted boxes through the air holes and watch the baby chicks peck through their shells and wobble wetly into the world. One newborn chick, the color of butter and fluffy as cotton, made its way into our Easter basket. Miss Drumstick, as she was named, became the center of attention. As our chicken grew, so too did the boxes in which she was kept, but nothing short of a cage could contain her. Droppings began to appear in awkward places, like the clothes closet, so Miss Drumstick was evicted onto the back porch.

When she was a baby chick, I kept a pocket full of cracked corn to coax her into tagging along, and before her pin feathers were in, she was following me uptown, to the train station, old Henry's shack, to my friend Charlotte Dominic's house, or wherever I went, leaving her signature everywhere. At two months, a rooster's comb appeared on top of Miss Drumstick's head, and the "Miss," was dropped from her name. From then on it was just plain Drumstick.

Drumstick wanted to go where the family went, even when we went places in Grandmother's Model T, so to accommadate the traveling chicken, a newspaper was spread on the open lid of the glove compartment. The instant Dad cranked the motor into action, Drumstick half-ran, half-flew for the car, jumped onto the seat, and up to his perch where he rode clucking contentedly, sometimes dozing with an eye half open.

One day, the family went into the grocery store in Chillicothe and left Drumstick sitting on the glove box lid. When we arrived home, Dad got out of the car and carried a sack of potatoes up the steps. "Oh my God," gasped Mom, "look at the leg of his pants!"

Sis snickered. Mom clamped a hand over her mouth.

Mom was afraid to tell Dad about the large blob of chicken poop he was wearing and wouldn't have except he started to sit down on the flowered settee in the living room. She grabbed his arm. "Come sit with me in the kitchen and keep me company, Honey."

"Naw, I get tired of those old hard-back chairs."

"Well you can't sit there."

He looked at her for a long moment then down at the settee. "What's the matter with sitting here?"

"You've got a mess on your pants."

He twisted first to one side then the other. Momma eased back a step. He spotted the streak of manure. "By God," he roared, "you'd better do something with that damned rooster."

I ran outside and took Drumstick to grandmother's henhouse. Mother said I'd better keep him away from the house. But he escaped and that night was roosted on the railing of the back porch. Evidence that he'd been there was splattered all over the porch, some of which was tracked into the house. He always pointed his rear-end towards the door so he wouldn't miss anything in our yard. Rags couldn't match his alarm system, a menacing cluck, followed by an ear-piercing squawk whenever a stranger approached.

To make matters worse, an hour before sunrise, which in the summer meant 4:00 a.m., Drumstick issued his version of reveille. There were times when Dad didn't get home until almost daylight, and complained to Mom about the damn rooster waking him up at the beginning of each day.

On this morning, before I had a chance to rub the sleep out of my eyes, Mother seated me at the kitchen table, and said, "I'm sorry, but we're going to have to do something about that rooster. He poops everywhere and keeps Dad awake."

"What do you mean?" A knot jumped into the pit of my stomach. It sounded scary, her referring to Drumstick as "that rooster."

She took my hand, pulled me to the back door, and said, "Come on."

"Where're we going?" I tried to pull back, but she held on, and down the back steps we went. Drumstick came running across the yard. "Stay away, Drumstick!" I yelled, but he kept coming. I waved my free arm. He ran up and poked around my pocket for cracked corn.

Without a word, Mother snatched him by the neck and swung his body around and around. I grabbed her leg and screamed. Then Drumstick's head was in her hand, his body flopping on the ground splattering blood on my bare feet.

I stayed at Grandmother's house the day they ate him.

It seemed there was always a shortage of fresh meat in our house. Dad, who loved to hunt, told us that when fall came he would remedy that situation. He was proud of the double-barreled, twelve gauge, hammerless, hand-engraved Ithica shotgun his mother had given him before he married. She had also outfitted him with a canvas jacket with built-in game pouch, an ammunition belt, hat, hip-boots, and the rest of the gear required by the serious duck hunter. He might have stepped off the cover of *Field and Stream* in his fashionable hunting cloths. The expensive gun was slung casually across his shoulder, as he left the house to hunt the marshes and wetlands along the Grand River. There'd be plenty to eat on the table tonight.

That evening we gathered in the kitchen as Dad stumbled up the back steps, and, with hat askew, came through the door. Mom mouthed to Sis not to say anything to upset him. There was a detached look in his eyes, one I would come to dread in later years. We watched wide-eyed as he emptied his hunting pouch. There fell upon the kitchen table a half dozen or so scrawny blackbirds. He stood back with his hands on his hips looking first at Mom and then at us kids.

After a long silence, Sis said, "Yuk."

I said, "What're those things?"

Mom said, "What in God's name am I supposed to do with them?"

"Cook 'em," said Dad.

In her most non-offensive voice, Mom said, "Honey, where'd you get the money to buy whiskey?"

He slammed his hand down on the table so hard it caused Sis to jump a foot off her chair. I clapped my hands over my ears. He growled, "If I have to go through some kind of interrogation every time I come in this house, I'll find somewhere else to spend the night."

That did it. The prospect of Dad spending the night away from home was the last thing Mom wanted. "Please, Honey, don't get upset, it's just that we don't have anything much to eat, and I was just wondering." She picked nervously at the cuticles around her fingernails.

"You're about the most ungrateful wife in this town. There're lots of people who'd be glad to get their hands on the meat I laid on your table. But no, not you."

"We're grateful, aren't we kids?" Mom said, giving us a look.

"Yes, Momma," we said in unison.

"I'll cook the game you shot," she said. "Go get out of those clothes and into something comfortable." After he left, she began plucking feathers on her drain board, and muttered about how stupid her mother-in-law was for giving Dad money for shotgun shells and liquor when she knew there wasn't food on the table. Within minutes the birds were boiling in a pot with a few limp vegetables. Later, Mom hollered, "It's ready, come and eat."

"I'm not eat'n that crap," Dad said. "You've ruined those birds—they should've been baked." Then he launched into a harangue about how the birds he brought home were a delicacy if she had known how to prepare them. Hadn't she ever heard of blackbird pie?

Mom and I ate blackbird stew. It wasn't all that bad. Sis kept pretending she was going to throw up, so Mom let her fool around with her fork without putting any in her mouth.

Twelve years later, at The Great Lakes Naval Training Center, I found out I had made the highest score in my Company on the General Qualifications Test. The reward was another physical exam, which, if passed, would qualify me for admission to the Naval Academy at Annapolis.

A week later, I was told I had failed the physical. I supposed it was because of my flat feet, or it could have had something to do with my hands. As I was leaving the medical examiner's office, after being told of the rejection, he asked if I knew I'd had rickets at some time in my life and that it had caused a minor deformity of my breast and leg bones.

That weekend I called home. "Mom, did you know I was malnourished when I was little?" There was a long period of silence. "Hey, Mom, you there?"

"I didn't know," she said. "But it doesn't surprise me, I'll explain it all to you someday."

I said, "Well, I don't know if rickets—whatever that is—had anything to do with it, but that and a few other physical oddities cost me four years at the Naval Academy."

She did tell me why her parents refused to help us when we were hungry. Will and Lillian Sherman retired from farming and moved to Utica a few years before we moved back from Detroit. Their house was within a quarter-mile of Doctor Carpenter's office. Will Sherman said he'd see his daughter and her children starve rather than help. Hadn't he warned May about that hoodlum she married?

My father was tall, dark, and Rudolf Valentino handsome. He inherited the rugged features of his father, H. H. Myers, and the smoky complexion of his mother's Cheyenne Indian ancestry. A star basketball player and president of his senior class, Speck Myers, as his friends knew him, was popular among his peers and the teachers at Utica Public School, until the end of his last year, when two incidents changed everything, including his reputation.

Miss Barrington, a young teacher, came to Utica to teach English. She was auburn haired, and green-eyed, a lovely thing, and enthralled the boys of Utica High as she recited poetry of Keats, Barrett, and Kipling. But their minds and hearts were focused, not upon the lilting poems quoted, but by the tantalizing upward tilt of her bosom, nipples outlined against her blouse.

There was an eruption of testosterone in the glands of the senior boys, and numerous snide remarks from the mouths of Utica's young ladies.

Toward the end of Speck Myers's senior year, the Calvary Baptist Church held its annual cake auction. The church basement was full of Utica's most prominent citizens when Miss Barrington descended the steps, walked across the room to where Speck stood, and to everyone's shock and amazement, took a long, languid lick of his ice cream cone. Dalton Pepperton, one of the Deacons, remarked that the English teacher had the most beautiful tongue he'd ever seen. His wife, Elsie, took him by the elbow, marched him up the steps, and out the door.

The sale had been going pretty much as usual until Robert Urstrom, owner of the Utica Grocery and Mercantile Store, and Grand Dragon of the Livingston County Ku Klux Klan, paid the outrageous sum of ninety-cents for Gracie Kimball's light-as-air, lemon layered, angel food cake. Everyone applauded the generous price bid by Mister Urstrom, which someone said was the highest in the thirty-year history of the event.

The Reverend Cranston Littlefield rapped the rostrum. The last item of the evening would be Miss Barrington's cream-filled, devil's food cake, topped with fresh strawberry icing. The women of Utica sat sullen as the seductive pastry was lifted high above the reverend's head. Who would start the bidding at a quarter? The men coughed nervously. The women turned to those sitting next to them and engaged in small talk. After a long pause, Preacher Littlefield cleared his throat and said, "Who will start the bidding at a dime?"

My Grandpa, Will Sherman, raised his hand, but at the same time, in the back of the room, Speck Myers stood up and said, "Hell, I'll give a dollar for that cake." There was a collective intake of breath. Folks hurriedly left the basement, while Speck went to the rostrum and collected his prize.

At the School Board Meeting, called for the purpose of firing Miss Barrington, several citizens confirmed that when Speck Myers bid for the teacher's cake, she leaned forward, and smiled sexily at him. At the same time, he reached behind Melvin Peavy, and patted his English Teacher on her well-rounded bottom. The vote was unanimous. This loose woman, who had come to Utica and led one of the its outstanding young men astray, had to go.

At daybreak on the Monday morning before graduation exercises, Carrie Walz got up and walked sleepy-eyed to the shed out back to tend her milk cow. She yawned, rubbed her eyes, then rubbed them again. She came suddenly awake and gawked. A Livingston County road grader, fully assembled, was setting on top of the school building. The figure asleep in the driver's seat, with an empty pint bottle of Four Roses beside him turned out to be Speck Myers.

When Dad finished high school, Doctor Carpenter sent him to the University of Missouri at Columbia to study pre-medicine. But his love affair with liquor flunked him out at the end of the first semester. In 1919, he joined the Navy, spent three months on an island in San Francisco Bay, and was discharged when the Great War ended.

Mae Sherman was in the ninth-grade when Speck Myers left Utica, and already had a crush on him, as did most of the girls in school. When he returned after his ninety day stint in the navy, he strutted around town and hung out at Urstrom's, a man of the world who had been all the way to California and back. The girls in town were aflutter.

One night after supper, when the coil-spring in Will Sherman was beginning to unwind, Lillian seated herself beside his chair and said, "Will, I want to talk to you about Mae."

He lifted his head from the back of the chair. "Well, what are you waiting for?"

"I don't want you to get upset," she said.

"It must be bad, else you'd go ahead and say it."

She placed her hand on his arm, a gesture from the remote past, and said, "Promise me you won't fly off the handle."

"How can I make such a promise?" he asked.

"You have to, or I won't tell you."

"Okay. I won't fly off the handle—whatever that means."

"Will Sherman, you know exactly what it means. I don't want you doing something you'll regret later."

"My God, Lillian, if it's something bad, quit beating around the bush, 'cuz I'm entitled to know." But Lillian closed her lips. They sat staring silently at one another until he said, "Okay, okay, I won't lose my temper."

She tightened the grip on his arm. "Mae told me she's got a date to go to the Utica Ice Cream Social."

"Why should I get upset about that? Who's it with?"

"That Myers boy, the one they call Speck."

Will Sherman jumped out of the chair and yelled, "Where's my gun?"

But he didn't get a gun. Later that evening, Will sat quietly on the front porch, his hands folded neatly in his lap, and said to the Myers boy, "I expect you to have my daughter home here by 10:00 o'clock, is that clear?"

"Yes, Sir," said Mae's date, as they walked off the porch and headed toward town. He was true to his word. At five-minutes before the dead-line, Will Sherman, sitting in the dimly lit front room, heard the screen to the front door open, and the muffled voice of his sixteen year old daughter. He waited until Mae was in the house, then walked to the door.

"Where you going, Papa?" she asked.

"You go on to bed. I'm going to have a little talk with your friend, Speck Myers." He took the young man by the arm and led him around behind the cowshed out of earshot of the house. "I don't want you coming around my daughter anymore."

Speck, one leg behind him propped against the shed, a cigarette dangling from his mouth said, "Why not?"

"Because you're a grown man, and she's only sixteen—too young for someone who's been around as much as you."

"Aw, I won't hurt her. She and I have a lot of fun."

"Maybe you didn't hear what I just said. I want you to stay away from Mae. Is that clear?"

Speck pushed away from the shed. "Wait a minute. You can't tell me what I can and can't do."

In an instant, Will Sherman pinned Speck to the side of the building with his forearm and put a knife to his throat. "Now listen, you smart aleck know-it-all. When it comes to my daughter, I can tell you anything I want, and I'm telling you, if you don't stay away from her, I'll cut your goddamned throat. Is that clear enough?"

So, when the Myers boy made arrangements for he and Mae to elope, Will Sherman vowed he'd never be allowed to step foot in his home—and he kept that oath until he went to his grave.

CHAPTER 3

The Night of The Cyclone

Saturday afternoon, July, 1935. My sister and I were invisible, hunkered down in a culvert grown over by a thicket of wild roses. The bushes hummed with bees. Butterflies floated from one fragrant blossom to another, their languid flight slowed by the summer's sultry heat. We were on a secret mission. Go uptown, stay out of sight, and see if Dad was hanging out at Urstrom's Grocery Store.

We had been crouched down for only a minute when the pollen from the roses made me want to sneeze. I stuck a finger up each nostril. Sis, who never missed anything, hissed, "Don't you dare sneeze!"

I stuck my fingers in further. "Why nod? Nobody cad hear us."

"Yes, they can. Everybody in this whole town would hear you. Now be quiet."

Insects crawled on our bare feet. Sis didn't seem to mind, but I stamped up and down. It didn't do much good. "There's sometheg crawling ub my leg," I whined.

"My God. You're the biggest baby I've ever seen. Here, let me look. And take your fingers out of your nose." She pulled my pant leg up.

"It's higher ub than that," I said. "If I take my fingers out, I'll sneeze."

"Well, whatever it is, it won't hurt you, so shut up for one minute."

From the culvert, we could look over the edge of the sidewalk and see the entire length and breadth of Utica's main street. To the left was the barbershop, on the right Urstrom's Grocery and Dry Goods Store, the only businesses that had survived the crash of '29. Other buildings were boarded up this way and that, like a giant hand had crossed them out.

Dad and his friends hung out at Urstrom's, wiling away the days with stories about the good times. The few customers who actually wanted to buy a grocery item caused a pall to fall over the store when they entered, and the minute the screen door slammed behind them, knee-slapping laughter could be heard at the post office, two blocks away.

Mom said sometimes you could smell home-brew fermenting in Urstrom's storeroom. Maybe that's what gave Dad the idea that he could make his own beer. He lined the shelves in our fruit cellar with quarts of amber-colored stout; said it would be the best and strongest in Livingston County. About a week after he finished bottling, we were in bed when the first fruit jar exploded, then the second, and third. The chain reaction sounded like a war under our floor. Dad leaped out of bed in his underwear and bound down the steps, but was afraid to open the cellar door for fear of being hit with flying glass. All he could do was lean his head against the door and listen as his dream of beer abundance blew itself to perdition. Mom worked for a week cleaning up, but Sis and I could tell from the satisfied expression on her face, she was glad the stout was gone.

In addition to beer, if a man had a nickel, he could get a snort or two of bathtub gin at Urstrom's anytime, day or night. It was what you couldn't get at Urstrom's that made Mom hope Dad was there, rather than at Greely Bonder's place on the river.

So Sis and I waited in the rose bushes. Nothing moved except the bugs on my legs and a scraggly looking mongrel walking bowlegged toward us. Sis hissed to the dog to get on out of there. The critter sauntered past without a pause.

The screen door of the store squeaked and slammed. Old man Satterfield stepped out and stood on the porch for a long moment blinking in the bright sunlight, his hands tucked in the front of his bib overalls. From the center pocket, he took a wad of something, stuck it in his mouth, stepped off the porch, and nonchalant-like crossed the dirt street to the sidewalk.

Sis was as motionless as a lizard watching a gnat. The bug on my leg reached my crotch. I squirmed and tried to scratch through my pants, and would have jumped up, but Sis gave me one of her, "I'll brain you if you do," stares. I was afraid to tell her I had to pee.

Old man Satterfield, tobacco juice running out the corners of his mouth, walked down the sidewalk until he was right above us, then looked down and with a sneer said, "I see you Myers brats. You're not fooling anyone. Go on home where you belong."

I almost wet my britches. Sis's face blushed to the color of the roses. "Mind your own business," she said. "We're not bothering you."

The old man squirted a stream of tobacco juice between her feet.

"Don't you spit at my sister," I piped.

She looked down at the stains splattered on the inside of her ankles. "You . . . you, you nasty old . . . bastard!"

Satterfield snorted and said, "You're lucky I don't come down there and slap your smart mouth. Now get on out of here." He turned and walked back toward Urstrom's, while we scrambled up on the sidewalk and ran for the house.

Sis would soon be ten years old. On the way home she kept saying over and over, "Oh my God. Oh my God, everybody will know we were sneaking around spying on Daddy."

We had been discovered, and it would be the talk of the town. When we got home, Sis washed her feet under Grandma's pump, ran up our back-steps, through the open door, and started crying. Mother came out of the kitchen, swept damp hair out of her eyes, and wanted to know what was wrong. Sis made a flying dive onto the sofa, buried her face in a pillow, and wailed, "We got caught."

"And old man Satterfield spit tobacco juice at Sis," I added with indignation. I'd been slapped just a day or two ago by Sis for spitting at my friend, Charlotte.

Mom, started picking her cuticles. "Did Dad see you?"

Sis lifted her face out of the pillow. "No, but old man Satterfield did, and that's worse 'cause he'll tell everybody in town."

"I have to go pee," I said and started crying.

"What are you crying about?" Mom said.

"Something bit me on the thing."

She pulled my pants down, and an ant fell out of my underwear. "See," I said to Sis, "I told you something was biting me."

"Oh, shut up. It was 'cause you made so much noise that we got caught."

"It was not!"

Mom jerked me by the shirt. "Both of you be quiet. Maybe Dad won't find out."

"Ain't you going to tell old man Satterfield not to spit on Sis?" Mom acted like she didn't hear me. I could tell by the look on her face she believed it was my fault we got caught.

Later that afternoon, Dad borrowed Grandmother Carpenter's car so we could go to the Old Settler's Picnic in Chillicothe. Mom started out happy—Dad was taking us somewhere. Then she became real quiet when he said he wasn't going to the picnic after all, but to the pool hall for a few games, and would pick us up before dark.

The park was full of people. Baskets of fried chicken, smoked ham, baked beans, pickled beets, potato salad, bread and butter pickles, peaches marinating in brown sugar, and cakes of every kind, color, and size were on every table. Watermelons, in tubs, their backs rising above ice-cooled water like green hippopotamuses were scattered though the park.

Uncle Vern and our cousins Weldon and Wanda brought an ice cream freezer with liquid sloshing around inside. Weldon carried a block of blue ice from Gleasen's Ice House on his shoulder, which turned his work shirt two different colors. He chipped and stuffed the slivers between the wooden bucket and the metal cylinder, then poured salt on the ice, and told us nobody got ice cream unless they helped turn the crank. Sis took the first turn. Weldon added more ice and salt.

"Let me turn the handle," I said, to make sure no one could deny me a helping.

"You're too little," Weldon said. He was the oldest of the cousins and bossed us around.

I was about to sully up when Sis said, "Come on Brother, you can help me." I grunted and tugged on the handle. Sis winked at Weldon. "See how strong he is?"

Uncle Vern stood around watching the kids struggle with the crank. Everyone started moaning about how tired they were, and how the ice cream was never going to be ready. Mom said she and Vern would finish while we ate. Ever so often, Uncle Vern pulled a big watch out of his bib-overalls, studied it, and put it back without saying anything. Every time he'd pull out the watch, all the kids would stop whatever they were doing and stare at him. After what seemed like the hundredth time, he said, "Let's see what we've got here." He unlatched the top to the bucket. The cover of the inside cylinder pushed upward and ice cream ran over the side like an eruption from a volcano. "Okay, kids," he said, "come and get it."

Everyone cheered. We danced around celebrating the magic of the liquid turning solid, and being through with the crank.

Full of cake, ice cream, and watermelon, the kids scattered, while the parents exchanged bits of gossip and fanned themselves. One of the Old Settlers gave me a green and white kite. Sis and Weldon put it together. I ran as fast as I could, with the kite bouncing along on the ground behind me. A weak breeze caught and danced it upward, then, like a bass trying to throw a hook, the kite shook itself in the windless sky, convulsed, and nose-dived into a tree. When I tugged on the string, it broke. I ran back to the picnic table, got Sis by the hand and pulled her to where she could see what had happened. "Can you get my kite down for me?"

Sis put her hands on her hips. "You've already ruined that kite—lasted about two minutes. I'm not climbing that tree, but if you'd asked Weldon maybe he'd do it."

The kite hung listlessly, then made a slow loop around the limb, and another a little faster, and then like an airplane propeller, started spinning like a whirligig.

A sharp gust of wind kicked dust off the dry grass, and bucked tablecloths, making them snap. Those not weighted down by baskets or half empty jugs, skittered off the tables. Napkins and paper sacks danced in circles, shot straight up, and hung in tree limbs like my kite. People ran about grabbing chairs and other belongings. Mothers called for their children. Black and green clouds reared up over the southwestern sky, swallowed the sun, and gave daylight a yellow pallor. Tongues of lightening flicked. Someone yelled, "There's a cyclone coming."

Uncle Vern, herding his crew in front of him, yelled, "Come on May, I'll give you a ride."

Mom's skirt whipped to her waist. She yelled, "Go ahead, we have to wait for Keith."

Torrential rain slashed across the park. Within minutes the area was deserted, except for a woman who ran by with a baby clutched to her breast and carrying a paper sack. She said something about lightning and to stay away from trees. Mom must have misunderstood, because we dashed for the tree. Howling wind sucked breath out of my lungs. The kite shredded and flopped like Drumstick the day Mom twisted his head off. The woman's sack broke, spilling remnants of the afternoon onto the ground, but she ran on and disappeared into a car parked at the curb. As she drove away, another car pulled into its spot.

Mother cheered. It was Dad. We splashed through ankle-deep waer. Mom took one of my hands, and Sis the other so I lifted my feet and skimmed along like a water bug. Mom jerked the passenger door open and shoved Sis and me into the rear seat. It was as dry and warm as a cocoon. We laughed with relief as we tumbled in, thankful to be out of the storm. "Thank goodness you got here," Mother said, as she dried her face on the hem of her petticoat. "We were scared to death." The wind and rain beat against the windshield. Dad slouched in the seat, both hands on the wheel. Mother quieted.

The engine rumbled loud then soft. Dad turned in his seat and stared at Mother, eyes not quit focused. The threat outside began to pale. Without a word he jammed the car into gear; it jerked away from the curb, and careened down the highway, the windshield wipers flapping impotently. The headlights barely penetrated the deluge, as we headed west into the storm.

Mother, white as a sheet, said in a pleading voice, "Dad, whatever you do, don't harm the kids."

Sis screamed, "Please, Daddy, please don't be mad at us. Please don't drive fast!"

A howling wind lurched the car from side to side and lifted one set of wheels off the road. "My God, you're going to kill us all," Mother said. She grabbed his shoulder. "You've got to pull over 'til the storm passes."

"Shut your mouth," he said. With his right hand, he pushed Mom away from him and pinned her to the passenger door. "You sent the kids to spy on me, and by God I'm going to teach you not to do it again."

Sis screamed, "I won't spy on you anymore, Daddy, I promise. Don't push Momma out of the car." Outside lightning flashed and struck a power pole next to the road, the thunder clap shook the car. The highway disappeared beneath swirling brown water, and we were surrounded by a giant lake. Sis crawled onto the floorboard, covered her eyes, and prayed, "Please God, don't let us go in the river." The only benchmark of the road was the outline of the wooden skeleton of railings and support beams of the bridge illuminated by the continuous lightning flashes. The river boiled on both sides. The car rolled onto the wooden structure. Water pushed against the fenders, ran under the doors and across the floorboard as we passed over the river.

For the remainder of my sister's life, she would never again cross a bridge in a car without screaming and cringing on the floorboard with her eyes covered.

In Grandmother's driveway, Dad reached across Mom, opened the passenger door, and pushed her out sideways into the mud. She jumped up, herded Sis and me into the house, and closed us in the room where we slept. We stood breathless at the door fearful of the storm raging within, no longer caring about the one outside. When quiet settled through the house, Sis put me to bed. It took a long time to fall asleep, and when I did, I dreamed about the green and white kite flopping around on the tree limb, and the black water of the river. My cot bumped across the floor and I woke up thinking we were still in the car. But it was Sis pulling my cot snug against her bed; then she took my hand and said, "It was just a bad dream. Everything's going to be alright."

The next day when I got up, Dad was gone, and Mom was busy in the kitchen. Sis had gone to Rosemary Potts's house. The rain from the night before left everything muddy so I had to stay in the house.

In the former waiting area of Doctor Carpenter's office—now our living room—there was an old piece of furniture, a settee, covered in a multi-colored floral pattern, the fanciest thing in our house. I ran my hand over the intricate design which included a garden filled with bright yellow flowers, one of which was stained a dull beige, perhaps the result of a spill as a patient waited to see the doctor. Whatever the cause, it needed to be fixed. I climbed down, found a set of water colors, scrambled back up on the settee, spit on the brush, and painted the dull flower bright purple.

Sis hadn't been back from her friend's house five minutes when mother saw the purple flower. Everything we used for daily living, including the settee, had either been loaned or donated by Grandmother Carpenter and her husband—a bitter pill for a woman of mother's industry and frugality. Her reaction to my artwork was hysteria, so I feigned complete ignorance. Someone would pay dearly for this act of inconsiderate vandalism, she declared, and the only other person in the house who might have done this was my sister. But having just arrived back in the house, she knew nothing about the cause of Mother's rage until she was marched to the settee and had the offense pointed out. Then we were set down, not too gently, and told we would stay there, not for hours or days, but forever, unless one of us confessed. The episode might have ended sooner had mother said how the guilty party would be punished, but she knew about fear of the unknown, and refused to tell us of her intentions. I sat in terror imagining the worst, my vocal cords paralyzed. After a final burst of outrage, mother returned to the kitchen leaving us alone.

As soon as she was out of sight, Sis hissed, "You little monster! I have to sit here for the rest of the day for something you did. I'll get even, don't you worry . . . you'll pay for this." She made mean faces at me for awhile, but in this situation I was more afraid of my mother than her, so she changed her tactic. "Please Brother, tell her you did it. She won't do nothing much."

"Then tell her you did it," I said.

"You brat!"

The back door banged. Dad came striding through the house. Mother rushed out of the kitchen to greet him. "Did you find a job?" she asked. The smile on Dad's face was a hopeful sign.

"Naw, the crops are so bad, no one needs farm labor. But Vern said if I'd help him castrate his shoats and put up silage in the fall, he'd give us a hog when it's time to slaughter. That ought to keep us in pork for the winter."

Mom took his arm. "That's wonderful, Honey. Come in the kitchen and I'll pour you a cup of coffee."

Dad jerked his head toward Sis and I as we sat glaring at each other. "What's with the kids?"

"Oh, it's nothing for you to worry about. You kids go on outside and play so Dad and I can talk."

I bounced off the chair like a firecracker had gone off in my pants.

Sis, right behind me, said, "Got out of that one didn't you? Just don't forget what I said about getting even."

"I was afraid," I said.

She put her arm around my shoulder. "What's there to be scared of? Come on, let's go down to the depot and see what's going on."

My sister was fearless about most things, but there was a new look in her eye. It had been there since the night before when Dad drove us across the Grand River bridge.

CHAPTER 4

The Magic Stick

Mom and Grandmother Carpenter were whispering a mile a minute. Empty coffee cups decorated the table. The faster they talked the closer their heads got. When I walked toward them, their heads drew back. The space between them expanded and contracted like the bellows in an accordion. I pretended I was going into the living room, then snuck in and heard Greely Bonder's name mentioned.

After I listened for awhile, Mom told me to go get some more lemonade. I had already drunk a gallon, so I crawled under the table and pretended I was asleep. I listened for a long time, then Mom must have seen my eyes blink. She nudged me with her toe and told me to get myself outside.

"I have to go to the bathroom," I said and looked with longing through an open door at Grandmother's new porcelain privy. I crawled in that direction. Grandmother made a sound like a bullfrog croaking. Mom grabbed the back of my shirt and told me to use the two-holer outside. Said I didn't know how to use an inside toilet.

I figured just because I hadn't ever done it, didn't mean beans. I could see myself perched on that beautiful white throne doing my business without having to hold my breath. No flies or spiders, and soft paper instead of catalogs or corncobs. But no amount of arguing and griping could persuade them to let me have my first indoor experience. Out I went.

I held my breath and let loose with a stream of used lemonade that knocked a spider off its web at the bottom of the hole. An aim like that made me wonder why the porcelain bowl would be any harder to hit. I banged the door behind me, expelled my breath, and grinned—hadn't smelled a thing. Feeling cocky about hitting that spider, I walked around to the shady side of the hen house, sat down, and thought about what I'd just heard concerning Greely Bonder.

Grandmother said when corn got down to fifteen-cents a bushel, eggs three cents a dozen, pork twenty-cents a hundred weight, and the Farmer's Bank in Chillicothe closed, Greely said to hell with it and quite farming. Like many of the other folks in Livingston County, including Grandfather Myers, when the bank went bust, he'd lost his life savings, so Greely sold his mules and what was left of his equipment, and used the money to bring two down-on-their-luck girls from Kansas City to his shack on The Grand River, where moonshine flowed like flood waters in an April downpour. Dad told Dyke McCoy that the repeal of something called prohibition, didn't hurt Greely's moonshine business one bit, because what he was making was better than bonded. I wondered if all that whispering in the kitchen had anything to do with Dad not coming home last night.

There was no one to play with, so I wandered down to Grandma's rickety old chicken coop, climbed up on an empty crate, and squinted through the wide cracks. It was too murky inside to tell what was going on. The outline of several hens roosting on bleacher-like poles, and a hen with baby chicks scratching on the dirt floor was about all I could see. Might be a lot of things to do in there. I jumped off the crate and on my tiptoes turned the latch-board on the door, and stepped in. A rusty spring pulled the door closed behind me. The floor was a minefield of chicken droppings and corncobs. The brood-hen squawked, herded her chicks to the far end of the coop causing powder-dry dirt to swirl. Above the nervous clucking of the hens, there was a faint humming sound.

I edged my way toward the nesting boxes on the opposite wall. The farther I advanced, the louder the hum became. I squinted through the settling dust, and saw a spongy looking thing with several wasps perched on it hanging from a rafter. A whole swarm was flying about, and the air was filled with the whirl of their wings. Grandmother did not want those pests in her hen house. Lying at the toe of my shoe was opportunity—a large corncob. If I rid the place of wasps, Grandmother might let me sleep over. I knew when Dad came home there was going to be a lot of yelling at my house, and, Grandmother would let me dunk toast in a cup of coffee when I got up in the morning.

I took aim and let fly. The corncob bounced wide. The wasps paid me no mind. The second missile turned end-over-end, and blam!—a direct hit. Before I had a chance to celebrate, a wasp also scored a direct hit on the back of my neck. I yelped, whirled, and hit the door going full speed. I bounced back and landed on the floor in the middle of the dust, corncobs, and poop. The old latch-board nailed to the outside of the door had flopped cross-wise and I was trapped.

It was a hot summer day, so Grandmother's back door was open. She and Mom were within earshot of the chicken coop and heard me caterwauling. Mom banged through the coop door, scooped me up, and ran back out as fast as she could. Within minutes, my head, arms, and hands were covered with marble sized welts. Mom only got stung once. The attention I got that day was sure not the kind I'd been looking for. Mom put me to bed on Grandmother's couch and covered the stings with baking soda. For the rest of the day, Grandmother let me use her indoor toilet, and that night she let me sleep in her bed.

Later that summer, we spent the weekend at Uncle Vern's farm. Even though it was only three miles from Utica, it seemed further. The road to the farmhouse was rutted, hilly, ran through deep woods and crossed two running streams. Mom packed a change of cloths for everyone in a paper sack. Dad brought some home-brew. Sis and I brought toys and my tricycle for me to ride over the pine floors.

Saturday morning everyone got cleaned up to go to Chillicothe, ten miles to the east. Mom wanted to look for a bolt of cloth to make Sis a dress for school. Uncle Vern, Weldon, and Dad were going to the livestock auction. Uncle Vern gave Sis thirty cents to take Wanda and me to the movie.

The feature presentation at the matinee was *"The Keeper of the Bees."* The part I saw, when I wasn't running up and down the aisles to the bathroom, was where the hero approached a beehive with nothing on but a bathing suit. He stood like a statue in a meadow until honeybees covered all of his body parts. It was like what Idgie would do many years later in the movie, *"Fried Green Tomatoes."* But unlike Idgie, all this guy did during the entire film was let a horde of bees climb around all over him.

When we got back to the farm, Sis made a big deal out of the movie. She told the story over and over to the adults. With every telling it got better and she'd say, "Isn't that right Brother?" I nodded my head as fast as she talked. She told about stuff in the movie I couldn't remember. I figured those were parts I'd missed while I was in the toilet.

She told about the hero saying anybody could handle bees without getting stung. It's fear that gets people in trouble. If you're not afraid and walk right up, reach in and take a handful of their honey, the bees won't bother you at all. That's the way Sis told it. After awhile, I started remembering the things she was big-eyed about. After the third telling, the adults, exhausted from the sheer volume and intensity of Sis's story-telling, let her know they'd heard all they cared to hear. That was when she said, "Come on Brother, we're going outside." Out we went, down the hill in front of the farmhouse we marched. Straight to the beehives.

"All you have to do is show them you're not afraid," she said, and gave me an encouraging smile and a gentle push toward the hives.

It had only been a month or so since my encounter with the wasps in Grandmother's chicken coop. My recollection of the hurt a wasp can put on your body was still vivid, and I explained to Sis how I had learned my lesson at the expense of great pain and discomfort.

"Naw," she said, "There's no comparison. A bee's real gentle. A wasp is mean. And they are especially mean . . ." She gave me one of those you brought it on yourself looks, ". . . when someone attacks them with corncobs." She took me by the shoulders and said in her most wheedling voice, "You know perfectly well your sister would never tell you to do something that would hurt you, now don't you?"

"Well, if bees are so gentle, why don't you do it?"

She hesitated for only a second, leaned over, looked me right in the eye, and with the authority of Moses added, "Brother, don't you remember? In the movie it was only *men* who could go near the bees. There was not a single girl. Not one."

True—and this was different. My Sister was the last person who would put me in harm's way. So despite my skepticism I edged a few feet toward the hives, attention fixed above the box where the air was alive with activity. Five feet away, there was the hum of hundreds of bees minding their business. Two feet from the hive—still no bees bothered me. Some came close, circling overhead. I turned to my sister. "Are you sure they won't sting me?"

In her most soothing voice she said, "Lift the cover up slowly, and they won't hurt you. Just don't let them get the idea you're afraid." Then she changed to her commanding voice. "Now, go ahead and do it!"

The instant I lifted the lid, a bee whacked me between the eyes. I let it slam shut, and a cloud of bees landed on my head. I started running, flailing my arms thinking that when I reached my sister she would somehow save me. But the place where she'd been was no longer occupied. The door of the farmhouse slammed behind her.

The rest of the weekend, I rode my tricycle around the house careening off the walls and doorframes with both eyes swollen shut.

Dusk, August 3, 1935. A white frosted cake sat gleaming in the center of the kitchen table, ten candles sparkled in the dusty air. Sis gripped the edge of the table, bent forward, and took two practice breaths.

Mom said, “Don’t forget to make a wish.”

Charlotte and I jumped up and down and yelled, “Yeah, make a wish.”

Grandmother Carpenter, perched like a Buddha on a stool too small for her rear-end, said, “Shirley Jean, you’re going to set yourself on fire if you get any closer.”

Sis pretended she was deaf, closed her eyes, and then with a mighty puff blew out all ten candles. Everyone cheered.

Mom cut the devil’s food cake topped with powdered-sugar frosting, and dished up large portions.

With my mouth full I said, “What’d you wish?”

Sis gave me a look and said, “I’m not telling. If I did, the wish wouldn’t come true, isn’t that right Momma?”

“That’s right, Honey,” Mother said.

I puckered and said, “Okay, then I’m not going to tell you my wish.”

“It wouldn’t hurt you to whisper your wish in your little brother’s ear, would it?” Grandmother said with a frown.

Sis paid Grandmother no mind and laughed. “Brother, you’re so dumb. Your birthday’s not for another month. You don’t know what you’ll wish for.”

“I do so. I’m going to wish for a pony.”

Sis slapped her forehead and squealed, “I can’t believe it. You just told your wish.”

“I did not. I was just pretending. I know I can’t have a pony, ‘cause we don’t have no money.”

Sis, her eyes bright, said, “Grandmother, may I open my present?” A single package lay on the table next to the leftover cake. No one said anything, so she untied the ribbon and ripped the paper. She looked first at Grandmother, then at Mom who avoided her eyes.

“What is it?” I said, all excited. Charlotte and I left our cake and ran to see Sis’s present.

Grandmother sniffed and said, “Those are school supplies that your parents won't be able to afford when you go back to school in the fall." She struggled off of the stool, set her empty plate on the table and said, "Happy Birthday, Shirley Jean." To Momma she said, "Mae, I have to use the toilet so I'm going home." She held out her arms to me. "Come here little Darling and give your granny a kiss." When she bent forward, her breasts hit me on top the head. "Let your grandmother see those old bee stings." She gave Sis a withering look, then held me out in front of her. "Looks like they're about all gone. Goodness sake, my boy's had a hard summer."

Mom, in the middle of wrapping the remains of the cake in wax paper, turned around, and said, "Thanks for coming, Anna." Then to Sis. "Tell your grandmother thank you. Dad will be home any minute and I don't want any noise in here, so take these kids outside."

Sis, still staring unbelievingly at the spiral notebooks, muttered, "Thanks, Grandma." Then she put her hands on her hips and said, "I don't want to baby-sit. I want to go over to Rosemary's."

"Well, you're not going—unless you want to take these kids with you."

Sis stamped her foot. "I'm not taking these brats to Rosemary Potts's house. Meredith might be there. Besides, Brother looks like he's got marbles stuck on his face."

"Then you can stay home. And don't call your brother and Charlotte brats."

The summer had been torrid. The Chillicothe paper reported the hottest July on record. And, as if the landscape hadn't been punished enough, hordes of grasshoppers swept across the drought stricken corn belt and ate the lawns, the flowers, the gardens and all the crops—everything that had ever been a vegetable, including curtains, rugs, and clothes. They were everywhere, the sidewalk, the lawn, and dozens clung to the screen door of the house.

Sis herded Charlotte and I out the back door to the sandbox. The still evening air pulsed and throbbed with the mating calls of the cicada, katydid, crickets, and tree frogs. Fireflies flashed on and off across the yard like miniature beacons. She brushed several grasshoppers out of the way and stood against the side of the house with her arms crossed and a sour look on her face.

Charlotte and I stacked buckets of sand four high, and then tunneled through making several levels of miniature corridors and windows. We stepped back and decided we had built a castle.

Sis said, "I guess you know you're playing in cat-poop. Grandmother's cat made a mess in your sandbox this morning."

"I thought I smelled something nasty," said Charlotte.

"Grandma's cat died a long time ago," I said.

Sis giggled. "Well, maybe that's where her dead cat's buried. And there was a cat digging around in that box a couple days ago."

A car door slammed in front of the house. The sound of men's voices rose above the throbbing of a motor. Car lights moved on, and Dad walked around the corner of the house carrying a paper sack.

"Daddy, Daddy," sister said, and ran across the yard.

He scooped her up and said, "How's my little angel?"

"Did you bring me a birthday present, Daddy? Is that what's in the sack?" He carried her up the stairs and through the backdoor without answering.

In a minute, she came back and sat down on the side of the sandbox. "Look what I've got." She dropped ten partially burnt candles on the sand.

"Is that your birthday present?" I asked.

"No, Stupid. Daddy can't afford to buy me a present now. But when he gets a job, we'll have lots of money and he'll buy me anything I want."

"What was in the sack?"

"How should I know?" she said and kicked sand at me. "Just shut up."

"What are you going to do with the candles?" I asked.

"Move over, Lumpy, and I'll show you." She sat down in the sand, fished around in her dress pocket, and came out with kitchen matches.

"We're not supposed to play with matches," I said.

She exhaled a long sigh. "We're not *playing* with matches.

Watch." She struck one against the side of the sandbox, lit candles, and set them in each of the several passages and rooms of the sand castle. The tenth she placed on the tip-top.

A summer breeze slipped through the tunneled spaces, moving the flames, dancing the shadows. Charlotte and I were hypnotized. "It's beautiful," she whispered.

"Like magic," I added.

My sister backed away from the box until she was hidden in the shadows. Her black hair blended with the moonless night. An occasional flicker of candlelight flashed in her dark eyes. "Speaking of magic," she said in a mysterious voice, "did you tell Charlotte?"

"Tell her what?"

"About the Magic Stick."

I had never heard of a magic stick, but I knew from her tone there was a plot afoot, and it would be best if I went along. "I forgot," I said. Anything that noncommittal should get me off the hook.

"We do have a Magic Stick, don't we Brother?"

"Sure," I said.

"Why didn't you tell Charlotte about it?"

Whoops. My sister wanted me to say something, but what? She was in no mood for me to come off sounding insolent. From the day I was born she'd been my caretaker. If I didn't do whatever she had in mind, I'd get another lump on the side of the head and it wouldn't be from a bee sting. So with a flat voice I said, "You can tell her better than me."

I could feel her staring at me through the darkness. Then in a spooky voice, she said, "Charlotte, the Magic Stick will do anything I tell it. Do you understand? Anything."

Charlotte leaped out of the sandbox; said she had to go home.

Sis stepped forward into the flickering light of the candles. From behind her back there appeared a stick—the same twisted hackberry limb I'd found down at old Henry's and carried home that very afternoon—but in the dark, the knots appeared as bulging eyes staring straight at Charlotte. "You're not going anywhere until the Stick tells you to."

Charlotte froze in her tracks.

"Jump, Stick, jump!" Sis said. The Stick jumped up, turned in the air, and landed back in her hand.

By now it was pitch dark, and the candles were burning close to the sand. Charlotte was paralyzed.

Sis's voice—barely audible: "What do you want her to do, Stick?" The Stick quivered in the hand of its mistress, then spoke with a baleful rasp, "Charlotte, Charlotte," it intoned, "eat the candle that just went out. Hurry, eat the candle that just went out."

Charlotte hesitated.

The Stick shook as it tried to reach Charlotte, and its voice said, "If you don't eat that candle, I will beat you bloody!"

Charlotte ate the candle, wax, wick, sand and all.

But the Stick was not satisfied and commanded, "Charlotte, catch a grasshopper." The Stick followed her as she trotted to the side of the house and came back with a large grasshopper. "Now eat the grasshopper!" the Stick commanded.

She bit the insect in two, gagged; but the stick was unrelenting and told her to swallow. She gagged again. The stick threatened to gouge out her eyes if she didn't chew and swallow all the parts. Charlotte ate the grasshopper.

Later she said that was the worst birthday party she'd ever attended, and it was a long time before she would come back to my house.

Sis twirled the lead-end of a pencil around on her tongue wetting it over and over, a clean sheet of notebook paper spread before her. At the top she had written, December 19, 1935. "Okay," she said, "what do you want Santa to bring you?"

"I don't know," I said, fidgeting around in a straight-backed chair and pulling at the crotch of my pants.

Exasperated, she said, "Mother told me to help you write a letter to Santa. Now you have to tell me what you want, otherwise he won't bring you anything. Do you have to go to the toilet?"

"No."

"Well, stop wiggling around. Now what do you want?"

"Let me write it," I said.

She exhaled loudly. "That's the stupidest thing I've ever heard of. You don't know how to write."

"You could show me."

"I'm not going to sit here all day and try to teach you to write, you'd never learn anyway, you're too dumb. Now you either tell me what to put down on this paper, or I'm leaving, and you won't get nothing." She tapped the pencil on the table.

"I want a nigger baby-doll."

"A what?"

"A nigger doll."

"You're nuttier than I thought. I'm not writing that down."

"Okay, then I don't want nothing."

Sister pushed the paper aside and adjusted her chair so she was looking straight at me. "Brother, why in the world, when the *Sears and Roebuck Catalog's* full of toys, would you want a nigger doll?"

"I just do, that's all."

"You've been down to old Henry Crain's place again, haven't you?"

There was no sense lying, she'd find out one way or the other. "I want a doll the same color as Henry."

"Why?"

"Cause he tells me things—teaches me stuff."

Hands on her hips, she said, "Tell me one thing, just one, that old Henry Crain has ever taught you."

"He told me not to kill dung beetles 'cause they clean up the messes left by Mister Romeiser's mules."

"That's it?" she asked, slapping the table and laughing.

"No. He told me that Mister Urstrom and Reverend Littlefield drowned Lester Parsons in the Grand River, or know who did."

Sis jerked back from the table, her eyes wide as silver dollars. "Don't you ever repeat that to anyone, you hear me? Give me that paper." She began to scribble furiously, "Dear Santa: All I want for Christmas is a nigger doll. Signed H. K. Myers." She threw the pencil down. "There. My God, Brother, how can you be stupid enough to listen to that crazy old nigger? You probably carried those bed bugs we got home from his house."

"Don't you call Henry crazy! Momma says we got those bugs from Doctor Carpenter's patients. And I don't want you to write to Santa for me. I'll get Momma to do it."

"Don't you listen to nothing? I told you Momma said I should do your letter. And besides," she leaned toward me and lowered her voice, "there's no such thing as Santa Claus." She pushed away from the table and hurried out of the kitchen.

"There is so," I said. But she was gone.

Mom, Sis, and I were at my Grandmother Carpenter's house on Christmas Eve. Dad had to run up town to get sugar so Grandmother could bake oatmeal cookies.

While he was gone there was a great commotion and jingling of bells on the front porch. Then a loud knock. My mother threw the door open with a flourish, and Santa Claus walked right into Grandmother's house like he owned the place. His voice was hoarse and raspy, and he said it was from hollering at the reindeer. I could barely understand him when he told me to come sit on his lap. With Mom and Sis encouraging me, I whispered in Santa's ear what Sis had helped me write in my letter. And as though by magic, old Santa reached down into his pillowcase and produced a chocolate colored baby-doll. I knew then that my sister had lied. There really was a Santa Claus.

The doll was eight inches long and the color of a Hershey candy bar wrapper, with hair done up in miniature pony tails, and had the most beautiful face I'd ever seen, with soft brown eyes and a pink mouth fixed into a permanent pout. I jumped for joy, and told Santa she was exactly what I had always wanted, and that her name was Mandy. "Why Mandy?" someone wanted to know. I had seen Raggedy Ann and Andy in the Sears Catalog and somehow turned their names into Mandy. Grandmother Carpenter had tears in her eyes. My sister shook her head and smirked when she saw

Mandy, but she got a lot happier when Santa handed her a box. Inside was a soft baby doll with silken blonde hair and over-sized blue eyes that opened and closed, and said, "Waaaaa," every time she was picked up.

None or us knew that 1935 was to be our last Christmas in Utica.

I carried Mandy everywhere. If someone had told me little boys didn't play with dolls, I wouldn't have believed them. I played with my sister and Charlotte all the time. Mandy was perfect, dressed in a beautiful dress with tiny purple flowers in the pattern.

Betsy Sue, my sister's doll, was laying next to Mandy on an orange crate draped with an old towel. We were under the back porch in a playhouse created by nailing cardboard around the back steps. The door was built from wood salvaged from an old packing crate.

"My goodness," Sis said with a heavy sigh, "Betsy has had a time of it."

"What's the matter with her?" I responded in my most fatherly four-and-a-half-year-old voice.

She paused for a long moment, listening to Betsy Sue's breathing through the stethoscope pressed against the doll's upper chest. Then she turned, and in a very serious tone while mimicking the good Doctor Carpenter, said, "There's no doubt, she has the whooping cough. But she's going to be alright now."

"What about Mandy? Is she okay?"

"Mandy, get up here on this table for me so I can take a look at you. Hmmmmm. Well, it looks like she's going to have to have a shot." The syringe and needle were held upward momentarily. "This will sting for just a minute. Please hold her still." I gripped Mandy and held her down while Sis mimicked Dr. Carpenter and administered the dreaded shot.

"There now," my sister said, "that wasn't so bad was it? Mandy will be just fine."

"What about Betsy Sue," I asked.

"As I said, she has had a rough time of it, so I do insist you continue lots of fluids, and you must keep her in bed, but in a few days she'll be just fine. Do you have any other questions?"

Betsy Sue must have been a lot sicker than my sister thought, for in just a few months, we would bury her in a place far, far away from Utica.

CHAPTER 5

A Positive Forecast

June 19, 1936. It was too hot indoors, so Sis let me get out of my damp bed and took me out on the porch. She swept the grasshoppers off the swing and lifted me onto the platform. A feeble breeze dried the sweat on my forehead.

Mom set the radio in the front window and turned it up high, then she and Dad went out in the yard and sat on a blanket. It was too dark to see anything except the red glow of two cigarettes floating in circles where they were sitting. Night creatures filled the air with a hum like a universal motor. A scratchy voice and a lot of static came out of the radio. It was long past my bedtime, so I laid my head on Sis. The rocking motion and the swing's chain squeaking rhythmically put me to sleep.

I woke with a start. Dad was begging. "Get up, please get up!" He sounded like he was on the verge of crying. "Come on Joe, you can do it. Get up . . . damn, he's not going to make it."

The voice from the radio: ". . . eight, nine, ten! Ladies and Gentlemen, Max Schmeling has just knocked out the Brown Bomber with a vicious overhand right. Louis never knew what hit him."

"What's the matter with Dad?" I asked.

Sis put her hand on my arm. "Nothing . . . I mean nothing we did. Some German guy just knocked out Joe Louis."

"What'd he do that for?"

"Shhhh. Dad's upset. Two guys were boxing. You know, fighting—one was from Germany, and the one named Louis was from our country. They just announced it over the radio, the German won."

Later that summer, after Sis told Charlotte the Magic Stick had died, she came over to play under the back-steps. Sis and her boyfriend, Meredith McDowell, came out of the house and told us we were all going to the depot.

The WPA had been busy building sidewalks in Utica, so we wouldn't have to dodge sharp rocks and mounds of manure left by Mister Romeiser's mules on the dirt road, or cut through the fields to get to the depot.

In the summer, the lot next to our house belonged to the banana spiders. They built webs strong as gates across the footpath, where, sentinel-like, they stationed their fat, yellow and black striped bodies. By July, they were the size of silver dollars with long, black legs.

My Grandma Carpenter kept telling me what a big boy I was, and how when I had my birthday in the fall I'd start school. But, it didn't matter how big or how old I got, I wouldn't touch a banana spider—or its web—not even for a Baby Ruth candy bar, especially after Sis told me how they wrapped people up in sticky stuff and sucked out their blood.

When Charlotte and I ducked our heads and came out from under the steps, the thick summer wrapped around us like a mustard poultice. Charlotte, red-faced and sweating, pulled the front of her dress up and wiped her forehead.

Meredith hooted.

My sister snapped, "Charlotte! Where are your underpants? You ought to be ashamed."

Charlotte tugged the dress down in front. The hem had come unstitched and hung six-inches lower in some places, but not in back. When she bent forward, her rear-end flashed like a pair of cue balls. With the back of her hands she rubbed away tears and said her momma ran out of material to sew, and they didn't have money for store-bought.

Sis put her arm around her. "I've probably got a pair or two I've outgrown. They might have a hole here and there, but that's better than none. Come on." She jerked Charlotte up the stairs, and at the top hollered they'd be right back.

On the way to the depot, Charlotte kept pulling her dress up to show us her new-to-her-used panties. At the corner, we turned west, continued past old Henry's shack, and jumped down three steps onto the station platform.

There was no one around except a man and woman sitting on a bench in front of the waiting room. They stared. All four of us were skinny as straws. We must have looked like children whose parents lived at the county infirmary. The yellow and white dress Sis wore had been washed on a scrub-board so many times, you could barely tell the difference between one color and the other. She was the only one of us wearing shoes, a pair of worn-out high-top sneakers. The soul was half gone on one, the other was tied at the top with a broken lace.

The elastic in the legs of Meredith's corduroy knickers had stretched as big as muskmelons and sagged to his ankles. The cord was worn from the knees and seat, leaving shiny spots. The sleeves of his denim work-shirt were cut off at the elbow, and the chest-pocket hit him just above the belly button.

Grandma Carpenter bought my short pants a year ago for me to wear to have my picture taken in Chillicothe. They were the only pair I had with pockets, and I had jammed my hands in and out so much it'd worn holes in the bottoms. A whittling knife my Uncle Gus gave me disappeared through one of those holes, and Mother said I couldn't have another one until I learned how to take care of things. I cried for two days. Now the pants, two sizes too small, were wedged up the crack of my butt causing me to chafe and to pull at them all the time.

Sis gathered us in a circle on the platform. "Here's the game. When the afternoon express comes in, the one who stands closest to the track without flinching wins the prize. Just don't try to touch the engine, you might get hurt."

We jumped up and down. "What'll the prize be?"

"An oatmeal cookie and half a soda-pop."

"You ain't got no cookie," I said. "If Grandma Carpenter had baked cookies, I'd of smelled 'em. And you ain't got no pop either." A bottle of soda pop cost three pennies.

"Brother, don't say ain't, and shut up or you can't play. You don't know anything, but you're always talking."

"Where'd you get the pennies to buy soda?" I asked.

"I didn't buy it, smarty-pants. I found a half-drank bottle on the front steps of Urstrom's."

"What kind?" Charlotte asked.

"Pepsi."

"Where is it?" I wanted to know.

"It's none of your business—unless you win—and everybody knows you're not going to."

Meredith wrinkled his nose and said, "What if a nigger or somebody spit in it?"

"Nobody spit in it, silly." Sis stuck her chin out. "I watched Lattie Davis come out of Urstrom's with that bottle, she took a few drinks and set it next to the post. As soon as she was gone, I ran over and got it."

"Can I have a taste?" I said. The only soda I'd ever had was a swig from a bottle of Higgin's Orange-Pineapple that my cousin Weldon gave me at a picnic. Except for a Baby Ruth Candy Bar Grandmother Carpenter gave me, it was the most delicious thing I'd ever put in my mouth. The saliva flowed. I spat on the station platform.

"You can't have anything unless you win. And you're such a big baby, it'll never happen," Sis said.

Just a few minutes later, the Chillicothe to Kansas City Express rounded the bend a mile up the track. Porters and loaders ran out of the station and scurried about the platform—this train would waste no time in a town the size of Utica. The couple on the bench stood and hugged, the woman dabbed at her eyes. Other passengers came out of the waiting room carrying suitcases and cardboard boxes tied with strings. We dodged people trying to get in position near the track.

A half-mile away, smoke and steam shot from beneath the engine, and sparks flew on both sides of the track as the wheels dug in. It sounded like the cat fight from hell. The steam whistle screamed, and I stuck my fingers in my ears. Bells clanging, the train slid in. My stomach tightened, and the hair on my neck prickled as I edged closer and closer toward the path of the monster. I didn't want the others, especially Sis, to think I was a fraidy-pants. Besides, I wanted some of that Pepsi, so I closed my eyes and held out my hand.

"Are you kids nuts?" a voice yelled. I was swept up by a pair of arms, carried under the overhang and set down hard. Mister Talbot, the station master, said, "I don't ever want to catch you kids out here when a train comes in again, you hear? Where's your folks?"

The engine ground to a stop on the far side of the station, groaning and expelling steam like an exhausted athlete. Passengers hurried on and off, while porters handled luggage and unloaded a small bag of mail. Mister Talbot told us to get on out of there, then he turned and ran toward the engineer who was swinging down from the cab.

A white man with a billed cap, pushing a cart full of boxes and canvas sacks said, "Get out of the way 'fore you get hurt." My sister stuck her tongue out at him. He shook his head and wheeled the cart into the station.

"Who won?" I said.

"Yeah. Which of us got the closest?" Charlotte asked.

Sis closed her eyes like she was trying to figure out who the winner was. "It was a tie between Meredith and me."

I stamped my foot. "You're just saying that so you don't have to give me and Charlotte any." I puffed up. "I'm going to tell Momma you stole Missus Davis's soda-pop."

"I didn't steal anything. She left it there."

"Yeah. Missus Davis is fat as a pig. She's not going to leave anything as good as a soda-pop half drank."

"If your going to be a tattle-tale, crybaby, I'll say it was a four-way tie and everyone gets a bite of the cookie and a sip of Pepsi—but only a sip, you hear?"

The Express let out a scream, spun its wheels, and grunted out of the station toward St. Joe. We forgot about the prize and ran out on the tracks, waving at a man hanging on the back of the caboose with one hand. We kept on waving until the train rounded the first curve and disappeared. By then, the platform was deserted. Mr. Talbot was nowhere in sight, so Sis said we might just as well go inside where it was cool. Through the door and into the waiting room we went. "Pee-yewww," I said, and held my breath. The disinfectant used in the toilets was so strong it burned my eyes. The depot's inside toilets were the only ones in town until Grandma got hers. Sis and Meredith took turns reading the signs above the doors. They said, "LADIES," "GENTLEMEN," and "COLORED USE OUTSIDE TOILET."

"How come the colored can't use the inside toilets?" I asked.

"Shush," said my sister.

"How come the ladies and gentlemen don't use the same hole?" We did at my house, and sometimes two of us sat side by side.

"Brother, be quiet. I'll tell you all about it when we get home."

Charlotte and I went into the toilets together, flushed, then stood outside the door to see if someone carried a pail of water in to fill the water closet. How in the world did the water get in that tank near the ceiling and how did it stay the same depth in the bowl after every flush? When nobody showed up we pulled the chains again to see if the tank was full.

"How does the water get in those tanks?" Charlotte wanted to know, but Sis and Meredith just looked at us like we were dumb, so I guess they didn't know either.

We couldn't figure out the toilets, so we went over to study the water bottle. A sign above it said, "WHITES ONLY." Seemed odd that my friend, Henry, who was colored and got just as thirsty as anybody else, couldn't get a drink from that bottle. I thought about that while Charlotte and I filled paper cups, and watched big bubbles start from the bottom of the bottle and gurgle to the top. We drank all we could hold, then got on opposite sides of the bottle and pressed our noses and tongues against the glass while we crossed our eyes. We laughed so hard we had to run in the toilet to keep from going on the floor.

Sis emptied the drinking bottle by filling her cup and dumping it in the slop bucket while Charlotte and I watched the bubbles. Pretty soon, all the cups, and all but a few drops of the water, were gone.

The ticket clerk, surly in the heat, leaned out of his cage to see what all the commotion was about. His face turned as red as the heart of a ripe watermelon when he saw the empty bottle. "Hey!" he said, "You kids get yourselves away from there. That's for passengers; you've got no business in here."

Sis and Meredith thumbed their noses at the clerk, while we ran between the benches, and out the door. On the tracks we played the tight-rope game, a contest to see which one could walk the farthest without falling. Sis' sneakers gave her a better grip and kept the bottoms of her feet from getting burned. She walked like one leg was longer than the other to keep the bottom of the foot in the torn sneaker off the hot rails. I jumped off to let my feet cool, but everyone hooted, so I got back on. We waggled down the tracks like floppy-armed scarecrows, except Sis who was flapping her arms and bobbing up and down at the same time. She lost her balance and fell off, then wiped her forehead with the back of hand and said she was thirsty for soda pop, and we should go to the house for the prize.

We had turned around and started back, when we saw the dog. It came from the direction of the depot, and was headed straight for us. A lop-eared mongrel loping along cock-eyed between the rails, like a car with its frame knocked out of alignment, its head down, and its tongue lolling within an inch of the cinders.

Sis jumped straight up and hollered, "Mad dog! Hydrophobia," then started running like there was a hot poker in her pants. Meredith was behind her, but the legs of his knickers slapped together so hard he was losing ground.

Charlotte, who was afraid of bugs, animals, adults—everything—caterwauled and hit the cinders sprinting. I had no idea what "hydrophobia" meant, but "mad dog" sounded scary, especially with Sis running flat out and looking back over her shoulder.

The old mongrel arrived at the uphill turn the same time as Charlotte and I, so we cut the corner and barely got out in front.

No matter how hard I tried, I couldn't keep up and the dog closed in behind, panting on the backs of my legs. Sis was ten strides ahead and nearly to the corner, but instead of staying on the sidewalk, she cut through the field and mowed half an acre of banana spider webs down. I let out a bellow heard all over Utica. If my sister was scared enough to run through a nest of banana spiders, there had to be something bad chasing us, and it was only one step behind.

Charlotte and I followed Sis and Meredith through the path they cleared and tumbled up the steps to the front porch. In Utica in the summer, doors were always wide open, but today you could have heard ours slam all over town. We yelled, pounded, and begged to get in. Finally the door cracked and my sister peeked out. Satisfied the mad-dog had not followed us onto the porch, she threw the door open and yelled, "Get in here!"

We fell on the floor bawling.

Everyone except me lined up at the front window. They watched the old dog lope along up the hill past the blacksmith shop, and on out of sight. Sis said she saw the dog foaming at the mouth, and told us we were lucky she had saved us from the dreaded hydrophobia.

I wouldn't go to the window, or get near my Sis for the rest of the day. I was afraid there might be banana spiders hanging on her clothes.

Sis didn't cry often, so I knew something terrible must have happened. I could hear her sobs from the kitchen. I crept into the bedroom and crawled up beside her. "What's the matter?" I asked. Mom was in the kitchen peeling potatos, so I knew she was okay. Must be something wrong with Dad. He had gone off to someplace called Detroit. Maybe he wasn't coming back. Sis kept on bawling, so I laid my head on her shoulder and cried with her.

"What in the world's the matter with you two?" Mom said, standing in the bedroom door, her hands on her hips. "You'd think somebody died."

I raised my head. "Sis," I said, "did you hear, he's still alive."

Sis sat up, rubbed her eyes, and between jerks, said, "Bro . . . ther, whaa . . . t you talk . . . ing . . . bout?"

"Daddy's still alive," I said.

Mother frowned. "Sonny, for God's sake, make sense. Of course he's alive. You two ought to be celebrating, not bawling."

Sis said, "Why couldn't he have gotten a job here, or Chillicothe?"

"I've told you a dozen times—there are no jobs here that pay enough for us to live."

"I'm glad he got a job," I said.

"Oh Brother, shut up!" Sis yelled. "He's going back to work in Detroit and we have to move, and I don't want to leave Meredith and Rosemary. Besides, I hate Detroit." She had gone through her first five years of school in Utica. She dove back into the pillow and wailed. I didn't want to leave my grandmother, and Uncle Vern, and Charlotte, and especially old Henry, so not to be out done, I let out another bellow.

"I've never seen such ungrateful children in my life," said Mom. She turned on her heel and was gone.

Sis rolled over so I could lay my head on her stomach. She ruffled my hair. "Before you were born, we lived in Detroit on a street called Cousins. There was this girl—Pearl—she had long dirty fingernails and used to scratch my face everyday and the scratches would get infected. Mom said if I came home crying with scratches one more time, I'd get a spanking, so the next time Pearl came after me, I grabbed her by the head and pulled out all of her hair. She never scratched me again."

"Did you really pull out all her hair?"

"Well, not all of it, but I brought home two hands full, and she had bald patches on her head." She lay quiet for a minute. "Maybe it won't be so bad. Momma says Dad rented an apartment on the third floor of a building that has an elevator."

"What's that?" I asked. She told me stories about when there was only her and Mom and Dad, and they lived in a place where there were all kinds of stores and movies and stuff to do, but I still didn't want to leave Utica.

Sis went off to school. We waited for a letter from Dad about when to come to Detroit. Charlotte had gone to school too, so when Mom told me to go out and play, I took my doll, Mandy, and set on the back steps. After a while I went to the sand-box and scratched around. The blinds were drawn at Grandmother Carpenter's house. She hadn't come home from visiting a sick friend in Chillicothe. I looked at her chicken coop—sure wasn't going back in there. That left the train station, or my friend, Henry.

I pulled my wagon to the corner. From there to the depot was one block—all down hill. Dad had given the wheels of my rust covered Red Flyer a squirt of oil, so it ran quiet and fast on the new sidewalks. A few pumps for a fast start, and away I went with Mandy in my lap, feet braced against the front, both hands on the tongue, and the wheels thumping across the separations in the sidewalk.

We went rolling so fast I hardly had time to look toward Henry's house before the wagon jumped the three steps down to the station, hit the platform, and catapulted Mandy across the brick paving. I cut hard to keep from going onto the tracks and went through a crowd of people. A fat woman threw her purse straight up in the air and let out a shriek heard clear uptown. Mister Talbot, the station master, grabbed the tongue of my wagon and said, "I'm going to tell your folks. How many times you have to be told, this is no place for a kid to be playing."

"I like to ride down the hill, and I can't stop my wagon," I said.

"What're you doing here by yourself?"

"My sister's in school."

"Well, you stop that wagon before you get to the station. Now git on out of here."

"I've got to get my doll." I got out of the wagon, picked Mandy up, and brushed the dirt and soot off her dress.

"Where'd you git that nigger doll?" he said.

I didn't like the way he said "nigger," sounded different than when I said it, made Mandy sound dirty. I sullied up, and mumbled, "Santa brought her to me."

Several people on the platform snickered. A woman said, "Oh, isn't he just adorable."

The fat lady, on her knees gathering the contents of her purse, said, "Adorable is as adorable does, if you ask me."

Mister Talbot said, "Santa didn't bring no white kid a nigger doll."

"He did so 'cause I asked him to."

"You and that sister of yours are white trash, and I don't want either of you down here. Now get on home, and don't come back."

I tried to figure out what my sister would have done if she'd been there. One thing for sure, she wouldn't let Mister Talbot boss her, or keep her from riding down the hill, so I pulled the Flyer to the top and started down again. I'd find out whether I could stop or turn before I got to the station. I was going faster than a blue-healer on scent when Henry Crain stepped out on the sidewalk, and snatched me out of the wagon. "Whoa dere Little Speck, one ah deese days ya gonna crash dat wagon an hurt you bad. Or you gonna run out in front a train. Then there won't be nothing left of yous cept a grease spot."

Everything seemed okay when I was with Henry. I squeezed his neck, and said, "Don't forget Mandy."

He carried me and the doll to his porch and sat us all down in a rickety old chair. With me balanced on a knee and Mandy on the other, he peered over the wire-rimmed glasses, and said with a wide smile, "Now den Lil Speck, tell ole Henry what you been doin?"

"Riding my wagon to the train station."

He coughed and said, "I could see dat. Now, you listen ole Henry." He put his finger on the end of my nose. "Yous not old enough to go there by yourself. Hear?" Henry's forehead was folded in deep wrinkles between his hairline and wide nose. A wiry, gray beard matched the color of the thin hair remaining on his head.

"My sister's in school, so she can't go with me. How come you got so many creases in your head?"

"I mean maybe yous oughtn't go there at all." He reached across me and jerked a rusty knife out of crooked pole that held the roof of his porch up, bent forward, and speared a potato out of a kettle beside his chair. He made a continuous curlicue out of the skin. When he finished, he cut a slice off the potato and with the point of his knife put it in my mouth.

"There's nothing else to do while my sister and Charlotte go to school. Can I come to your house? That potato sure tastes good."

"Yous come to ole Henry's anytime yous want. You like raw taters? Here." He put half the potato in my hand.

"Can I stay here?"

"Well now, there's a big question. Why you ask such a thing?"

"'Cause my momma says in a little while, we're going to a place way far away, and I don't want to go."

"A chile has to go where his family go."

His answer sounded good in a way, but I'd have to think on it some more. I said, "Them Romeiser boys been mean to you Henry?" I studied his eyes, fascinated by the whites, almost completely brown, which matched the color of the few teeth he had left.

"Oh, they's some bad boys! I's can't go out on dat sidewalk for mor'n a little bit fors dey shoot'n at me wi dat BB gun." He took my hand and put it on the back of his neck. "Feel dat?" My fingers passed over two large knots near the base of his scull. "BBs.," he added.

The Romeiser's barn, across the street, was less than a hundred feet from the sidewalk in front of Henry's place. I heard Dad and Mom talk about how Romeiser's two teenage sons lay in ambush for Henry in the hayloft, and when he came out from under the trees that shaded his house, they took shots at him. "Henry." I hugged his neck. "I don't want them to shoot you anymore."

"Now doe'n you go to crying. Ole Henry not go'n out on dat sidewalk less'n he has to."

"Can't you make them stop?" I asked.

He let his glasses slip off his nose and dangled them on one ear. "Henry," I said laughing. "You look funny."

"Can't keep these derned things on." He fussed for an unnecessarily long time perching his glasses back on his nose. "Doe'n you be worr'n none bout ole Henry. Some day, dey get tired of shooting, or maybe when those boys get older they lose some of their meanness. Maybe not."

We sat for a long moment. "If I lived with you, I bet they'd stop shooting at you!"

"Yous can't live with me, and that's final."

"Then take me to the cistern Henry. Please!" I said with a mouth full of potato. Mom had told me not to go near Henry's cistern. But if I could go to the depot and the railroad tracks, why not Henry's cistern?

"Your mammy and pappy be mighty put out wid ole Henry if he take you where dat cistern be."

"I won't tell, Henry, I promise."

He got up, opened the door to his house and came out with a rusty bucket. "No sense wast'n a trip."

I walked through the woods and brush, holding one of his gnarled hands, and swinging Mandy with my other. The light filtered dimly through the dense foliage. The pungent smell of damp and decaying flora lay heavy in the stillness. "How come the Station Master said Santa wouldn't bring a nigger doll to a white boy?"

"Mister Talbot say so?"

"Uh huh."

"That sompin hard to splain to a young-un. When yous get a little older asks your daddy and momma, they tells you."

"What's it mean when someone says you're white trash?"

We stopped. Henry picked me up, looked in my eyes. "Chil', whatever it is, yous ain't none. Sometimes folks say things bout chil' and doe'n know what they's talk'n bout. That chil' goes along believing somepin not true at tall, jus 'cuz some big person say it. Yous believe yous bad, most likely yous gonna be bad. Same's true bout good. Now stay here til I fills this bucket, then I'll brang yous to the edge."

He struggled with a moss-covered lid. It slide partially to one side creating a black half-moon in the ground. He tied the bucket to a rope and dropped it in the hole. There was a loud whack, and an echo as the sound bounced off the damp walls. He motioned for me to come, then held me over the edge. I peered for a long time into the darkness. After a while I could make out the jagged stone walls covered with green moss, and roots from surrounding trees sticking out between rocks into the cavern like twisted arms reaching out to each other. "Henry, what's that?" I pulled back against his leg. A large blob floated on the water with two pinpoints of light on top unblinking in the darkness.

He chuckled and said, "Dat be Mister Frog, he be da boss aw dis place. See his eyes? And dere his head. He jump off dat rock. I guess he doe'n like my dropp'n dis here bucket in his pool." The frog floated spread eagle on the top of the water. "Bout ever otha bucket dat ere frog, or one his pollywog, gets a ride to the top."

"When you catch a frog, would you save it for me Henry?"

"Naw, you doe'n wan to take Mister Frog home, Chil', 'cuz your folks would know you been to this here well. Yous doe'n wan to git ole Henry in trouble do you?"

I shook my head. "But what do you do with them?"

"I throws em back. I catched some of them frogs when they was pollywogs and I catched them again when they was bull frogs." He grinned as he pushed the lid back on the cistern.

"You sure are lucky, Henry, to have all them frogs."

He picked me up and hugged me. "Lil Speck," he said, "when you go away, remember what ole Henry say—yous ain't no white trash, never will be."

PART II

Detroit and Hazel Park, Michigan

1936-1945

CHAPTER 6

Trouble In Motor City

I unlatched the screen on the kitchen window and swung it out far enough to stick my head over the sill. On the sidewalk three stories down, people scurried about like they were looking for a privy. A streetcar, bell clanging, sparks shooting from wheels and tether, ground to a stop at the corner of Livernois Avenue and Finkel Street sending such vibrations through the ledge I was leaning on it made me wonder why the building didn't fall down. Horns blared. A vendor jingled a bell and at the same time sing-songed, "Eskimo Pies, Creamscicles, Raspberry Popscicles, three cents!" Under an umbrella decorated with the picture of a bottle of beer, a man sold apples, hot dogs, bagels, and para-mutual tickets. The west side of Detroit looked like a carnival this Saturday morning.

A dapper man wearing something on his head like a black bowling ball with a feather stuck in the side came around the corner. He swung a cane jauntily, reminding me of the bandleader who had waved his baton in circles and jabbed it up and down like a sword fighter the last time Sis and I went to an ice cream social in Utica. From the opposite direction, a fat lady with a full shopping bag bounced down the sidewalk with a dead dog wrapped around her neck.

"What're you doing?" My sister asked.

"Watching."

"You are not. I saw you spit out the window."

"It didn't hit anybody. What's that fat woman got around her neck?"

She took the back of my collar. "Don't lean so far. Momma would kill me if you fell out the window."

"What is that?" I repeated.

"It's a fur piece. Don't you know anything?"

A horse-drawn cart with a picture of a smiling cow on the side came around the corner. I couldn't read, but I knew it was the milk wagon.

To get Sis to let go of my collar, I rested my elbows on the soot-covered sill.

She peered over my head at the people below. "I've got an idea, instead of you spitt'n, I'll get the modeling clay, and we'll make bombs."

It was late September, 1936. I'd been five years old for two weeks, and Sis had turned eleven in August. Mom said she was old enough to boss me, but she'd already been doing that for as long as I could remember. Dad had gone back to work at a factory spraying paint on new cars. He'd been laid off the year before I was born, and had not worked again until two weeks ago. When Henry Ford said my Dad could come back to work, Mom, Sis, and I stayed in Utica until he found us a place to live, then we took the train to Detroit. The only thing I remember about the trip was that a skinny gray-haired lady made a fuss over me, and said I looked cute carrying my little nigra doll.

The apartment Dad found for us in Detroit had only one bedroom, so Sis and I slept on a bed that came out of a hole in the living room wall. Mom was always yelling at us to get out of the kitchen, but I had a hard time telling where the kitchen ended and my bedroom started. When we sat at the table, the four chairs were out in the living room or hitting the wall. Even with the chairs crammed as far under the table as they would go, it was still crowded.

The bathroom was next to the bedroom. It had a tub with spigots that Sis said were for hot and cold water, but both were cold most of the time, so Mom would heat a bucket of water on the stove to take the chill out of a tub of water. The toilet was by the tub. Whenever Sis took a bath, I'd say I had to go to the toilet.

She'd yell at me and tell Mom I was being a brat, but Mom couldn't tell whether I was lying, so she'd let me go, especially if I said I was about to mess in my pants. Sis would have to get out of the tub and unlock the door. Then I'd climb up on the pot, fart, and make faces at her.

A glob of clay the size of a quarter ricocheted off of the bowler. "What the hell," the man said, peering into the sky with his cane braced on the sidewalk, his hat in hand. He glanced down at the brim, then up at the pigeons roosting on the top of our building. Sis pulled the screen toward us until there was only a tiny crack. We covered our mouths to stifle laughter. Several pedestrians slowed and looked upward. I chortled through my fingers.

Sis gave me a dirty look. "Brother, shut your mouth. Don't you dare let him hear you!" The screen was ajar just enough to allow a view of the perplexed gentleman. He shook his head and started down the avenue, took two steps, and stooped to pick up the clay projectile. Sis eased the screen open so we could see better. Abruptly Mister Hat turned and looked up. Sis jerked the screen closed. The force of the slamming jumped the hinges out of their brackets and it tumbled end-over-end, careened off of the building, and crashed onto the sidewalk barely missing the lady with the fur around her neck.

"Oh my God, you're in for it now," Sis said. We leaned over the windowsill to see what damage the falling screen had done. The fat lady, directly below, looked at the broken screen at her feet, then at the two heads sticking out of the third story window.

Mister Hat turned and walked back toward the screen juggling the lump of clay in one hand and jabbing toward us with his cane. "You kids are going to hurt someone or fall out of that window and kill yourselves," he called.

The fat lady stood with one hand on her hip, the other on the back of her head to keep a tea-cup sized hat in place, and squinted into the sun.

I was trying to figure out why it was just me who was in for it.

A man carrying a block of ice between a pair of tongs, stepped up on the curb, hesitated for a moment as he looked at the broken screen, and then walked toward the apartment entrance with one of his arms stuck straight out.

Mister Hat said to the fur lady, "Don't worry, I'm going to tell the manager of that apartment what's going on up there." He walked around the corner in the direction of the lobby.

"Get rid of the clay!" Sis ordered.

"But what'll I do with it?" I asked, my feet moving in four directions.

"I don't care—hide it somewhere. Just get rid of it. Now!"

What to do with a wad of gray modeling clay the size of a tennis ball? I bolted for the bathroom. This was self preservation. Sis was sure to tell Mom and Dad it was me who did it.

Thirty minutes later, Mister Curinske, the manager, a squat, shallow man with tufts of hair on his chin, and wearing a dirty Detroit Tigers ball cap, stood outside our door and lectured Mom about something called "liability," that could happen to us and the apartment house if a screen bounced off of a pedestrian's head. Sis swore she knew nothing about the origin of the clay projectile that the manager had in his hand, nor the cause of the fallen screen. Fearing Sis's wrath more than Mom's, I said I didn't know nothing about nothing.

At 2:00 a.m., Dad got up to go to the bathroom. When he flushed the toilet, it overflowed and leaked into the apartments below. The manager was up and down the stairs the rest of the night. The last time he knocked on the door, he held a gooey mass in his hand. "Anybody with any sense ought to know you can't flush stuff like this. Maybe you people never had an inside toilet, but that's no excuse. If it happens again you're gonna hafta move."

Truth was I'd seen inside toilets, one at my Grandmother Carpenter's house and two at the Utica Depot, but no one ever told me you couldn't stuff clay down them. I figured anything soft and the right shape to fit in the hole was fair game.

Sunday morning. Mom looked at the bare spots on the soot covered window-sill, then looked at our soot-streaked arms. Before Sis could blame it all on me, Mom pushed us both into her bedroom and said to stay there the rest of the day. I'd have sooner gotten locked in a hen house full of wasps as to have to stay in one room all day with my sister.

I'd learned my lesson, but not Sis. She would have thrown more stuff out the window except she thought the screen would fall off again. It wasn't Mom or Dad she was afraid of, or much else. When she got older, she would hide in the closet and cover her ears when there was lightning or thunder, and wouldn't cross a bridge without ducking her head or laying in the floorboard of the car. Most of all she would have nothing to do with airplanes. But when she was growing up she was fearless.

Custer Elementary School was five blocks from our apartment. My parents decided that Sis was old enough to be responsible for getting me to and from school. On my first day, she dropped me off at kindergarten, and said she'd be back to get me when school was over.

The teacher took me around the room and introduced me, then set me at one of the tables where a half-dozen other children were bent over their coloring books. In the center of this table, a cigar-box full of crayons was the object of much activity. Hands were in and out, digging around, selecting particular colors or shades, and replacing those already used. I tried to time my searches when no other hands were in the box. An orange crayon was what I needed for a sunset I was coloring. During a lull in activity I reached into the box, and a second later, while I was still digging around, a freckle-faced girl went for a crayon. Her hand brushed against mine. She jerked back like she'd been burned, eyes wide. That's when I noticed that one of her eyes was half green and half brown. I stared, not because of the two different colors, but because she was the most beautiful person I had ever seen. There was sure nothing like her in Utica, Missouri.

At snack time she looked at me with that two-toned eye, took a bite of her cookie, and said, "You have funny hands."

The other kids at the table giggled.

No one in my family had ever said anything about my hands, nor had Charlotte Domineck, so I hadn't really thought about being different until that moment. I looked at all the other hands around the table then at my own. My ears turned red.

After school, when I told my sister about the incident she was steaming. "Don't pay any attention to brats like that. Tell her you're just as good as she is." She drug me along at a pace that required I trot every few steps to stay up with her. "And I'm going to tell your teacher tomorrow."

"Please don't say anything," I said.

"Why not?"

"'Cause. I just don't want you to." I didn't dare tell her I was in love with the girl that had a multi-colored eye. She'd have laughed herself sick.

The most direct route to Custer Elementary was across several empty lots. Mother had told Sis to come "straight home" after school, and she followed the instructions to the letter by cutting across what appeared to be a completely vacant lot. We were half way across when the earth bowed and caved in around us. Sis said, "My God there's an earthquake." We scrambled to climb up a slippery incline while sand, boards, cardboard, and sheet metal fell in around us. Sis pulled me up to solid ground and stood there scratching her head, then started laughing. "I think we just walked across a dugout."

That's when we saw the boy running full gait toward us. He was yelling at the top of his lungs, "How'd you like to have your asses kicked?" He skidded to a stop on the opposite side of what was now a gaping hole in the ground. "Jesus Christ! Look what you've done to our bunkhouse!" He stepped back two paces, took a running jump, and landed right in front of us. He was a head taller than Sis, wore glasses over a pug nose, and snorted like an English Bulldog.

I hid behind Sis's leg. She didn't budge. Looking down with a smile at what was left of an underground clubhouse she said, "How were we supposed to know where your stupid hole was?"

It sent the boy into a rage. "What's so funny? Huh? What's so funny?" He gave her a push.

She stumbled backward and went down hard in the sand on

her behind. She looked straight in his eye as she pulled her skirt over her skinny legs. "Better not touch me again, Mister!"

"Yeah, what're you going to do about it Miss Fart Face?" He smirked as he stood over her, hands on his hips.

"My father's a policeman and he'll put you in jail for being a juvenile delinquent. That's what!"

I was standing a few feet back, shaking. This kid was going to beat us to a pulp and my sister was making up something about Dad being a cop. If he was, it was a well-kept secret.

The boy hesitated, like he had to think about his next move. "I don't believe you." Then he backed off a few inches and said, "Even if he is a cop he can't do anything to me."

Quick to recognize a weakness, Sis took the offensive. "Touch me again," she said. "Go ahead, lay one finger on me, and you'll see whether he can do anything or not." She put her hand behind her in an effort to get up, and there, under her hand was a broken brick.

The boy turned, put his hands in his pockets, and started walking away. Over his shoulder he said, "You'd better not let me catch you around here again if you know what's good for you."

Sis gained her feet, and without taking her eyes off the boy's back she whispered, "Brother, start for home."

"I don't want to go without you," I said.

She was in no mood to argue. "I told you to start for the apartment and I meant it. Now get!" The most I could bring myself to do was walk backwards, so I'd at least know whether she was going to be killed. The brick was behind her back. The boy meandered along, cocky-like. At half the distance between a pitcher's mound and home plate, Sis hollered, "Hey four-eyes!" and threw the brick like she was trying out for the Detroit Tigers. He turned, and the projectile hit him in the center of his forehead. He went down like a sack of wet cement. "Run Brother, run!" she screamed. I was going full out when she came alongside, grabbed my wrist, and away we flew.

That night, the boy who had pushed my sister down, stood in our front hall with his mother and father. He didn't look near as sinister with his head wrapped in a bandage. I hid behind Sis while she peeked around the corner of the kitchen to listen to the boy's parents argue with Mom about a doctor's bill and the cost of broken glasses.

After the boy with the bandage left, everyone was happy and laughing. Dad had gotten his first paycheck in six years. He poured shots out of a quart bottle of Imperial setting on the kitchen table and kept saying, "Let's have a party." More people came into our apartment, and Mom put me to bed in her room. I griped about having to go to bed when Sis didn't.

I woke up drenched in sweat. It felt like an ice pick was probing my ear. The slightest movement made it worse. I didn't want to get up and I didn't want to cry out, so I laid there hoping someone would open the bedroom door to check on me. A steady rumble of voices, punctuated by episodes of shrieking laughter, came through the closed door and made my ear throb. The walls vibrated from the volume of a radio. I changed my mind, I had to find Mother.

There was a thick haze in the apartment, and the living room and kitchen were crowded with people. I didn't see anyone I knew, so I stood at the edge of it all with one hand over my ear. It had been a mistake to get out of bed. I had never seen these people before, and I didn't even recognize this strange place I was standing in. The din was so loud, no one heard me crying. I turned around and started toward the bedroom and ran into Dad pulling Mother by the arm.

"What's he doing up?" Dad asked, looking at me, but talking to Mom.

She kneeled and asked, "Why are you crying?"

"My ear hurts."

"Well, you should be in bed if you have an earache."

I wailed. I was going to end up back in bed, and both Mom and Dad acted like I had done something wrong.

A strange man with breath as rancid as mule piss, bent over in front of me and made some comment about what a cute little boy I was and that I should quit crying. Dad picked me up under his arm and headed for the bedroom. Mom tucked me in, then she and Dad backed out of the room. I increased the volume of my bawling. Back they came, "Sonny, I want you to try to go to sleep," she said.

"But I can't go to sleep, my ear hurts. I want my sister!"

"She's visiting a friend."

"My ear hurts—real bad."

Mother sat down on the side of the bed and felt my forehead. "Dad," she said, "he might have a little fever. Stay with him while I get an aspirin."

In a few minutes, she was back with a glass of water and a pill.

"Will it make my ear stop hurting?" I asked, as she offered me the medicine.

"Dad, blow some smoke in his ear. Maybe that'll make it stop hurting."

Dad sat on the side of the bed, and lit a Camel.

"What are you going to do?" I screamed.

He pulled my hand away from the side of my head, took a drag on the cigarette and blew a mouth full of smoke into my ear. I twisted and turned, but he held me and did it several more times. I coughed, wheezed, and gasped for breath. "There," he said, "that ought to do it."

The next morning, I woke up in the pull-down bed in the living room. Sis was sitting beside me, her legs folded in front like a Buddha, and a magazine across her lap. "You Okay ?"

"My ear hurts. Where's Momma?"

"They're still in bed."

"Where'd you go last night?"

She flipped a page of the magazine. "What do you care?"

"Did you go to the picture show?"

"If you must know, Mr. Nosey, I went downstairs to Sarah's."

"What for?"

She slammed the magazine closed. "Would you please shut up?"

"I'm hungry."

"Thought you were sick." She reached over and put the back of her hand on my forehead, then turned it over. "Sarah and I listened to her radio, she's got one of her own in her room."

The front door buzzed, sounding like a one-winged cicada twirling on a hot sidewalk. Sis jumped up and ran to the door in her pajamas. Without removing the night chain, she peeked through the crack.

Mister Curinske's voice: "Go get your parents."

"They're still sleeping," said Sis.

"I'd hate it if they missed lunch, so get 'em up."

Sis slammed the door in the manager's face as Mom came out of the bedroom putting her arm into a housecoat. "What's going on out here?"

Sis lowered her voice and pointed her thumb to the door. "It's that Mister Curinske. Says he has to talk to you and Dad."

Mom took the chain off and opened the door. "Good morning Mister Curinske," she said. "What can I do for you?"

He pulled at a tuft of hair on his chin, stepped inside, and surveyed the carnage. Empty bottles and cigarette packages littered the floor. Catsup spilled on the kitchen table was dripping off the oilcloth. "I'll tell you what you can do for me, Missus Myers. You can get out of this apartment. And I want you to vacate no later than next weekend. You people have been nothing but trouble since the day I first laid eyes on you." He handed Mom a paper.

"Our rent is paid," she said. "And we have a deposit up."

"Yeah—you're paid until next week. Read the eviction notice and you'll see what happened to your deposit." He turned on his heel and was gone.

Bacon sizzled on the stove. I blew on a piece of buttered toast with hot milk poured over it. Sis looked at her magazine. Dad stared blurry-eyed at the paper Mister Curinske had given Mom while he sipped a cup of coffee. "Listen to this," he said. "That bastard charged us a dollar and twenty-nine cents for a screen. What screen?" Sis stuck her nose farther into the pages of the magazine. I put my finger in the milk to see if it was cool enough.

Mom said, "The kids were looking out the window, and a screen fell off."

"And look at this—five dollars for plumbing. What a crook.

And the rest of the deposit he says will go for cleaning. Four dollars to clean this place?"

Mom brought Dad and Sis plates of bacon and eggs. "I can clean this apartment in an hour and a half. We have to have at least part of our deposit back if we're going to find another rental."

"Well I don't like this dump anyway," Dad said, diving into his breakfast. "There's no privacy. I'll find something else."

CHAPTER 7

To Wish Upon A Gum Ball

The "something else," Dad found for us was a one-car garage converted into two rooms with an outside toilet on Vassar Street, in a suburb of Detroit called Hazel Park. It was smaller than the apartment we had just left, and everything inside and out was so dilapidated no deposit was required. It would be real hard to damage this place.

The room where Mom and Dad slept had long ago been finished with stained, unpainted wallboard, and was barely large enough to accommodate their bed, a small night stand, and a slop jar. The other area served as both living room and kitchen and came with a relic of a couch whose cover had been lacerated exposing rusty springs. At night, it was where Sis and I slept.

Not long after we moved in, Sis said she was going to take me to Hazel Park's business district. I got excited, and shook all the money out of my piggy bank—two pennies and a nickel. Sis begged Mom for a nickel so she could get an ice cream cone, but she said we wouldn't have any money until Dad got paid. I told Sis I'd split my ice cream with her, so she agreed to go. When we got to Nine Mile Road, the business section of Hazel Park, we walked along the street peering in all the shop windows. "Wait, I want to go in this one," I said pulling her hand toward the door of a candy shop next to the Hazel Park Theater.

"Don't spend your money in there. I thought we were going to the dairy for an ice cream cone—you can't have both, so make up your mind." She started on down the sidewalk. "Let's look in more windows. You go in that place and there'll be a million things you'll want."

"I just want to look. Can I, please?"

She grumbled and came back, opened the door, and pushed me in. The man behind the counter wore a dirty apron and was picking his teeth with a matchstick.

The store smelled so good it made my stomach growl. The glass cases were full of black and red licorice twists as long as my arm, Gumby Bears, malted milk balls, chocolate peanut clusters, Milk Duds, peppermint patties, and all kinds of candy bars, including chocolate clusters with maple centers, and Baby Ruth's. Sis pulled me aside and whispered, "You're not buying anything in here, there's flies inside the candy cases."

I started to argue. That's when I saw the gum-ball machine, a glass globe the size of a soccer ball, full of different colored gum balls, including a few that were speckled. "What's this say?" I asked, pointing to a sign on the machine.

Sis stuck her nose close and read: "Gum Balls One Cent. If You Make a Wish and Get a Speckled Ball, Your Wish Will Come True, *Plus* You Win a Dime!"

"Let's do it," I said jumping up and down. "Please, let's try to win a dime!"

She looked at the globe, walked all the way around it with her hands on her hips. "There's some speckled balls in there all right, but I'll bet they're all on top."

"No. Look here." I pointed to a spot near the neck of the globe where the balls dropped into the chute. "There's some near the bottom."

"Okay. But just one penny, and don't say I didn't warn you."

I grabbed her around the waist and hugged. "I can win, I know I can. What should we wish for?"

"Wishes don't come true," she said.

"Yes they do." I put the penny in the slot, closed my eyes, and twisted the knob.

There was a metallic click as a gum ball fell into the chute. I opened my eyes and lifted the latch. A green ball fell into my hand.

Sis stomped her foot. "See, I told you that thing was a waste of money, now come on."

I put the green gum in my mouth. Lordy, it was nasty, but I wasn't about to tell Sis. "Let's put my other penny in."

"I told you no."

"Please. We'll still have a nickel and you can have most of the ice cream cone, I'll even let you pick the flavor."

"Okay, if you want to throw your money away, go ahead. But don't come crying to me after it's gone."

I put the penny in, closed my eyes, and turned the knob. The ball hit the slot, and I opened the latch, then barely opened one eye. There laying in my hand was a beautiful speckled gum ball. I jumped straight up. "I got one . . . I got one!"

"Let me see," she said. "My god, you did!"

"I told you we could win."

"You sure did. Give it to me and I'll collect your dime." We walked to the counter where my sister stuck out her hand. "My brother got a speckled gum ball." I could tell she was proud.

"Okay," said the man behind the counter, "go ahead and pick yourself out a dime's worth of candy."

"We'd rather have the money," Sis said.

He took the matchstick out of his mouth. "Well, I'm sorry, you have to take merchandise." He bent over to continue restocking one of the cases.

"It doesn't say that on the sign, and we don't want candy."

"Why not?" came the voice from below the counter.

"'Cause it's got fly shit on it."

The man stood up and looked first in both directions and then at Sis. "You'd best watch your mouth. If you don't want to take your prize in candy, get on out of here."

I started crying. Sis jerked the back of my shirt and said, "Stop that whining." Then she turned back to the man. "Listen Mister, you'd better give my brother his dime, or I'll tell my father. He's on the Hazel Park Police Force, and he'll close your shop."

She sure knew how to scare people. The man punched the cash register and handed me a dime. We danced all the way to the dairy store. While we waited for our triple-dip cones, she said, "What'd you wish for?"

"If I tell, it won't come true."

"It won't anyway, so what'd you wish?"

I figured she was probably right. "That Dad wouldn't drink anymore whiskey." Sis got real quiet for awhile.

On the way home we cut up, and took turns licking each other's ice cream. "Brother, lick on the other side, it's running down your arm! Now it's running down this side. Hurry up. My God, I've never seen anyone so slow." She laughed when the sticky stuff ran down my arm and dripped off of my elbow. She skipped away. "Don't come near me. You're nasty."

After the ice cream was gone, we had a contest to see who could make the ugliest face. She won by pulling her eyes down and pushing her nose up at the some time. Then she taught me some dirty words. The one I liked best was, "shit-for-brains," which was what she said the man in the candy store had.

I was still laughing when half a block from the house a loud scary voice boomed from the direction of our house. It was Dad, and he sounded like he was fighting for his life. He yelled, "I'll whip your ass all over Detroit." Sis and I ran through the front door. She headed straight to the bedroom where his voice was coming from, but I was scared and tiptoed past our sleeping couch, and peered around the corner of the doorsill expecting to see Dad engaged in mortal combat with a burglar or pervert.

Mom almost knocked me down coming out of the room. "He's gone crazy," she said. "Must of gotten hold of some rotten gin."

Dad stood against the wall with Sis's doll, Betsy Sue, in one hand held just high enough to keep Sis, who had climbed up on the bed, from reaching it. She was crying and begging him not to hurt her doll. It didn't matter that she was skinny as a straw, she fought like a tiger, arms flailing, her hands opening and clenching in an attempt to rescue her doll. Dad's eyes were unfocused, and he babbled about not letting some son-of-a-bitch get away with something. The first thing I thought of was the speckled gumball. *I knew I shouldn't have told Sis. It put a hex on my wish, and that's why it didn't come true.* He swung the doll outward in a curve, then back and smashed it against the wall. Sis screamed. He shook the wounded doll like a dog shaking a sock. Pieces fell to the floor.

Mom stuck her head around the door and handed Sis a large thermos bottle. In the next instant my skinny, eleven-year-old sister, whose arms were as big around as a noodle and who couldn't have weighed more than sixty pounds, raised the thermos, and with a wood-chopping motion slammed it down on Dad's head. The metal skin of the bottle collapsed and the glass lining exploded. I started wailing. Mother and Sis screamed, and Dad was cussing at the top of his lungs. It sounded like a massacre, but in our neighborhood no one would pay the least bit of attention.

When the thermos shattered, Dad didn't blink but he let out a roar, and slammed the doll again. A leg flew off. He swept Sis off the bed as though he were brushing away a cobweb. She went flying and smashed into the wall. Mom ran, grabbed her, and pulled her away, leaving an outline of her skinny body in the crumpled plaster board.

An hour after Dad passed out, Mom laid down to rest. Sis and I gathered up as many pieces of Betsy Sue as we could find, and put them in a shoe box. I took my doll, Mandy, and the three of us went out the back door to an open area behind the toilet. Sis dug a hole large enough for the shoe box, placed the make-shift coffin in the ground, and filled the hole with dirt. I started toward the house. "Wait," she said. "I think I should say something about how we will all miss Betsy Sue. You know, like how much fun we had with her . . . or something." I stopped and stood there behind the toilet staring. She stomped on the spot where the shoe box was buried pretending to pack the dirt down, then looked up and said, "God, how come you let my dad destroy Betsy Sue? She never did nothing to him, and I don't think I ever did anything to You. I won't ask anything else, but could you please let my brother's wish come true? And You'd better hurry before he does this to one of us."

* * *

June 2, 1937. It was like a bad dream—someone was trying to knock the front door down. I poked Sis until she woke up. We were sitting in the dark wondering what to do when Mom rushed past our bed. "Who is it?" she said through the door.

"Telegram," a voice said.

Mom opened the door and signed something. We followed her back in the bedroom and sat on the edge of the bed while she tore the envelope open. Grandmother Carpenter had died.

Before daylight, the car was packed and we were on the road. This would be our first trip back to Utica since moving to Michigan the previous September, and we would do it nonstop.

Seven-hundred-twenty-five miles of rutted roads with unmarked detours wasted dozens of miles and several hours of driving. It would be a test for the 1928 Model A Ford, given to us by the grandmother whose funeral we would attend, and for Dad's nerves stretched thin from lack of sleep and want of alcohol. The mood was anxious and fearful, everyone trying hard not to do or say something that would cause Dad to stop and buy a bottle. We traveled west and slightly south across Michigan to Chicago, then on to Joliet, Bloomington, and into a soupy fog at Springfield, Illinois, where I was jolted upright by Mother's scream.

Dad had been driving with his head out the window cursing the night and the gods for the thick fog. Mom was doing the same on the passenger side. The headlights shot milky beams ten feet into a thick mist and then disappeared. Suddenly Mom grabbed the steering wheel causing the car to swerve onto the shoulder. A truck sped past, its horn blaring. The Model A bumped to a stop. Dad said, "Where in blazes did that truck come from?" We had been driving the wrong way on a divided highway.

When we came to the Mississippi River Bridge at Hannibal,

Missouri, Sis fell to the floorboard and screamed all the way across. The last leg took us across the top of Missouri through Macon, Brookfield, and seven miles past Chillicothe to Utica. Twenty-seven hours to complete a journey that in those days should have taken nineteen.

Grandmother's living room was full of strange people crowded around a shinny wooden box. Everyone was talking so low I couldn't hear what they were saying. Dad lifted me up so I could look into the face of my dead grandmother, and Momma told me to give her a kiss. I understood I would never see her again, so I bent my head and touched my lips to her cheek—it was so cold it gave me the creeps, and made me shudder. I remembered the times when it was cold outside and I was playing by myself, she would tap on the kitchen window and motion for me to come inside. I loved it when she picked me up and held me tight against her warm, soft stomach and then fixed us steaming cups of cocoa with marshmallows on the top in a kitchen that always smelled like something good was baking.

One of my first memories in life was of Grandmother Carpenter's gentle hands when I was jolted awake by the wailing of the nightly passenger train to Kansas City. The train, with a full head of steam, roared through the Utica Crossing a few hundred feet from where we slept, its wheels clickety-clacking, the house shaking. The sound of my cry would blend with that of the engine's whistle as the train sped along the edge of town, and past the darkened station. Over the years, the sound of a steam engine's whistle at night, evoked strange emotions—fear, loneliness, and the need for human contact. The morning after sleeping at her house, I would shuffle into the kitchen sleepy-eyed, and be lifted onto a pedestal made special for me by Grandfather Myers out of a block of solid cherry wood. My favorite breakfast was hot sugared water with a touch of coffee for color, lots of fresh cream, and cinnamon toast for dunking.

The night of the funeral, the big people sat around talking about Grandmother and eating Mom's fried chicken. Some of the stuff they said made me sad, so Dad took me outside and stood with me by the pump. The only light in Utica came from dimly lit windows of a few scattered houses. It was a clear and moonless night. Every star in the Milky Way glittered. "What happens to a person when they die?" I asked.

Dad didn't say anything for a long time. Then he said, "I don't think anyone knows. A lot of people think they do, but I doubt it."

"Did Grandma go to heaven like the preacher said?"

Dad moved the pump handle up and down, causing it to squeak. "The preacher is one of those who says he knows."

"Do you believe in God?" I asked.

"Yeah, I think I do." He took a rusty cup off of a hook made from a clothes hanger, filled it from a thin stream of water, then held it toward me. "Drink?"

"Huh uh. Would that be heaven?" I pointed to the glittering night sky.

Dad took a long drink from the cup. "Nothing like Utica water," he said, and emptied the remaining drops onto the ground. He looked up at the path of stars. "Could be heaven—probably is."

"Sure looks pretty," I said.

In the months following our move to Detroit, I had dreamed of returning to the rolling, wooded hills of northwestern Missouri. The dream had come true, but on this trip there was no joy, no return to the familiar, as I had imagined. I didn't get to say hello to old Henry or Charlotte, or spend time at Uncle Vern's farm. The day following the funeral we headed northeast. Dad had to get back to Detroit for fear of losing his job.

I said goodbye to Utica and to Grandmother Carpenter, whose death would play a major role in my survival . . . one she could not have anticipated, and one I wouldn't recognize until many years later.

CHAPTER 8

Santa Claus Cometh

In the days and weeks after our return from Missouri, there was a whirlwind of activity. We were in and out of Sears & Roebuck, Montgomery Ward, and Penney's dozens of times. We even went to Hudson's Department Store, downtown. I guess we tried on every piece of clothing in Detroit shopping for new wardrobes. Next, Dad came home from work with a brand new Ford car and parked it outside the garage apartment on Vassar. Lots of people came by to look at it. There weren't many cars on our street, let alone new ones.

A week later, the night of June 22, 1937, Joe Louis Barrow, also known as, The Brown Bomber, from Detroit, Michigan, knocked out James (Cinderella Man) Braddock in the eighth round to become the Heavyweight Champion of the World. Everybody in Detroit was celebrating except Louis. At the press conference following the fight, the title holder said he didn't want anyone calling him "Champ," until he beat Max Schmeling, the German, who had defeated him the year before.

And then the most remarkable thing.

It was Saturday morning, the first weekend in July. I was zooming back and forth, and up and down, like a bird high above my sister's head, balanced on a pillow. She was on her back, the pillow on her feet. My favorite thing for Sis to do—the airplane ride. On one of the up-swoops, I went higher than the window sill and caught a glimpse of Mom getting out of their new car. Dad stayed behind the wheel. When the car door slammed, Sis let me crash into the bed.

Maybe they had brought us candy or something, I sure hoped it wasn't more clothes.

Momma stuck her head in the door and said, "You kids get dressed, we want to show you something."

Sis and I sat forward, leaning on the front seat of the new car so we could watch the speedometer. We begged them to tell us where we were going, but they were quiet with smug expressions on their faces. After we drove a few blocks north on John R. Avenue, Dad turned west on Browning Street. The houses were all shapes, sizes, and ages. Those on the end of the street where we turned were old, many dilapidated and run down. The entire street consisted of two long blocks sandwiched between John R. and Stephenson Highway. The closer we got to Stephenson, a divided highway, the more vacant lots there were, and the newer the houses. Some were built of brick.

Dad pulled the Ford into the driveway of a vacant house with a "For Sale By Owner," sign in front.

"What're we stopping here for?" Sis asked.

"We want to show you something inside," Mom said.

We walked up the steps. The entry door was shaped like a church window, its top curved, and had a small window too high up for me to see through. Dad took a key out of his pocket and opened it. When we walked in, Momma's heels made a clicking sound, and echoed off the shiny oak floors. To the right was a huge living room, to the left stairs led to the second floor. We turned right. I could see the porch, the street, and north to where Stephenson Highway curved and turned back into a two lane street.

They led us though something called a dining room, two-thirds the size of the living room, lined with windows on the east, and which connected to the kitchen through a solid oak swinging door. Sis, real excited, kept asking why we were going through an empty house. But Mom and Dad wouldn't say a word.

A breakfast nook in the kitchen looked out onto a long, narrow backyard. Next to the kitchen was a room for either a study or an extra bedroom with a window opening onto the driveway. A doorway on the side of the kitchen led down three steps to a landing where you could continue on through an outside door to the driveway, or turn right and go down into a full basement.

"Okay kids, this is really what we wanted to show you." Dad said, and headed up the stairs.

There were three large bedrooms, and across the hall was a bathroom almost as big as Mom and Dad's bedroom on Vassar Street. The basin and stool sparkled. Ceramic towel racks matched the white tile floor, which continued a quarter of the way up the wall. The tub was large enough for a six-year-old to swim in. "I have to pee," I said.

Momma jerked my arm. "Say number one."

"I have to go number one."

"Wait just a minute," Dad said. "Come here kids." We gathered in the hall outside the white bathroom. Dad pointed toward two of the three bedrooms. "Shirley Jean, this will be your room, and Son, this will be yours."

"We gonna move again?" I asked.

Sis was standing there like Saul's wife who, according to my Sunday School teacher, had been turned into a salt shaker.

"Yes," Mom said, "But this will be the last time 'cause we bought this house."

Sis started crying. "You don't mean it. I was hoping you'd say this was going to be our home. I started hoping you'd say it from the minute we entered this beautiful place, but I didn't dare say anything 'cause I thought it could never be." She grabbed Dad around the neck and boo hooed real loud, then said, "You're not fooling us or anything are you?"

Momma started crying. She blew her nose and through the tissue said, "We signed the papers this morning. It's ours. From now on our home will be at 428 W. Browning Street."

"That's a beautiful address," Sis said clasping her hands.

"I don't want to move here," I said.

There was silence. Then Dad shook his head. "Be damned if I know how to please him."

Mom dabbed at her eyes with the tissue. "Why not Son, why wouldn't you want to live in this wonderful house?"

I pointed to the room Dad said would be my separate bedroom. "'Cause I want to sleep with Sis."

Sis started laughing. "Is that all? Don't worry Brother," she patted my head. "If you get scared at night, I'll be in the room right next to you."

The idea left me cold, but everyone else was happy, and I couldn't deny that compared to what we'd been living in since arriving in Michigan, it was a palace. "Now can I pee?"

"Yes," said Mom, looking at Dad to see if he was still upset, "if you'll say number one."

But it was too late, I was already making a stream in our new toilet. "When can I take a bath?"

Everyone, even Dad, started laughing.

Sis said, "Boy, there's a good one. Brother wants to take a bath."

In August, 1937, we moved into the house on Browning Street. I was at the east end of the porch trying to stay out of the way, watching movers struggle up the three front steps onto the porch with our new furniture. The lots the houses were built on in this development were narrow like someone had been afraid of running out of land. On the west, a house was close enough to spit on. On the east, the neighbor's driveway was only a few feet from our property, so I had a clear view as Vivian and Wayne Schmidt came out of their front door, cut across our lawn, and climbed the steps to where I was perched on the railing. Vivian, a round-faced girl with Nordic features, appeared to be about nine years old. Wayne, like myself, would have his sixth birthday in less than a month. Their older brother, Kenneth, was the same age as my sister.

The only friend I'd had in Missouri, was Charlotte, so I was ill at ease with the prospect of meeting this boy and his older sister.

We exchanged names and stood around awkwardly for a few minutes. Then Vivian asked me what my father did for a living.

I knew Dad worked in a factory for some man who built cars. That wasn't very exciting. My sister had impressed me with the results she had achieved with a lie told in two different emergency situations since we had moved to Detroit. I had learned that a fiction carefully placed is strong medicine.

"He's a policeman," I blurted, hoping this nine year-old girl would be impressed with the newcomer on the block. Maybe she was, but not for long. The first time I went to the Schmidt's house with Wayne, his mother wanted to know which police force my father worked on. I stuttered and hem-hawed around and said I couldn't imagine where they got the idea my dad was a cop. It was my word against Vivian's. She would never speak to me after that.

Most of the kids my age on Browning Street, went to Martin Road Elementary School. Two families, the Pearls and the Browns, sent their children to St. Mary's Catholic Academy on Nine and One-Half Mile Road.

The day after Labor Day, 1937, Mother walked me to school. She kept reminding me to pay attention, so I'd be able to find my way home. She would not be able to come and get me. Dad's workday started at seven a.m. and concluded at 3:30 p.m., which was the same time school let out. Driving time from Ford's Highland Park plant, where he worked, to our house was twenty minutes, which meant Mom could either walk to school and escort me home, or be at the door to greet Dad when he pulled into the driveway.

On this morning, Mom and I stayed on the sidewalk along Stephenson Highway to Nine and One-Half Mile Road, turned west on the graveled road adjacent to an open sewer, went another two blocks, and there it was, Martin Road Elementary, a two story structure shaped like a saltine cracker box with a dirty brick veneer.

Mother had insisted I wear my new clothes which were supposed to be for Sunday School. The first time I wore that outfit in the neighborhood, I almost got beat up. The kids called me a sissy. I told Mom about the reaction the new outfit caused, but she insisted I put them on, so I showed up for the first day of school, dressed like some rich geek in a room full of impoverished kids whose clothes looked as though they had come from the wardrobe of the play, *Dead End*.

Miss Borchec, the First Grade teacher, spent half the morning writing rules on the blackboard under her name, reading them to the class, and making us recite them back to her. "Rule No. 1: We will not talk during class unless we get permission from our teacher. Rule No. 2: We will not go to the lavatory without first getting permission. Rule No. 3: We will not chew gum in class. Rule No. 4: We will bring the following items to school: a box of tissues or a clean handkerchief and cover our mouths and noses when we cough or sneeze; a padded oil cloth to lay on during our rest period; 40 cents for a years subscription to the *Weekly Reader*, 10 cents each week to pay for snacks." And on through the list. When we finished our recitation, Miss Borchec handed each of us a paper with all the rules to take home for our parents to sign.

I was sure glad when we finished reciting and the teacher said we could go out for morning recess. There were three other kids from Browning Street in my grade, but on the playground they disappeared into small groups of strange faces. I sauntered out the door and stood on the high steps looking across the soccer field. Not a blade of grass anywhere. Mister Parrish, the school janitor, who, on Sundays, was also the pastor of the Calvary Baptist Church, had covered it all with a thick layer of cinders. There was no gymnasium and no physical education program, only the cinder-covered playground with a set of swings, a slide, and a teeter-totter. This was where unsupervised mayhem occurred during two recesses and a lunch period for all six grades, each school day.

Leo Bradford was stocky, three inches taller than me, and wearing a beat up old leather helmet. It was strapped under his chin and was supposed to make him look like a World War I aviator. Instead, with the cap pulled down over his pointed head, he looked like a walking bullet. Leo's sidekick, Red McCauley, was paper-thin, with a face like a freckled weasel, and endowed with a shock of carrot-red hair growing too close to his fiery eyebrows.

Leo and Red were slouched against the building, their hands dug into their pockets, and matchsticks dangling from their mouths. Maybe they had been waiting for me. They pushed away from the building with their shoulders and made a motion with their heads for me to come down off the porch and join them. They seemed friendly enough.

As I came off the steps, I remembered the girl at Custer Elementary, with the two-colored eye, and put my hands in my pockets.

"Wha'cher name?" the carrot-topped one asked.

"H. K. Myers," I said.

"Naw, not your initials, yer name."

"Well, my name's, Hiram, but I get called lots of different things."

Leo and Red hee-hawed. "Yeah, with a name like Hiram, I'll bet you do," said Bullet-Head. "What grade you in?"

"First."

"Ol' Red and me, we's in the Third and kinda have our way around here." He looked at my clothes. "How much money you got?"

"I ain't got none," I thought of my sister. "I mean I haven't got any."

"Where'd ya git that southern talk?" One of them asked as they guided me toward the center of the playground. "Those sure are fancy rags. You sure you ain't got some money?" By the time we stopped, Red had disappeared.

Leo grabbed my wrist and pulled my hand out of my pocket. "What ya hiding in there?" He forced me to open my fist. It was empty, but he looked for a long moment, held it up and displayed it to several kids standing around and asked, "What's the matter with your hands?"

I couldn't think of anything to say. Several other kids meandered over to see what was going on. Soon there was a small gathering in a circle behind Leo. One of the newcomers said I was in their class and that Leo ought to leave me alone.

Leo pushed him back and said, "Git on out of here and mind your own business. Little Hiram will jist have lots of fun with me'n ol' Red, won't he?"

Nobody replied, so I half-heartedly nodded. He grinned and gave me a push. I went into a backward somersault over Red McCauley, who had knelt on his hands and knees behind me. I landed with a thump and got up crying. I put my hand on the back of my head. It came away bloody.

"Now wasn't that fun? If yer a good li'l hillbilly, we'll play the same game tomorrow, that is, unless you bring some money."

"I'm going to tell my sister," I said.

"You hear that, Leo?" Red asked, roaring with laughter. "He's going to tell his sister." They walked away chuckling, with their arms slung casually over each other's shoulders. Then they turned like they were part of a chorus line and said, "If you go to blabbing—you know, being a big mouth, we'll meet you after school every day and beat the living shit out of you. Understand?" I nodded. They turned around and walked back into the school. When the teacher asked why I'd been crying, and what happened to my head, I told her I had fallen off a swing. She sent me to the office where the school nurse picked some cinders out of the wound, dabbed on some Mercurochrome, and sent me back to Miss Borchec.

When school let out that afternoon, I stood on the steps to see if Leo and Red were lurking around. By the time I felt it was safe, the other kids from Browning Street were gone. I hurried away from the building and glanced over my shoulder as I walked, thinking about having to go to school every day with Leo Bradford and Red McCauley. Suddenly it occurred to me that nothing looked familiar. I was on a street with stores and shops I'd never seen before.

Several blocks later, I stood against a building, rubbed the back of my head, and tried to figure out what to do—keep going and watch for a policeman, or turn around and try to find my way back to school? What if it got dark? The more I thought about it, the more bewildered I became. I screwed up my face to keep from crying.

A lady with a shopping bag passed, then came back and asked what was wrong. My dad had told me to never speak to strangers, so I stood there chewing my lower lip. "Where's your mother?" she asked. I said nothing. "Don't be afraid. I won't hurt you." Her voice was gentle, like Grandmother Carpenter's during the nights when the train shook our bed. After a minute, she said, "Okay, if you don't want to tell me I'm going to leave."

"No. Please don't go," I blurted. Then I told her I couldn't find my way home from school, and that some kids had pushed me down, and I was afraid they were going to beat me up again.

Did I know my address, she wanted to know.

With great relief I recited what my sister had pounded into my head, "Four Twenty-Eight West Browning Street."

"That's not too far from here, so don't you be worrying." She picked me up, gave me a hug, and put me in her car.

We rode in silence for several blocks, then her car slowed in front of a strange house. Panic boiled in my stomach. She's like the witch in Hansel and Gretel, and will take me in this house and kill me. I had to escape. So the instant the car stopped, I'd jump out and run for it. The car slowed and I opened the door. A woman who looked like Mother came running down the steps of this house, swooped me up, and carried me around to the driver's side. She thanked the lady for bringing me home. I looked at the house in amazement—I hadn't recognized my own home. Mother was bent over, looking down through the open window, when the lady said, "If you don't mind my asking, how did your son end up alone with a cut on his head."

Mom curtly thanked her again, instructed me to say goodbye, turned on her heel, and carried me to the house. I got in trouble for two reasons. I had told Mom I knew how to get home when I didn't, and I got in a car with a stranger. "But what was I supposed to do?" I asked.

"You should have stayed at school and told someone there you didn't know your way home. Sis or someone would've come to get you."

"I thought I knew." Maybe my wound would elicit some sympathy. "Look what someone did to my head," I said.

She looked. "Well, it's been doctored, so it'll be just fine."

Sis was at the dining room table doing her seventh grade

homework when I came through with my head down kicking an imaginary can. "What's the matter with you?" she asked.

"Two kids at school pushed me down," I said sniffing, feeling sorry for myself.

She looked up. "Don't be a cry-baby. What were their names?"

"I can't tell you."

"Why not?" she said chewing on her pencil eraser.

"'Cause they said they'd beat me up everyday if I told."

She went back to her homework. "Suit yourself, but don't come crying to me when they do."

I didn't sleep hardly at all worrying about whether to tell the teacher or Sis about Leo and Red. If I told, they'd beat me up, and if I didn't, they'd know I was afraid and then beat me up for not bringing money.

Next day was Friday. I pretended I had a stomach ache so I wouldn't have to go to school, and slouched around the house all day, until I smelled something baking, then I got well. Mom gave me a snide look while I was eating a big piece of her spice cake. She knew I'd lied my way out of school.

Saturday morning I went over to the Little Woods next to Carol Young's house. Wayne Schmidt, me and two other kids were going to build a tree house out of used lumber Carol's dad gave us. I bent over to pull a rusty nail out of a piece of plywood when something stung me right through my britches. I jumped a foot straight up squealing like one of Uncle Vern's shoats. Everybody laughed, and that's when I saw Red McCauley standing behind a tree cocking a BB gun. He pointed it at me, and I started running. The gun went off, but I guess I was running too fast 'cause he missed.

"Now what's the matter with you?" Momma asked when I came through the door bawling and rubbing my behind.

"Red McCauley shot me with a BB gun."

"Well be quiet. I don't want you waking Dad up."

"He what!" Sis said coming down the stairs.

"Red shot me with a BB gun."

Mom said, "Where?"

"In the behind," I said.

Sis started laughing.

I gave her a dirty look. "It's not funny."

"Let me see." Mom turned me around, while I unbuttoned my jeans.

Sis whistled. "Boy, he sure popped you good."

"What's it look like?" I asked.

"It's not bleeding, but it sure is a big welt." Sis quit laughing and said, "Where's your pump gun?"

"In the basement."

"And where's this McCauley kid?"

"Over in the woods by Carol's house."

"Is he one of the kids that pushed you down at school?"

"Yes."

"Shirley Jean," Mom said, "don't you do something that'll get you in trouble again."

But Sis was already down the stairs. When she went out the side door she was pumping the lever on the BB gun. I ran after her. "What're you going to do?"

"Teach somebody a lesson."

I had to trot to keep up, as Sis walked in a straight line toward the Little Woods.

She zeroed right in on Red. "Your name McCauley?"

"Yeah, so what?" he said, eyeing his BB gun leaning against the tree.

"You shoot my brother?"

"So what if I did?"

"This is so what," Sis said. She put the muzzle of the pump gun against Red's leather jacket and pulled the trigger.

Red screeched, and grabbed his stomach.

"And tell your friend, whatever his name is, that if either one of you lay a finger on my little brother again, I'm gonna pump this thing all the way and come looking."

Red snatched his gun and took off running like a banshee was chasing him.

Two hours later, a car pulled up in front of our house. Sis and Mom went out on the porch and left the door open. Dad was coming down from upstairs wearing a new white shirt. He went out on the porch too.

A deep voice said, "Some girl in this house shot my boy, Frederick."

I ran into the kitchen and hid behind the swinging door.

My sister said, "Does Frederick go by the name of Red?"

Deep voice: "Sometimes he does."

"I shot him," Sis said.

The deep voice: "I had to take him over to the clinic and have that BB dug out from under his skin. Cost three dollars."

Dad said, "What's going on?"

Mom started twisting her apron and said, "Shirley Jean shot this man's son with the pump gun."

Sis: "Did Red tell you what he did to my brother?"

Mom hollered, "Son, come out here."

I didn't answer. I just hunkered down behind the door. About that time Sis flung the door open and it hit me in the face. My nose started bleeding. "Good enough for you," she said. "Now come on out here like Momma said and show Mr. McCauley what his Frederick did to you."

"I don't want to."

"Well you're going to anyway, so come on." She took me by the arm and dragged me through the house with blood running down my upper lip.

Out on the porch she shoved me toward Mr. McCauley. "Take your pants down and show him."

"Whose Frederick?" I asked.

Mister McCauley, his hair the same shade of red as his son's, pointed to my nose and said, "Did Frederick do that to you?"

Sis shook her head. "No. No. I did that. Red shot him in the ass."

Mom said, "Watch your mouth."

Dad said, "What do you mean? Son, who did that to your nose?"

Mom reached around me and unbuttoned my pants. "Now turn around so Mister McCauley can see what his son did to you."

"What in the hell are you pulling his pants down for?" Dad asked.

Sis said, "See that welt? That's what Frederick did to him, and that's why I shot Frederick."

Mister McCauley said, "Anybody that'd bloody a little kid's nose like that ought to be whipped."

"I didn't mean to bloody his nose, but Frederick meant to shoot him in the ass."

Mom said, "I told you to watch your mouth."

"That's the trouble with this family," Dad said. "Nobody ever tells me anything. Now, I want to know what the hell's going on."

Mister McCauley took a few steps backward toward his car. "I think you're all nuts. I ought to report you for bloodying that kid's nose."

As he got into his car, Sis cupped her hands to her mouth and yelled, "Don't forget to tell them about Frederick shooting my brother in the ass."

We watched Mister McCauley's car drive down Browning Street. Dad said, "As soon as your nose gets better I'm going to buy you a pair of boxing gloves and teach you to fight like Joe Lewis, so kids won't be bloodying your nose."

"The door hit my nose, and I don't want to fight like Joe Lewis," I said.

"Yes you do. In this neighborhood, a boy's got to be able to fight."

After that things went a lot smoother at school. The next Monday I took my tissues, oil cloth, and money.

Our afternoon snack consisted of a cookie kept fresh in a cellophane wrapping and our choice of regular or chocolate milk. Every school day we laid down to rest for a few minutes after recess and the snack. Miss Borchec got mad at me because I couldn't sleep when I laid down so I would pretend, then as soon as she turned her back, I'd poke Barbara, Carol, or Wayne, the other kids who lived on Browning Street that laid their mats close to mine.

On this particularly warm and humid Indian Summer afternoon, we were all at the community tables eating our cookies and sipping our half-pints of milk through straws. The windows were open to catch what little breeze there was. A rain storm must have been coming because there were more flies in the class room than in Uncle Vern's pigpen. They came direct from the open sewer a half-block away. One lit on the edge of my chocolate milk. Fly phobia runs in my family. Dad, Mom and Sis, even Grandmother Carpenter—when she was alive—hated them. I eased my straw close to the pest. I would trap the nasty little rascal in my straw and shoot it like a pea at Wayne sitting across the table. The straw was only a quarter inch away from its disc shaped eyes. I sucked in. The fly went straight to the back of my throat. I vomited all over the table and the kids sitting there.

Miss Borchec ran across he room with a handful of tissues. "What's the matter H.K.?" I could tell from her voice she truly felt sorry for me as I finished emptying my stomach on the floor. When I was through, I wiped my nose and mouth. "There was a fly in my milk. See." I pointed to the sodden creature crawling through the mess on the table.

"Oh, you poor thing," she said and patted my head. "We'll get Mr. Parish in here to clean this up, and I'll call your mom to come and get you. Now go lay down on your mat till she gets here."

Carol, who had been sitting next to me and watched the whole episode unfold, was dabbing at her dress with a tissue, then lifted her head and smirked as if to say it was good enough for me.

CHAPTER 9

Demons In The Night

By 1938, the nation was coming out of its deepest and most prolonged depression. Some of the twenty-seven percent who had been unemployed were, like my dad, working again and soup lines were shorter. Roosevelt's New Deal was being implemented. Talk of revolution, socialism, and communism subsided. An aristocratic President calmed social unrest by delivering on his promise to implement reforms; he had told the nation's people they had nothing to fear but fear itself.

Happily, hard times had ended for the Myers Family long before the depression was over, but it had nothing to do with Dad going back to work. Our depression ended when, eight months after we left Utica, Missouri, Grandmother Carpenter died leaving Dad cash and property worth twenty-five thousand dollars.

In the summer and fall of 1937, Dad bought a new Ford automobile for four-hundred dollars. With three thousand dollars he paid for in full, a brick, three bedroom, one bath house with living, dining, kitchen, breakfast nook, study, and full basement with central heating which Mom completely furnished with new, expensive furniture, and name-brand appliances, for seven-hundred fifty dollars. In the year 2003, the car would cost forty-five times as much, the house fifty times as much, and furnishing it twenty-six times as much. To have the same purchasing power sixty-five years later, one would have to inherit between seven hundred thousand, and one million two hundred fifty thousand dollars.

By the fortuitous combination of a Separation Agreement and

the death of my grandmother two and a half years later, our family was lifted from poverty and transformed over night to a family of affluence. Had the property settlement agreement not been consummated, Dad would have received nothing at her death because she owned nothing.

It is not unreasonable to infer (although it will never be known for sure), that the separation and consequent property division were caused, at least in part, by Anna's son bringing his family home to roost on the doctor's door-step from 1930 to 1936. It would be an understatement to say such circumstances would put a strain on even the most stable of marriages. Dr. Carpenter was known as a frugal, industrious professional who cared for and was loved my many, if not most of the people in Livingston County, Missouri. It must have been a bitter pill for him to have to support the step-son whom he had given the opportunity to attend medical school, who drank to excess, was a notorious philanderer, and worst of all indolent. It is one of the supreme ironies, that Dad's presence probably caused the separation which enabled him to inherit the doctor's money. Not quite six years old when Grandmother died, I understood none of this.

Toledo, Ohio, was sixty-five miles south of Detroit, less than a two hour drive. During the decade of the Thirties it was a wide open place where a person of means could have anything—everything had a price, and with the death of his mother, Dad had the means.

My father was five-feet-eleven-inches tall, and thick through the arms and chest. His nose, masculine but not large, was set over lips thick enough to suggest a pout. Hazel eyes, were a blend of his parents brown and green. The Indian heritage from his mother was evident in his dark complexion and coal black hair, which he wore in the style of Rudolf Valentino. Women could not resist a second look. He divided many of his weekends between the Detroit Race Track, and the temptations of Toledo. In the meantime, Mom cooked, cleaned, and looked after us kids, pretty much like other working-class housewives, and continued to believe her husband would play the role of father and husband. Unlike most other women, she was willing to give up everything, or do anything to keep him.

August 3, 1938, my sister, celebrated her thirteenth birthday. She was a teenager, and still Daddy's darling. Outside of her responsibilities as babysitter, she was allowed to do anything she wanted. The only disciplinarian she ever encountered in her life was Doctor Carpenter with his hypodermic needle, but that had been eight years before. With no threat of punishment, she rebelled about spending time with her brother. It was one thing to look after a sibling when she was also child-like, but the onset of puberty put an entirely new slant on the duty. There was an inevitable clash between Mother's pursuit of her husband, versus Sis's need for freedom. Mom continued to conscript my sister into service as babysitter. To vent her frustration, Sis declared war on me.

Bill Young, the son of the contractor who built our house, lived across the street. He became Sis's first Browning Street boyfriend. I ran to Mom and tattled about their every gushy activity. "Sis and Bill were holding hands on the way home from the store." Or, "I saw them kissing on the front porch." Sis had a memory like an elephant and kept books like a C.P.A. No matter how insignificant the mischief, retribution was certain.

Mom and Dad had left for Toledo on Saturday morning and promised they'd be home early Sunday. But by dark on the appointed day, they hadn't returned. It was bitter winter, too cold to do anything outside, so I nagged Sis to play with me. She refused. To make matters worse, Bill was hanging around which made me jealous, so I wouldn't let them out of my sight. She got testy and kept looking out the front window for Mom and Dad, hoping they'd show up so she and Bill could go off somewhere without me tagging along.

After dark, and still no sign of Mom and Dad, Bill and Sis decided to go for a walk. For a seven year old, a walk on a snowy winter evening was a great idea, but it meant putting on boots and layers of clothes and for that I needed help. I could tell Sis was in a cranky mood. She jerked my boots over my shoes, then yanked the zipper on my snowsuit so hard she hit me under the chin. Everything I had on was two sizes too big, meant to last longer than one winter. The hood of the jacket kept slipping down over my stocking cap and covering my eyes. I walked with one hand on the hood to keep it from blinding me. My hands were encased in a pair of heavy mittens, and my shoes slid around inside galoshes big enough for Bill.

The lovebirds took off down the steps and turned toward Stephenson Highway. With a hand on my hood and feet moving near a trot, I stayed within ten or fifteen steps of the hormone-driven pair. So far so good. I suspected they wanted to put some distance between them and me so they could engage in the very activity I'd been wondering about. Couldn't let that happen.

It was dark on Browning Street. At the end of the block, we passed the last house which cast a feeble light through swirling snow. A gust of wind blew the hood over my eyes, and by the time I got it back up, I was alone. I called out, "Sis? Where are you?" No answer. I knew the way back to the house, but stayed where I was, not wanting to admit what I knew in my heart. I hollered again, but louder.

Sis stepped out of the darkness and said, "Shut up you little brat! All you do is follow us around then run and tell momma."

I was so relieved to see her, I didn't pay any attention to the harshness of her words. "I didn't know where you were and got scared. Mom said you're supposed to take care of me, so you shouldn't leave me behind. I won't tattle any more, I promise."

She stepped closer, bent to within an inch of my face, and said, "I hate you." Then she started off into the darkness.

"Wait, don't leave me Sis." I started after her.

She turned. "Don't you dare follow me, do you hear?" She said this with such venom that I stopped in my tracks. The snow blew in gusts between us making her a dim outline against the blackness.

"What should I do?" I asked.

"I don't care what you do, just don't tag after me. Go home."

"But there's no one there, and I'll be alone." I said. There was no answer, so I trudged back to the house, turned all the lights on, and fell asleep waiting for someone.

Despite the growing tension between us, Sis was still the person I depended on when I had a problem. Browning Street was checkered with empty lots, and in the summer of 1938, as the construction industry came out of the doldrums, someone started a new house on the corner of Browning and Palmer Streets, two houses down from ours. Snooping around on the construction site, I picked up a piece of white pine. The weight and heft of it felt good, and it smelled like the trees along the banks of the Grand River, and it was perfect in size and shape for whittling, or for a sword or a rubber gun, or just about anything a boy with a pocket knife could imagine.

Kenneth Schmidt, older brother of Wayne and Vivian, was standing in their driveway when I passed with my new stick. "Where'd you get that piece of lumber?" he called.

"On the corner, where they're building the new house."

"Who told you you could have it?"

"Nobody. It was in the scrap pile." I kept on walking, set the stick on our porch, and went inside to go to the bathroom. When I came back out, Kenneth was still in his driveway, except now he had my stick. "Hey. How come you took my stick?"

"It's not yours."

"I want it back."

"Well, that's too bad, 'cause it's mine now."

I ran back in the house bawling. Sis was on the floor in the living room in front of the radio listening to *The Guiding Light*. "Where's Momma?" I said between wails.

"Shhh!" she said, "Can't you see? I'm listening to the radio." I increased the volume of my bawling. She gave me a hateful look. "It's impossible to do anything with you around. What do you want with her? And how come you're crying?"

I went on through the dining room and stuck my head in the kitchen.

Sis yelled, "She's not in there. She's in the basement doing the wash."

Sniffing, I said, "I need to talk to her."

"Go upstairs and blow your nose before you make me sick. And if you'll wait two minutes this will be over. Now be quiet."

When I came back downstairs, she was turning the radio off. "Okay cry-baby, what's the matter?"

"Kenneth Schmidt took my stick." I told her the story. "He says the stick is his."

"We'll see about that. Come on, we'll pay Mr. Potato Chip a visit." Sis started calling Kenneth that soon after we moved to Browning Street because his shoulders were covered with large flakes of dandruff. She took my hand. Out the door, down the steps, and over to the Schmidt driveway we went.

Kenneth was waiting. The same age as my sister, but more than a half a foot taller, he towered above us and stood there dropping the stick into the palm of his hand. "That's far enough!" he said when we were close. "Don't come on our property."

"Why not?" Sis asked, "You came on ours and took that stick."

"Well the stick belongs to that construction site, not to your brother."

Sis's eyes narrowed and flashed. I'd seen that look before. "Since when are you the policeman of the world?" She dropped my hand and took a step forward.

Kenneth also moved forward a half step. There wasn't an arm's length between them. I was hiding behind Sis's leg. He brandished the stick and said, "You're asking for it.You put one toe over this line . . ." He scratched a long mark between the sidewalk and his driveway with the stick . . ."and I'll break this damned stick over your head."

For just an instant no one moved. Then Sis's toe wiggled over the line. Two things happened in a blur. Kenneth brought the stick up, over his shoulder, and slammed it downward. The instant the stick began to move, Sis started with her arm at her side and landed a looping right hand to the top of Kenneth's nose. At the same time, the stick cracked into an "L" shape across her head.

Kenneth's glasses made a popping sound and jumped off his face. A piece of broken glass embedded between his eyes, and with shattered lens, the rims dangled from one of his ears. He dropped the stick and made a bee-line for his house, blood running down both sides of his nose.

Sis grabbed my hand. "Let's get out of here."

Inside our house, she took me by the shoulders. "What's wrong with you now?"

"I wanted my stick back, and he broke it."

"Yeah," she said, rubbing the knot on the top of her head, "I know."

Sis told Mom the whole story. The next evening, Mister Schmidt showed up at our door with the bill for new glasses and an office call to the doctor. Mom made Sis lean forward so Mister Schmidt could see the knot on top of Sis's head, and claimed self-defense. We would not pay a dime. The Schmidts lived next door to us for six and a half more years. During that time, Wayne became my best friend, and we visited in each others homes frequently, but our parents never spoke to each other again.

June 22, 1938. Out of a shack in the cotton fields of Lexington, Alabama, he had come, an uneducated Negro, a man of color whose ancestry included Whites and Indians, whose father was confined to an institution for the mentally ill, and whose mother and step-father brought him to Detroit to start a new life. Soon after their arrival in the Motor City, his mother enrolled Joe Louis in a vocation school to learn cabinet making and started him on violin lessons. But Joe found he had talent for a different art. He would become America's first black hero.

On this night, the nation's mundane activities halted, problems temporarily forgotten. The people's collective attention was focused on the young man from Detroit, the one who had become known as The Brown Bomber, who the year before had beat Braddock to become the Heavy Weight Champion of the World. Radios were on, breaths held, and bets placed. Joe Louis, was entering the ring against the only man who had ever beat him—Max Schmeling, Hitler's representative of the so-called Aryan Super Race.

Dad, on the living room floor, turned the knobs on the Emerson cabinet radio. Green lights flashed across the glass front while he located WKYB Detroit and sipped Imperial Whiskey from a tumbler. He worked at getting the best reception. "There," he said. "Now listen. I want you to hear this. Louis is the greatest fighter ever born. Last year, he knocked Braddock out in the eighth round with a solid right cross—never knew what hit him."

"What were they fighting for?" I asked.

He jerked his head around and narrowed his eyes. When he realized I wasn't kidding or being a wise-guy, he softened a little and said, "To defend his title, to see who's the best in the world. That's why he's fighting the Nazi, Schmeling, tonight. Now be quiet, we've got to hear this."

A year before, true to his word, Dad had bought me boxing gloves and was teaching me to fight. With me, a puny fifty-five pounder standing dumbly in front of him with over-sized boxing gloves pulling my arms down to my sides, he repeated over and over: "Keep the left out in front, jab, jab. Keep your opponent off balance, keep that left in his face. Tuck the right hand under the chin, wait for an opening—no not yet, dammit, wait—dance, move. Keep the left shoulder up, chin down, jab. Now with the right, hard. Naw, you don't call that a punch do you? Put your shoulder into it, put your whole body in it. Hit with every goddamned thing you've got. Shit! You call that a punch:? Remember, if you don't put him down, he's going to beat you to death."

We did it once or twice a month. I didn't mind the lessons when he wasn't drinking—it was sort of fun being with him—but when he'd had a few belts he'd start hitting hard to make me cry, which was not too difficult.

"Here it is," Dad said, turning the volume up. Then he cupped his hand and yelled toward the kitchen, "Come on Mae; fight's starting."

Mom joined us on the floor in front of the radio.

The static eased. The Ring Announcer at Yankee Stadium went through the history of each fighter, telling in detail how, two years before, Schmeling had knocked The Brown Bomber out in the twelfth round. Then drawing out every syllable, the Announcer said, "Ladies . . . and . . . Gentlemen. The main event of the night. For the Heavy . . . Weight . . . Championship . . . of the World. In this corner, from Berlin, Germany, . . . weighing in at two-hundred . . . seventeen pounds, . . . the former World Heavy Weight Champ, . . . Max Schmeling!"

A sell-out crowd of seventy-thousand booed.

"And in this corner, . . . weighing in at one-hundred-ninety-seven pounds, . . . with twenty-six wins and . . . one loss, . . . the current Heavy . . . Weight . . . Champion of the World, . . . from Detroit, Michigan, . . . the Brown Bomber, . . . Joe . . . Louis!"

The fans went wild. Louis's one loss had been to Schmeling two years before.

The bell calling Round One clanged. Schmeling and Louis advanced into the center of the ring, touched gloves, and took their fight stance. Schmeling, bent forward, both hands in front. He jabbed with the left and Louis hit him with a pile-driver right hand. Schmeling's knees buckled, and he went to the canvas. The referee pushed Joe back to a neutral corner and started the count. One, two . . . Schmeling staggered to his feet. The referee backed away and Louis closed the distance. Schmeling tried to cover his head, but Louis was savage. He hit the German with a devastating left, and the former champ was on the canvas again. The fans were wild. But Schmeling grabbed the ropes and by the count of five had gained his feet. The media had wrongly characterized him as a Nazi, hyping the fight as Fascism versus the Free World, to incite the crowd—and it had worked.

Louis, ever the stalker, now sensing the kill closed, his knees slightly bent, he shuffled, bobbed, left hand leading, right tucked under his chin. They circled. Schmeling jabbed, feigned, blocked a punch, and backed away, but Louis kept coming. Suddenly, the Brown Bomber unleashed a lightning barrage of lefts, followed by a crushing right cross which connected with the German's cheek. The blow shook Schmeling. Louis jabbed twice more with the left and then, his right coming in a slight curve connected to the chin. Schmeling went down for the third time. The referee started the count. Schmeling rolled on his stomach, tried to bring himself to his hands and knees. The referee's count: ". . . six, . . . seven, . . . eight, . . . nine, . . . ten!" The announcer screamed, "Joe Louis has just knocked out Max Schmeling in a stunning victory!"

The fight had lasted two-minutes and four seconds. Louis, who had said he did not want to be called "Champ" until he beat Schmeling, had avenged his only loss, and won not only the most important fight of his career, but the heart of America.

Dad must have had a lot of money on Louis. He was so happy I thought he was going to cry. "I knew you could do it Joe, I knew it," he said over, and over, then celebrated by drinking himself unconscious. Sis and I helped Mom drag him down the basement stairs on a throw-rug, and put him to bed. As Mom pulled his pants off, he muttered, "Atta boy Joe, I knew you could do it."

The week after the Louis and Schmeling fight, Dad said he couldn't stand the paint he was breathing as spray-man at Fords, and quit. That same week, he bought a store on the corner of Garfield and John-R Streets, and opened a meat-market.

Sunday, October 30, 1938, Mom had her thirty-fourth birthday. Somehow she persuaded Dad to stay home with her. To celebrate, they both had a few drinks. Sis and I, on the floor in front of the radio, were having a cuss fight over whether we would listen to *The Lone Ranger,* or *The Romance of Helen Trent.* Sis had the tuner control and was running the stations. She hit CBS as the announce said, "My God! Martians have landed in New Jersey, the United States is under attack by the most gruesome creatures you have ever seen . . . horrible . . . . killers!"

Sis jumped up and ran to the kitchen, with me right behind her. "Martians are coming! It just came over the radio. They've landed in New Jersey, they're killing everyone, burning all the buildings. The Army's been called out. Nothing can stop them."

Mom said, "Sister, are you sure?"

"She's right!" I said, "The Martians are coming."

Dad slid out of the breakfast nook. "We'll fight the sons-a-bitches to the end." He zig-zagged unsteadily through the swinging door. In a minute he was back loading shells in both chambers of his Ithica double barrel. The handle of his .38 Police Special was sticking out over the top of his belt.

Mom headed for the door. "Let's go listen to what's going on."

Back in the living room, an announcer was saying, "Please remember, this is only a dramatization of H. G. Wells's, *War of The Worlds,* and is presented by Mercury Theater of The Air."

Mom started laughing. "Shirley Jean, you scared the pants off us."

"I'm not afraid of the fucking Martians," Dad said, and poured his shot glass full.

I sure was glad we would not have to rely on Dad to protect us from the Martians.

By 1940, my parents were hosting all manner and theme of parties at 428 W. Browning Street—poker, cock-tail, and costume parties were on the agenda whenever Dad was in town. This Saturday night it was costumes, adults only, in anticipation of Halloween coming next week. Sis had gone to the movies with Bill Young. Mom told me to stay in my room and go to sleep—a brilliant piece of advice considering the throb of the record player as Tommy Dorsey's band rattled the pictures on my bedroom wall. Downstairs, the front door opened and slammed every two minutes. I recognized the voices of several neighbors. Everyone was having a swell time.

The thump of the music got louder as the hour got later. Voices without words were intermingled with boisterous laughter and high-pitched squeals. I had to contrive a reason why I should go down and have a look. I could pretend I had a stomachache. But if I did that I wouldn't be able to have anything to eat and Mom might make me take cod liver oil or some other nasty remedy. Same for a toothache. Maybe I would tell Mom my plantar wart was hurting. That wouldn't work, she'd just say it was reason to be off my feet and in bed. How about, I left my new comic book in the kitchen? I would decide on which excuse to use when the time came. Maybe I could just go down, get something to eat, and bring it back to my room without Mom or Dad seeing me.

I eased out the door, and at the place where the staircase curved so you could see into the living area, I sat down flabbergasted. A woman was dancing with a bowl of fruit stuck on her head, and her partner, dressed like W. C. Fields, had a red nose stuck on his face. Dozens of people were dressed in costumes, some looked like Hollywood celebrities. There was also a chicken, a white rabbit, a skeleton, a pumpkin, and President Roosevelt. Some were dressed in street clothes but hid their identity with Lone Ranger masks. I made a mental note to try and swipe one of those. No one paid me any mind; there was too much going on.

Feeling invisible, I walked on down the stairs, and into the living room, threaded my way past the Fruit Bowl Woman, and her new partner, Tarzan, on through bodies weaving, bobbing, and twisting toward the dining room. A woman with Mickey Mouse ears and Mae West boobs walked past carrying a plate heaped with food. I recognized the boobs as belonging to Missus Burl, Dicky's mother. I forgot to look at her plate, and my stomach was rumbling, so I kept going toward the dining room to see what she'd been carrying. Before I could reach the entry, there was a yelp, a cross between a Comanche war cry and a Swiss yodel; a burst of laughter, and people pointing. A bed-sheet with one eye peering balefully from a hole flew across the room toward me. The crowd parted. The apparition's arms flailed the air with the sheet gripped in its fists, resembling a picture I had seen in our *Standard Encyclopedia* of a grounded gooney bird frantically flapping large white wings. Astounded, I stood riveted.

The sheet flew directly over me, and something stepped on my right foot. I screamed, took a deep breath and screamed again. Someone bumped the record player and the needle screeched across Count Basie playing his *One O'Clock Jump,* then the room went dead silent.

There I was, in the middle of a circle of bizarre costumes hopping around on one foot and squeezing the other. The space in the middle of the living room enlarged to avoid blood squirting between my fingers. President Roosevelt said, "My God, he's bleeding."

The bird-like thing stood swaying above me. The sheet slipped from its head, and there stood Dad. For a long moment he looked at me with a blank stare, either too drunk to recognize me, or not believing what he was seeing. The blood dripping on the floor finally stirred him. He took a handkerchief from his pocket and wrapped it around the injured toe. When Mother arrived, he stood up and said, "What's he doing up?"

The next thing I knew, I was setting on the edge of the bath tub with water running over my foot. When the wound was clean, I saw the cavity where Dad's one-hundred-ninety pounds had popped the entire core out of my planter's wart.

Next morning, Sunday, my foot felt better than it had in weeks. Everyone was still sleeping when I got up. In the kitchen, I fixed a piece of toast to settle my stomach. Mom showed up and said I should get dressed and go to Sunday School. I groused around mumbling about not wanting to go, but Mom insisted.

Church was held at Martin Road Elementary School. Missus Parrish, the janitor's wife, was my Sunday School teacher. She told us the new church building would be completed in about six more months. It was only three blocks from my house. The lesson that day was on how much God loved all his children. That confused me when I thought of what she said the week before about how God sacrificed his son by purposely causing his hands and feet to be nailed to a pole and left there naked to die. I sure hoped He didn't love me that much. But I stopped worrying about that and got all excited when Missus Parrish handed me a wrapped package and said it was a gift. I tore the paper off. It was a Bible. Inside the front cover, it said, "To H. K. Myers, For One Year's Perfect Attendance. 1939-40. Signed: Missus Parrish, Calvary Baptist Church."

That night I dreamed I was alone on a quiet and barren plain. The thick surface felt substantial; it was brilliant white, like a glacier. As I moved forward on solid footing, I felt confident, my spirit buoyed by a feeling of security and happiness. Then far in the distance, almost imperceptibly, a small and seemingly insignificant fissure appeared and made me uneasy. I walked on, but my attention kept going back to the crack. Somehow I knew its appearance would have a catastrophic effect on my life. I was transfixed. Suddenly it widened, opened like an earthquake fracture, shot branches at various angles, small at first, but growing. I stopped. Confusion enveloped me. I needed someone to explain what was happening, but there was no one, so I backed away, careful to keep my eyes on the widening separations. Then the surface under my feet trembled. I turned. The entire plain was churning, heaving. Broken pieces pushed and protruded upward, grinding like gigantic ice burgs moved by opposing currents. Panic replaced confusion. I tried to run, but my legs would barely move and then only with great exertion, like being waist deep in heavy syrup. Then it became clear—the surrounding chaos would consume me, as in the vortex of an earthquake, or the belly of an erupting volcano. Cognition of no escape sucked air from my lungs; I fought for breath. The dreamscape was Dante's Inferno, the displaced areas gaping mouths of blackness. The solid and unlimited place where I once stood, now heaved like the breast of a stricken beast and continued to shrink, leaving barely enough space for me to stand, its edges crumbling. With nothing left I lost balance, screamed, and fell into the abyss, down, down. I stretched my arms, spread my hands to break the fall. Below, at the place where my hands would land, was a pole with two sharp nails pointing up, waiting.

In 1940, Ted Childers started school at Martin Road. We were in Miss Tinder's fourth-grade. My seat was in the row by the windows near the front of the class. Ted's desk was next to mine. The closeness enabled me to know him, but not well. No one knew him very well. A loner, he rarely took part in any playground activities, spoke only when spoken to, and was not a part of the smart-aleck group. He was preoccupied and more introspective than most fourth graders. He had lived somewhere in Georgia, and his family had recently moved to the Detroit metro area to find work. I told him our family had also been real poor when we moved back to Detroit. Maybe that's why he talked to me more than to any of the other kids.

Ted was my height, but muscular in an adult way. His muscles looked older than his age, knotted like those of a heavy laborer. In the school picture, Ted's thick hair is a predominant facial feature, growing low on his forehead. The line above his nose was so deep it pulled the nostrils up creating a pug that permitted a look into his head. And his complexion was yellow, like he had been deprived of sunlight or was jaundiced. Dark brooding eyes under a wrinkled brow, gave him the appearance of a little old man.

Our desks were constructed of steel frames with wooden panels. The top opened to a deep well in which we kept books, tablets, rubber bands, jars of tad-poles taken from the open sewer, pencils, pieces of erasers, candy, bubble-gum wrappers, marbles, legless bugs, tacks, jack-knives, and other paraphernalia essential to the well-being of a nine year old boy. The desks were substantial, solid, built to last.

On the first day of school of the second semester, I bent over and stuck my head inside the cover of my desk so Miss Tinder could not see me eating a Butterfinger. Everything was noisy and disorganized, including the teacher as she rearranged seating assignments, and attempted to bring some semblance of order to chaos. The scream started as a growl, continued in an upward crescendo, increased in volume, and climbed into an ear piercing soprano. Domestic screaming, which I was used to, can be terrifying, but never had I heard anything like the animal sound now reverberating through the class room. My desktop slammed shut, the Butterfinger dropped to the floor, and I jumped to my feet. The scream slowly died and was replaced by a series of short, frenzied bursts like someone in the throes of unbearable pain gasping for breath.

It was Ted standing next to his desk, his head back howling like a wolf; then with a single movement, he gripped his desk, raised it over his head, and held it like a newsboy might hold a front page headline aloft. I scrambled to join the other fourth graders pressed against the opposite wall.

The girls were screaming and crying. Miss Tinder started toward Ted, but when he hoisted the desk, she stopped. No one breathed. For an instant he might have been a statute, his muscles banded in his neck, as he balanced the weight above his head. Then he began to sway, ever so slightly. The desk quivered. Ted moved, a stutter-step, and with a final burst of strength, and another bloodcurdling scream, he lunged. The desk and boy crashed to the floor.

Ted lay twitching and foaming at the mouth. Miss Tinder was at his side and Mister Clark, the Principal, entered the room and rushed to assist. When the desk hit the floor most of the kids ran into the hall. I stayed. My running away might add to Ted's embarrassment, or make him think I was offended by his curse. It didn't occur to me he would never know of my staying.

At home that afternoon, I described the episode to my mother. She remarked that Ted had had a fit and I should stay away from him. "Go outside and play and forget it."

Forget it? The image of Ted Childers holding that desk aloft was burned into my mind forever.

CHAPTER 10

My Friend Elmer

A new litter of pups at the Standard Oil Station caused a lot of excitement. The kids on Browning Street started pestering their folks to let them have a dog. The Gang was in and out of the station so often, the owner told us to go away unless we intended to buy one.

"Please, Mom, please. Let me have a puppy." I had repeated the plea a dozen times every day since the new litter arrived.

She swept spilled corn meal into a neat pile on the kitchen floor. "I don't have time for a puppy. Who will house-break it, clean up after it, feed and bath it? Not you. You'll get tired of it and then expect me to do it."

I skipped away in front of the broom. "I'll break it Mom, and do all the other things you said. I promise."

"Dogs make all kinds of messes. If Dad steps in dog poop, there will be heck to pay."

I thought of what had happened to Drumstick. "I'll clean up after it, Mom. Come to the station with me. They're the cutest things you've ever seen in your whole life. I'll pay for it out of my paper route money. Please let me have one." After haranguing, begging, and some general obnoxious behavior, I wore her down. She agreed to look.

The puppies were in a box of dirty rags under the gas station counter. There was a chorus of grunts, whines, and sucking sounds while we watched them compete for milk. There weren't enough dispensers. One, its eyes barely open, tried hard to get something to eat, but could never quite get past the tails and butts sticking up around the mother's stomach, who seemed content to let her nine babies solve their own food problems.

A sign on the counter said, "Females $1 / Males $2."

Mother, a former farm girl, had seen and cared for countless new-borns. She watched the activity for a few minutes. "They are kinda cute. What do you think about the littlest one?" She pointed to the one struggling to nose a sibling off of a teat. It was scrawny, wrinkled, and about half the size of the others.

"I don't know. You think it'll live?" I asked.

She smiled. "Sure, lots of times the runt turns out to be the smartest and the strongest of the litter."

I lifted it out of the box, and turned it belly up. A male. That was good. I couldn't have a female, and it had to be small, otherwise, I couldn't keep it in the house. The mother looked to be a little taller than a fox. The station owner, who bred her every six months, said the sire was a Terrier just a mite larger. Mom said it also had to have short hair, and I had swore an oath to be responsible for all its messes. He wriggled and squirmed around in my hand. The right side of his head, including the eye and ear, was covered by a light brown oval. There were two other brown spots on his back, otherwise he was white. He found my little finger and began to suck. From the smacking and grunting you'd have thought he had found the real thing. Mom said he sure sounded hungry.

I asked the attendant to show us the other males.

"All males 'cept that one's sold," he said.

That made me antsy. Someone might come along after we leave and buy this one. I wouldn't get a puppy out of this litter—maybe never.

"Can I have him, Mom?"

"I guess. Just remember what you promised." She paid the attendant two dollars.

I couldn't believe it. All of a sudden, the runt was transformed into the most beautiful puppy in the litter. He was my own dog. I pulled one of the other pups off the mother, and stuck his nose on her breast. Now, all I had to do was wait until he could be weaned. Four more weeks. A life time.

I asked the attendant everyday how much longer before I could take him home. Exasperated he said, "Look kid, I've got work to do. That pup can't leave here for three more weeks so go home and mark it on your calendar."

Every day, when the station opened, I'd hurry over and pick him up and hold him for as long as he'd let me without fussing. As soon as the owner or attendant went outside to take care of a customer, I'd pull another pup off the momma. When the station was busy, I could keep him sucking until his belly was tight as drum. After two more weeks, my pup got so strong I didn't have to help him get milk; he'd just nose right in there and get his share. Got so he knew when I was there and whined for me to pick him up.

On the day my dog turned six weeks old, I carried him home in a clean cardboard box and gave him his first bath to get rid of the fleas and the smell of gas and oil. You could hear him bawling all over the house. After he was dry and fluffy, I took him outside and showed him to every kid on Browning Street.

The next day, a Saturday afternoon, I was down on the living room floor playing with him. Dad was in his chair watching. I had spread papers to protect Mom's rug. The pup made a beeline for the dining room. I was on my feet and running. "Come Boy," I said. "Don't mess on Momma's floor."

Mom, on one of her frequent trips in and out of the kitchen, came through the dining room and stood watching. The pup ran to where Dad was sitting, grabbed one of his shoe laces, pulled, and shook his head. The shoe came untied. Mom, always happy at any sign of domestic bliss, went to the remnant box and got a rag for him to pull. Dad jiggled the rag, and the pup attacked, got tangled, and tumbled end over end, making Dad laugh. "What're you going to name him?" he asked.

"Let's name him something neat like Wolf, or Savage, or Satan," I said.

"Naw, he's too little for a name like that. He'll never be a fighter." Dad said as he filled his pipe from a can of "Half and Half Tobacco." If it was only half tobacco, I wondered what the other half would have been.

A lot of different names were suggested, but everyone agreed that names like Spot, Prince, and Pal were too common.

Dad said, "Why don't you name him Elmer?"

"Elmer!" I had to hold my mouth to keep from laughing. "That's a dorky name. Whoever heard of a dog named Elmer?" The Browning Street Gang would never let me live it down.

Sis stuck her head out of the bedroom and yelled, "Dorky! where do you come up with stupid words like that?"

I didn't want to tell I made it up. She'd have laughed, but it was true, I was always trying to think of new words, like *walunked*, which was what I called it when Dad was too drunk to walk.

Dad was talking. He said Daisy, the dog in the funny papers that belonged to Dagwood, had whelped a litter. The Bumstead's named the runt, Elmer. If it was good enough for the Bumstead's dog, why wasn't it good enough for ours?

I thought about it. I could tell the Gang my dog was named after a famous dog in the comic strips, and besides, I didn't want to upset Dad by telling him what I really thought. "Great idea, Dad."

He followed me everywhere. If I was out of his sight for more than a few seconds, he yelped, then let loose with a sorrowful howl. After he was house-broken, Mom changed one of her rules. Elmer didn't have to stay in the basement, except when he did something bad, like the time he chewed the heel off of one of her favorite dress shoes.

Mother had been right. Elmer was the smartest dog ever born—smarter than the performing terriers I'd seen at the circus. Within a few months he'd obey all of the commands I could think of—all the standard stuff. In addition, he would go to the basement, get under the chair, heal, and salute. And there were dozens of other things he understood from the tone of my voice. I never missed an opportunity to show him off, and despite his name, he was soon the envy of all the kids in the neighborhood.

That September, when I started back to Martin Road, Elmer couldn't understand why I left him at home. Mom said the first week he cried for an hour then laid around the house and sulked the rest of day. But after he got used to the routine, he'd wait in the front yard, or on the porch until he saw me coming through the Little Woods then run as fast as he could to meet me. The other kids I walked with thought it was great the way he licked my face and ran around in circles as if to say he was glad I was home.

Mom and Grandmother Sherman, re-upholstered an antique chair with a silky fabric of pale and dark green strips, then attached a skirt which hung to the floor. When company came, or when we didn't want Elmer hanging around the table begging, or yapping to go out and play, I would say, "chair," and under the stripped chair, on his belly, he'd go. After a few minutes, just the tip of his nose would stick out, and if no one spoke in harsh tones, the nose came out a little farther, and the progression continued until his brown eyes peeked from under the skirt with a forlorn plea that the sentence be suspended.

On winter nights, when he and I were restless and full of energy, we'd play a game we called, "Find Elmer." I'd lay on the floor, and he'd dive under the stripped chair. On one of the four sides, there would be a slight movement of the skirt, then the tiniest tip of his nose would appear. Using my thumb and forefinger, I'd flip him gently on the nose. The black spot would pull back, then re-appear on a different side. By the time I could get there, his nose would be gone again, only to poke out from still another location. Around and around the chair we'd go, for hours.

Our favorite outdoor game was hide-and-seek. The neighbor on the east of the Schmidts' had a four-foot high picket fence around their front yard. I would throw Elmer's ball as far as I could. He'd fly over the fence with a foot to spare. The instant he was gone, I'd scramble for a hiding place; behind a bush, around a corner, into a ditch, on top of a shed—somewhere out of sight. Coming back with the ball, he'd see I was gone, and the chase was on. In hiding, I'd hold my breath, but it didn't matter how quiet I was, there was no fooling his nose. Running like a rabbit, tongue hanging out the side of his mouth, and yapping with great excitement at the joy of the hunt, he would find me, jump up and down, and with a special bark tell me he was ready to go again. And we did, over and over, until I fell exhausted with Elmer panting and licking at my face. Then he'd lay next to me, always close enough to touch.

We were on the ground in the Little Woods, trying to catch our breath. "Elmer," I said, "help me figure out what to do." He cocked his head, and twitched an ear. "There's this girl at school, her name's Sharon—sits right in front of me. I'm not sweet on her, at least I don't think I am, but she does something everyday . . . it's hard to explain, and I'm not sure I understand it. She crosses her legs, stretches them straight out, and squeezes them together over and over. Yesterday when she did it, I got up and fooled around at the pencil sharpener so I could see better. She kinda worked her thighs, and at the same time closed her eyes. She did that for a couple minutes then her eyelids fluttered and she took her lower lip between her teeth. It got me so stirred up watching, I wanted to go in the toilet and do something, but I wasn't sure what. I don't know for sure what she's doing, but it has to do with sex and it drives me nuts. I think about it all day instead of listening to the teacher. And there's no one to talk to except you. I can't tell anybody at home, that's for sure, and I can't tell any of the gang, 'cause if they believed me, one of 'em might go up and say something to her, you know, something dirty. Besides, I ain't . . . I mean I'm never going to snitch on her—never, but I'm dying to know what she's doing."

Elmer hitched up his hind leg, scratched his neck, and made his collar jingle.

"What I really want is to walk her home from school; have her tell me what she's doing. Maybe I could help her, or maybe she and I could do something together, you know. I could write her a note. But I'd have to say who it was from, or it wouldn't do me any good, and I'm too embarrassed to do that."

Elmer got up, licked my face, trotted over to a bush.

"I saw you sniffing around Mitzi, that new female up the street, so don't be so darned prudish."

He came back, rolled over for me to rub his stomach. "I guess you've heard all you want. Let's go home and get a peanut butter and jelly sandwich."

Mister Burger operated a small convenience store across Stephenson Highway. It was a rare day when I didn't have to make a trip to his store for milk, bread, or something we needed in the kitchen. On this day, it was Calumet Baking Powder.

I jumped on my bike. Elmer, now ten months old, loped along behind. Stephenson Highway was busy as usual, so we stopped at the curb of each lane. "Sit Elmer," I said. Down he went. When traffic cleared, we crossed. At Berger's, I leaned my bike against the building, and told him to stay. He laid down by the door.

I found the baking powder, paid Mister Berger, and went out. Elmer was waiting. I whistled for him to come. Burgers' store stuck out toward the highway. I pulled my bike far enough out to check for on-coming traffic. There was an opening. I mounted and started across. When I cleared the first lane, I noticed Elmer was not at my side. I turned. He was sniffing at something on the pavement outside the store. He looked up, saw me across the street, and took off running toward me. A car, moving fast, was too close for Elmer to make it. I screamed, "Stay! No! No! Don't come boy!" But he knew he was supposed to be with me, so he came. The car hit him and never slowed down.

"Elmer! Elmer!" I screamed. I dropped the bike and ran into the road. He lay there with blood bubbling from his mouth, nose, and eyes. "Oh my God, you've killed my Elmer! You son-of-a-bitch, you've killed my Elmer!" I picked him up, and he whimpered. He was alive! "Oh Elmer, don't die. Please God, don't let him die." I begged and prayed all the way home.

Mother looked at him and shook her head. "He can't live with his skull fractured. See, the blow even knocked out several of his teeth, and from the looks of his eyes he's probably blind. It's hopeless."

"No," I cried. "I couldn't stand it if Elmer died."

I laid him in a box in the basement and stayed with him every day, and late into the night, for ten days. He couldn't move so I spooned water into his mouth and told him how much I loved him, and how important he was to me—that if he died, I would die too. On the tenth day, he turned his head and stuck out his tongue for more of the water I offered.

"Mother, Mother," I called up the basement steps. "He took a drink of water! You think he'll live?"

"How can an animal live with injuries like that?"

"Don't you understand? He has to live. Can't we take him to a doctor?"

"There's no point in wasting money, he's going to die."

I hated her for saying he would die. Under my breath, I said, "No, by God, he's not going to die, even if you don't care." I carried him choice bits of meat from our supper table. At first he refused it. Then one day, after he drank, he took a small offering. I jumped up and down. "He's eating," I yelled. Elmer always had swallowed most everything without chewing, so the loss of some teeth didn't seem to be a hindrance. Next day, his bowels moved in the box. I carried it outside and put fresh rags down.Toward the end of the second week, he tried to get up. The pain and stiffness caused him to whimper, but his will to live was strong. Finally, he staggered out of his box and began to heal.

For the rest of his life, his eyes watered. Elmer had survived without benefit of a veterinarian. Mom said it was because I gave him water everyday while he was down, but I think he lived because he knew how bad I needed him.

Our new car was packed to the dome-light as we sped along the Lake Huron shoreline on our way to Alpena for a two week vacation. Dad said next year we wouldn't have to go so far. We would have our own cabin, presently under construction, and only an hour's drive from Hazel Park.

Dad was in a foul mood. He drank until late the night before, got up early, and then Elmer had been car sick three times the first hour after we left. I leaned over the front seat and stared at the highway trying to figure out why we couldn't get any closer than half a city block to heat waves on the road before they disappeared.

Sis had her nose stuck in a magazine. I figured it had dirty pictures in it. Every time I'd try to see she'd jab me with her elbow. Without looking up, she said in her snooty voice, "Mother, will you *please* tell Brother to quit chomping his bubble gum, it's enough to make me want to throw up."

"Sonny, stop smacking your gum," Mom said.

I blew a bubble big as a tomato. It popped right between mom and dad. "I'm not chomping," I said pulling gum off my face. "How come she won't let me look at the pictures in her magazine?"

"Close your mouth when you chew and it won't make so much noise. Sister will let you look when she's through. Now be quiet."

I couldn't blow bubbles with my mouth closed. I gave Sis a hateful look. She glanced up from the magazine, smiled, and with the tip of the thumb and two fingers of one hand made a motion like a tiny mouth talking. It was the taunt, like giving someone the finger, only this was just between her and me. When one got the better of the other, we threw the taunt to rub it in. "Make Sis quit teasing me," I said.

Dad turned around in his seat. "If you two don't shut up you're going to drive me nuts."

Mom jumped in hard. "Okay. That's it. I don't want to hear another word out of either of you for the rest of this trip." Then to Dad in her soothing voice she said, "Look at all the blueberry bushes along the road, and they're loaded. If you'll stop, it wouldn't take the kids and me long to pick enough for a couple of pies."

Swell. If I couldn't chomp or blow bubbles, I'd save my gum for latter. I took it out of my mouth, rolled it into a perfect ball, and stuck it on top of the ashtray.

It was near noon when we stopped. The berry bushes were heavy with fruit. Mom had been right, the sweet, blue currants came off the branches by the hands full. Purple juice ran to my elbows. In fifteen minutes, I had filled my sack and ate almost as many berries as I picked.

On the shady side of the car, Mom poured water from the cooler over a napkin while Sis scrubbed at the stains on her hands complaining about her black fingernails, and that she didn't like berry pies anyway. I drew my lips back so she could see my purple teeth, growled like a bear, and stalked her with my stained fingers curled like claws.

"Don't you dare touch me with those hands you little brat!" She bellowed, and jumped into the car. There was an ear piercing scream. "Oh my God!" she said. "Look at my skirt."

"To hell with it," said Dad, "this is the last vacation I'm ever going on."

Mother, her anxiety alarm going off, dropped a sack of berries and said, "Sonny stop it!" and to Sis, "Don't call your brother a brat."

Sis, in her most mournful voice, said, "Daddy, look what Brother got all over me and the backseat."

He stuck his head into the hot interior. "Jesus Christ, look at my new car!"

I stuck my head around the seat. Long pink strands of bubble gum clung to Sis's skirt, the rest of the glob had run down the ashtray onto the upholstering. Mother said, "Now Dad, don't get upset, turpentine will take that off." Then she gave me a look worthy of Attila the Hun. "Sonny, get in that back seat and don't open your mouth again until we get to the lake."

Dad had rented a cabin with three rooms, an outhouse, and a private row-boat—a great place for a family of four to spend their vacation. What he didn't tell Mom was that he had also invited one of his favorite drinking buddies, Charlie Weatherup and Charlie's tubercular wife, Daisy, to join our family outing for a few days. When we pulled into the parking spot in front of the cabin, there they were. Good old Dad. He told Mom he only did it, ". . . 'cuz he thought the fresh air would help Charlie's wife get well."

On the trip from Browning Street, I hadn't seen any beer or whiskey in our car, but Charlie and Daisy solved that mystery, they had brought a case of Stroh's Bohemian Fire-Brewed Beer, and a quart of Canadian Club Ninety Proof Bourbon. Dad told Charlie he sure didn't expect him to bring such expensive whiskey.

That evening, Mom baked two blueberry pies. Dad and Charlie said they were going fishing. Mom helped Sis and me build a bonfire down on the beach. We roasted hot dogs and marshmallows, and ate blueberry pie while we listened to whoops and boisterous laughter coming off the lake. I was ready to go to bed when I got what Mom called the cholera marbles which is when you get sick at both ends at the same time. She said it was from eating too many uncooked blueberries.

I sat on one hole in the toilet and threw up in the other. When Mom came outside to check on me, she found Daisy staggering around the cabin with an empty flask in her hand. Mom tried to get her to go inside out of the damp night air, but instead Daisy walked down to the edge of the lake and started hollowing for Charlie to bring that bottle of Canadian Club back to shore. I couldn't figure out how she could yell so loud with her chest heaving and wheezing, while coughing and spitting every minute or two.

Sis went to the toilet. Everything was quiet, when all of a sudden she shrieked like she was being chased by a bear. Mom grabbed the flashlight and a butcher knife and ran to the outhouse. I still didn't feel too good so I stayed in the cabin. Pretty soon, Sis came stomping through the door, poured water from the bucket into the wash basin and carried it into mom's bedroom.

"What happened?" I asked when Mom came through the door frowning.

"You threw-up blueberry pie all over the toilet seat, and Sis sat in it. Why didn't you clean up after yourself?"

"I was too sick."

Sis stuck her head out of the bedroom door. "You're not half as sick as you're gonna be when I get through with you." Pretty soon she came out of the bedroom and started sniffing. "Momma, can't we just go home. This is a terrible vacation."

"She just wants to see that boyfriend of hers," I said with a sneer.

Just before we left for vacation, a football player called "Topper" had started hanging around our house. In a month Sis'd be fifteen years old, so going to a primitive cabin on an isolated lake was not high on her list of preferred vacation spots.

"You shut up. That's none of your business. Mother, do I have to sleep with this brat?"

"Now Shirley Jean, don't talk like that to your brother, he was sick."

Sis, Elmer, and I slept on the kitchen floor so Charlie and Daisy could have the spare room. Mom said it wouldn't be good for a skinny lady like Daisy to have to sleep where it was drafty.

The next morning I dunked a piece of toast in some warm milk, while Mom and Sis talked about what had happened the night before. I must have slept real hard 'cause there had been an awful lot of stuff going on in the kitchen.

Dad and Charlie hadn't come in off the lake until the whiskey was gone. Dad said Charley got turned around in the dark and rowed for a half an hour toward the other side, then he was too tired to row back so Dad had to do it. When they pulled the boat up on the shore and Daisy found out all the Canadian Club was gone, she started cussing Charlie; said he had no heart because he drank all the whiskey knowing she was sick and needed some to keep her from catching a chill.

After Mom finished telling about what had happened the night before, we all just sat quiet for awhile. Then she said, "Well, it ain't going to happen again today."

"Momma, 'ain't' isn't a word," chimed Sis. She would soon be in the tenth grade, and had always made high marks in English, so she did a lot of correcting around our house.

"Okay Miss Know-It-All, it's not going to happen again today," Mom said.

"What'cha going to do?" I asked, afraid there was going to be another fight. "Can't we all just go fishing?"

"There's still a case of beer in Charlie Weatherup's car and I'm going to get rid of it. I'm not getting in that boat with those three and a case of beer. Listen to 'em in there—all three snoring—sounds like a road grader without a muffler."

That was about the bravest thing I'd ever heard my mother

say. I tried to think of another time she'd stood up to Dad. There wasn't any, and I didn't believe she'd do anything this time. Seemed like she always made excuses for his drinking and more and more she was drinking with him.

Mom got up and put a sweater on. "Come on kids. We're going for a boat ride."

"Can I take my fishing pole?" I asked.

Sis perked up. "Yeah. Let's take the fishing poles. Maybe brother and I can catch something for supper."

The sun had almost reached the top of the trees behind the cabin when we loaded the anchor, a case of Strohr's Beer, two fishing poles, and a rusty Campbell's Soup can full of nightcrawlers. I pushed the boat away from the shore and sat in the back.

Big Bear Lake was spring fed, its water crystal clear, so as Sis rowed, I hung over the back and watched the bottom fall away. The water looked like clean glass. I could tell the color of every piece of gravel on the bottom which was at least ten or twelve feet below the boat.

After a few minutes, I yelled, "Stop! Stop." Elmer, his feet on the gunwale, started barking.

Sis almost popped an oar out of the oar-lock. "Brother, for God's sake, you scared me half to death. What's wrong?"

"Look." I pointed over the side. "See. There's a whole school of perch—big ones."

Mother, in the bow, let the anchor go.

"Bait my hook for me Brother," said Sis.

"Bait your own hook."

Mom, busy with the case of Stroh's, said, "Bait your sister's hook."

I pulled an eight-inch nightcrawler out of the can, broke it in two and offered half to Sis.

"Don't you dare touch me with that thing. Mom, make him stop." Elmer tried to grab it out of my hand, so I dug around in the can and gave him a worm.

Sis said, "My God, Mother, he's feeding the worms to Elmer. I think I'm going to be sick."

Chuckling to myself, and feeling fully recovered from the cholera marbles, I put a worm on her hook and threw her line over. The other half, I put on my own hook, but before I could get my line in the water she screamed, "Oh my God, I've got something." She jerked the pole around and wacked me across the head.

"Ouch," I yelled. Elmer snarled at Sis.

"Okay, *now* what's the matter?" Mom asked dropping two bottles of beer in the lake.

"Sis hit me with her pole."

"Oh my God, it's still on there," Sis screamed and swung her line over the oar and into the boat. A fat perch flopped down on the deck between her and me. It was sure a pretty fish, and I was jealous, so I put my line in the water hoping I could catch one a little bigger.

"What'll I do now?" Sis asked.

Mother gave her a look. "Take it off the hook."

"You take it off for me Mom, please," Sis said.

"Shirley Jean," Mom said, "don't be such a big baby. Put your foot on the fish, and pull the hook out."

Sis put her foot over on the fish. It flopped. She jumped straight up; I started laughing.

Mother said, "Alright, that's enough. Brother, take the hook out of the fish for your sister."

Something jerked on my line. "I've got a bite."

"Brother, would you please take the fish off of my hook?"

I couldn't believe my ears. That was the nicest my sister had talked to me in weeks. "But I've got a bite." I reeled the line up. The hook was bare, so I put another nightcrawler on, and took the fish off Sis's hook.

"Would you bait my hook again? Please brother. Just once more, and I promise I won't ask again."

"Okay, but just one more time."

I had just finished baiting her hook when we heard this loud noise from shore. Dad and Charlie had come out of the cabin in their underwear, opened the car door and then slammed it real hard. They were standing on the beach. Dad yelled, "Okay who's the wise-ass?"

Mom started pulling up the anchor. Sis screamed she had another fish and cranked her reel. I looked over the side. Sure enough, coming up through the water was another striped perch. It was bigger than the first one and had a beautiful yellow belly. Another thing I saw on the bottom of the lake, standing upright like play soldiers in a platoon, were twenty-four bottles of Stroh's Fire-Brewed Bohemian Beer.

Sis rowed us in with her second fish flopping around. "What are you going to tell Dad?" she asked, Mom.

"That I threw his beer in the lake. I don't intend to spend two weeks in this woods babysitting three drunks."

Sis shook her head. "But they'll just go buy some more."

Mom smiled. "Not today they won't. It's Sunday. Sonny, take the other fish off Sis's hook so she can show her daddy what she caught."

"Hey, Mom. How'd you make all those bottles stand up like that?"

"Son, those bottles are just like Daisy, they've got a lot of air in them."

Dad, Charlie, and Daisy moped around the cabin for an hour or so. Then Dad said he and Charlie were going fishing. He took Sis aside. "Where'd you catch those big perch?"

"Right out there in front of the cabin where you saw us, Daddy."

Dad and Charlie grabbed the fishing poles and ran for the boat. We stood on the shore and watched while Charlie rowed and Dad hung over the bow with his nose close to the water. Pretty soon he yelled for Charlie to stop. The anchor splashed. Charlie leaned over one side and Dad the other. They let their lines down, then maneuvered those bare hooks real careful like until they caught the lip of a cap, and slowly reeled the bottle up. When the first bottle surfaced you could hear them cheering all over the lake.

After awhile they got the hang of it and were pulling up beer faster than they could drink it.

Daisy came staggering out of the cabin and wanted to know what was going on; said she had a terrible taste in her mouth. Mom told her the men had gone fishing for beer.

"Are they catching any?"

Another shout went up from the boat. "Does that answer your question?" Mother said.

Daisy cupped her mouth and yelled, "Save me a couple of bottles."

I crossed my arms over the back of my head to ward off the blows. Sis had been hitting me for so long and with such force she was gasping for breath like a long distance runner. "You damned brat!" she screamed. "I hate your guts."

It had started when she caught me reading her "Dear Diary" with all the mushy stuff about her boyfriends and the part about Topper where it said she, " . . . longed for his caress." I was rolling on the floor laughing when she walked in our bedroom. She snatched the book, chased me through the house and rode me to the floor like a wrangler on a spooked dogie. "I'm gonna tell Mom," I said, concerned about her hitting me as hard as she could on the head. Not that she hadn't slapped me around plenty of times before, but not, it seemed with the same fury.

"You just do that," she snapped, "I'll tell them what a snoopy little creep you are, and that you spit on me." I guess she figured she could do just about anything she wanted and get away with it, knowing Mom and particularly Dad would believe anything she told them.

I hollered as loud as I could hoping the volume would hurt her ears. I glanced up and saw a scary expression in her eyes. I hadn't understood how infuriated and hateful she was—it was a look I'd seen only one time before—on the face of the man old Henry said was the big shot, or whatever you call the leader of the Livingston County, Missouri, Ku Klux Klan.

It had happened the day Mom sent me uptown to Urstrom's with a quarter to buy some turnips and a slab of fat back, the week before Lester Parsons turned up missing.

The quarter was wet and slippery, but I was afraid to open my sweating hand to let it dry for fear I'd lose it. There weren't any pockets in my britches, so I had no choice except to clutch for dear life what Mom said was the only money we had. She said I had to go to the store 'cause she didn't feel good, and Sis was in school, but I think it was so people wouldn't see the purple bruise under her eye.

My hand was cramping when Mister Urstrom tore a sheet of brown butcher paper from a roll, threw on a chunk of salt pork and laid it on the swinging scale. I watched a roach climb the side of the corn meal barrel and perch sentinel-like on the brim. "Few ounces over," he said. "But I'll only charge for a pound. What else you want? Tell your mamma I've got some fresh calf liver, butchered yesterday, and tell your daddy I've got something for him too." His grin pealed his lips back from teeth that matched the color of the yellow stains under the arms of his shirt.

I wanted to say, "Give me a nickels worth of turnips *and* a pennies worth of licorice drops, the ones covered with pink and white sugar sprinkles." But I didn't get a chance to answer before the screen door squeaked, slammed, and Lester Parsons was standing inside.

Mr. Urstrom squinted against the glare from the front window, scribbled .09 cents across my package, and strode toward the cash box. I followed in that direction, lagging at the candy counter to have another look at the licorice drops, knowing if I bought a pennies worth I'd be in big trouble.

Lester, shuffling his bare feet on the sawdust covered floor, was field dressed in a ragged pair of bibs with one strap looped over a shoulder wide enough to host a yard of momma's cotton muslin, the other flapping behind him for want of a hook on the front. The long hard muscles of his upper arms glistened with sweat. His head was topped with a tattered straw fedora pulled down so tight tufts of hair poked through like donkey ears, and was slanted across his forehead in a hell-take-the-hindmost fashion. What made Lester stand out though, and made the way he dressed seem unimportant, was the flash in his eyes like he was on the verge of laughing at the world's funniest joke, but he was looking straight at Mister Urstrom.

Mister Urstrom yelled, "Hey, boy! You come in this store, you take your hat off. What cho do'n in here anyways?"

Lester slid the hat off the side of his head and crumpled it in his hand before it disappeared behind his back. Mister Urstrom reached down and came up with a baseball bat which he set next to the cash box. It was one of those little ones, about the right size for me to play with. Then he leaned forward with both hands flat on the counter and said, "Get on out of here. You ain't got no money."

Lester, his eyes darting between the club and the floor, dug deep in the pocket of his overalls and brought out something wrinkled like a wad of green chewing gum, which he worked with until it took the shape of a dollar bill. He held it up in front of Mister Urstrom's nose. "I needs a pound of fat back."

Quicker than an eye blink, the bat came off the counter and made a slapping sound when the grocer brought the thick end hard into the palm of his hand. "When you speak to me, Boy, you say 'Sir.' Hear?"

It was in that moment, that precise instant, that I saw the look of pure hatred on Mr. Urstom's face, the kind that telegraphs violence, and speaks of the willingness to inflict unlimited pain, even to the darkest of all deeds. I'd never seen it before, and hadn't since—until I looked up into the eyes of my sister, with her jaw clinched, plummeting me with blows.

CHAPTER 11

The Handshake

From the maroon divan in the living room, Sis and I could see beyond the vacant lot across from our house, past Garfield and Annabelle Streets, all the way to where Stephenson Highway curved and became two-way. We leaned against the back of the couch and pressed our noses against the front window—the perfect place to watch for Dad.

Mom, reaming the center out of a bell pepper, came out of the kitchen, and peered over our shoulders into the dusk. "Tell me the instant you see him," she said, then spun and hurried back through the swinging door. Cars were turning headlights on as the traffic moved steadily from the manufacturing plants back to the northern suburbs of Detroit and rounded the curve on Stephenson at Nine and One-Half Mile Road. Night was beginning to settle, but we'd be able to recognize Dad for a while longer. He was driving a shiny new green Ford, and there would be traffic bottle-necked behind him. The drunker he got, the slower he drove.

Mother stuck her head through the door again and said, "Maybe he stopped at the store."

Yeah, I thought, *that will happen about the same time Hitler has a Bar-Mitzvah.* But in the years we'd lived on Browning Street, she had never stopped hoping that just once when Dad was late it would be because he stopped on some domestic errand. It never happened. Week after week we repeated the ritual, and the result was always the same.

"Here he comes, Momma, he's coming!" Sis yelled. The green Ford crept tentatively around the curve, weaving slightly as other vehicles sped past. We bounced off the back of the couch and away from the window so he wouldn't see us when he pulled into the drive.

Mother was beside us in an instant, hands clasped. "Are you sure it was him?"

"It was him Mother," Sis said with a touch of impudence, full of herself, and never wrong.

"Thank God," Mom said, and headed toward the kitchen, apparently too preoccupied to react to Sis's tone of voice. "Now don't you kids say anything to upset him, you know how he is."

Mom had her hand on the door when Sis muttered, "Sure hope none of my friends come over tonight."

Mom wheeled in her tracks. With a steely stare, she snapped, "You better remember what a good provider he is whenever you start feeling sorry for yourself."

It would be another twenty years before I would unravel the "good provider" myth she had just voiced. The car pulled into the driveway. "Now please, you know how he is . . ." She disappeared behind the swinging door.

The back door in the kitchen opened into a stairwell that went down three steps to a landing. From there you could go to the right and continue down into the basement, or go straight out the back door onto the driveway. I tiptoed across the dining room and pushed the door into the kitchen open just wide enough to see Dad come through the back door. Mom was holding the door to the stairwell open.

"Brother! Get away from there," Sis said, from the living room. "Dad might think you're spying on him."

I cocked my head so I could see what was going on through the crack and at the same time whispered, "I'm not going to say anything."

Dad paused on the landing as though indecisive about whether to turn and go to the basement or step up into the kitchen. Then he lurched up the steps where he braced himself unsteadily against the door frame, and muttered something unintelligible under his breath.

Mom's hands were twisted in the apron around her waist. She managed a smile and quietly said, "We were so worried about you. Where have you been?"

"That's none of your business." He said, glaring at her. His black hair hung lankily across his forehead, the unopened top of a whiskey bottle stuck out of a paper sack in his right hand. He used his left hand to apply torque and twisted the top off. The muscles in his jaw moved, his teeth made a grinding sound as he stared at Mom.

"Come and have some supper, Honey," she said while he manipulated the bottle cap.

"I want a drink."

She said, "I fixed everything you like—a pork roast, even a lemon meringue pie."

"Jesus! Don't you understand English? I don't want any goddamned supper—I want a drink, so get me a glass." The cap from the whiskey bottle fell to the floor and rolled under the table. The muscles in his jaw bulged and the grinding started again. Mother ignored the rolling cap and scurried to the cupboard. She thrust a shot glass in his hand. Dad would get falling down drunk several times a week, go unshaven and unbathed with clothes askew for days at a time, but would never, ever take a drink of whiskey straight out of the bottle. Mom said it was because when he was a teenager, some boys had offered him a drink of whiskey out of a brown bottle. It had been urine. He took the glass, steadied himself, and poured it full. Phenomenal nerves—hands steady as a rock. He could stay drunk for days, and after sobering up, not have a trace of tremor. It didn't matter if his body was as toxic as a present-day Superfund Site, nor that he would go through bouts of delirium tremors; his hands were always as steady as a brain surgeon's. He stood there, the glass level, teeth grinding.

Mother took a half-step toward him. "Come on, Honey, sit down over here and let me get you a bite to eat, you'll feel better."

He brought the shot glass to his mouth and threw back the whiskey, suppressed a gag, and dropped the glass. It shattered at his feet. Mother rushed to grab the bottle but he pushed her away and she stumbled backwards. He lurched away from the door and staggered to the breakfast nook table. Mother grabbed the broom and started gathering in the broken whiskey tumbler.

Sis leaned over my shoulder and whispered, "Tell Mother, I'm going over to Audrey's house to study for a test."

I wasn't about to deliver that message. I didn't want Mom or Dad to know I was anywhere around. Besides, Mom was absorbed in Dad's next move and not about to get involved in supervising children. I let the door close quietly, called to Elmer, and walked through the front of the house, and up the stairs to my bedroom. Directly above the kitchen, the rise and fall of muted voices came through the vents—obscenities from Dad and an occasional plea from Mom. I should have left the house like Sis, but I lingered too long.

Mom's voice came up the stairwell, "Sonny, Sonny, come help me get Dad to the basement—quick."

I wanted to hide, to stay as far away from what was going on downstairs as possible, but she needed help, so I hung on the banister, letting myself down each step slowly hoping something would happen. Maybe he'd pass out, and I wouldn't have to go to the basement with them.

"Hurry," she urged, leading me through the house to the kitchen door where we stopped. "Don't say anything to upset him. He's getting sick and we need to get him downstairs before he throws up. Where's your sister?"

"She went somewhere to study."

He was half-sitting, half-lying on one of the benches in the nook, his hair, black as coal, plastered against his forehead. The aroma of Rose Hair Oil and stale alcohol filled the kitchen.

I reached around to his back pocket and found his handkerchief. "Here Dad, let me wipe your mouth." He mumbled an obscenity and pushed me back. His eyes, unfocused, vacuous, stared past me. Saliva, the consistency of gravy, bubbled when he mumbled, "I can whip any sonfabitch in the world, you know it?" He repeated the boast until it trailed off lost, or used up. Being a southpaw, his left hand was naturally powerful, but was made awesome from squeezing the trigger of a spray gun everyday. When he clinched his fist, the skin in his palm squeaked.

"Dad, it's me, let me wipe your face, it's dirty." I swabbed the corners of his mouth with the soiled handkerchief.

Mom, on his opposite side, put her hand under his arm, tugged upward. He didn't move. At his weight, and walunked, there was no way we could move him unless he wanted to go. "Come on, Honey," she said. Let Sonny and I help you downstairs to bed. You'll feel better if you lay down." She gestured with her head and eyes for me to take hold of his other arm.

I stuffed the handkerchief back in his pocket and got a grip on his arm near the elbow. We pulled and coaxed until finally he struggled to his feet and stood swaying like a hickory tree in a cyclone. I draped his arm over my shoulder and grasped him around the waist. Mom did the same on the other side. Together, we moved toward the stairwell. We jostled and bumped through the door frame like three clowns in vaudeville slapstick. It would've been easier if he'd have passed out. We could've slid him down the stairs on a throw-rug. I thought of the twenty spelling words on a sheet of paper in my room that Miss Olsen, my teacher, had assigned for the next day. I felt guilty, and unconnected to anything tangible. Down three steps to the landing we went. A ninety degree turn to the right, and seven steps to go. At the third, Mom pushed Dad's head down to keep him from hitting it on the low ceiling that resulted when the builder saved a little on construction costs by leaving one course of cement blocks out of the basement walls. We made the bottom step without falling, stumbled past the basement toilet, past the furnace, past mom's Maytag with the manual wringers, and into the far corner where Dad went when he was drunk.

The three-quarter sized bed smelled musty. Snow melt and spring rains often flooded the basement with foul smelling water. Dampness and mildew took up residency year-round accounting for some of the bed's sour odor. An orange crate set on its end next to the bed was topped with a stained dresser scarf, an over-flowing ash tray, crumpled packages of Camel cigarettes, a book of matches—

too damp to strike—and a partially filled water glass in which a drowned bug floated.

He half-sat, half-fell on the bed next to the night-stand, and said, "Gimme a drink."

I reached for the glass with the floating bug. He grabbed my arm, his grip like steel. "I want a drink of whiskey." I tried to pull away. Mom, in her most placating voice said, "Now Dad, don't hurt Sonny. He was just teasing. I'll get you a drink."

That mollified him, and his grip relaxed enough for me to ease my arm loose. Mom hurried off up the stairs, and in a minute was back with the bottle and a shot glass. She poured from the pint of Imperial and handed it to him. He started the drink toward his mouth, stopped, and said he wanted a cigarette. I shook a Camel from a crumpled pack, Mom handed me a match from her apron pocket, and I lit up. After sucking a big puff into my lungs, I put the cigarette between his lips, stepped back, and rubbed the spot on my arm where he had dug in with his fingers.

At age nine I'd just started smoking, and was already liking it too much. My primary source of supply was Sis. When she started smoking, she plied me with a few cigarettes out of each of her packages to ensure my complicity and silence. But even if she hadn't supplied me, tobacco was always available at our house. Opened packages could be found lying around on the end-tables, the dressers, the kitchen counter, and refrigerator. Occasionally I'd lift a whole pack from an open carton and no one paid the slightest attention. After the war started, cigarettes made the rationing list, so I had to be a little more resourceful; I even learned to roll a cigarette from a sack of Bull Durham.

The cigarette I lit at the moment was intended as a chaser. A shot of straight bourbon and a pull on a cigarette was Dad's routine. But with the drink poised near his mouth, he said, "I've got to take a leak."

Mom nodded toward a white porcelain mug setting in the corner by the furnace with a lid in place. I groaned. The weight and heft of it told me it hadn't been emptied lately. I carried it around the corner to the stool, turned my head to the side, held my breath, and poured out the contents. By the time I got back to the bed, Dad was trying to stand up, with Mom steadying him. I sat the pot in front and started with his zipper, but Mom shook her head and whispered, "Undo his belt—take his pants off." I guess she figured that once his pants were off, any threat of him leaving was over. I unbuckled his belt and let his pants fall to the floor. Before I could get his shorts halfway down, he was peeing. Urine splashed off my hand, the side of the pot, and onto the floor—like an out-of-control firehouse. I finally got his penis aimed in the right direction. He must have drunk five gallons of beer without going to the bathroom. After an interminable time, I glanced over my shoulder at the two narrow basement windows at ground level. If a member of the Browning Street Gang would see me holding my Dad's pecker there'd be hell to pay. Urine splashed on Dad's foot.

"Watch what you're doing," Mom harped.

I took the pot to the bathroom and returned to the bed with a washcloth and towel which Mom used to clean him up. He still had the drink in his hand. When she finished his sponge bath, she lit him another smoke and inhaled a puff before surrendering the cigarette to Dad.

Instead of drinking his whiskey, he set it on the orange crate, put his arm around Mom's waist, and started the old refrain, "Just you and me and the kids, right? Just you and me and the kids. Together we can whip the world—the whole fucking world."

Mother beamed. This was what she lived to hear.

He looked in my direction, one eye on the ceiling the other on my right shoulder. "You don't believe that, huh? Well I *can* whip any som-bitch in the world." He reached out with his left hand, that big paw, clenching, unclenching. "Shake on it Son, put'er there."

He didn't need his strong hand to deal with me. I weighed in at eighty pounds, arms about as big around as a garden hose. I knew what was coming. I put my hand behind me. "I don't want to shake."

Mom gave me one of her looks and said, "You shake hands with your dad."

I stuck out my hand. He took it, gentle at first, then wrapped his forefinger around my extra knuckle like it was a pistol grip and started squeezing. The pressure came slowly while he looked at my face. Maybe he imagined I was one of the adversaries he had to whip. Maybe he knew it was me, and wanted to see how much I could endure. Or maybe he was just plain mean. I stood there, my knuckles popping, him babbling about how tough he was, and how invincible the family was—if we stuck together. All the while I wanted to scream and ask him why he was hurting someone who loved him so much. The tears started. There was the pain, and humiliation, and I wanted to tell him I hated his guts because he was hurting me. Instead I said, "Dad, please stop, your hurting me." He didn't stop. He acted like he didn't hear me, but in my heart I knew he did. So I stood there, trying without success to stem the flow of tears streaming down my face, and wondering when it would end.

Mother chimed, "You didn't drink your drink, Honey." She sounded like we were at some happy social gathering. She took the shot glass from the orange crate and offered it to him.

He looked at the liquor, then at me, chose the drink, and relaxed his grip. I escaped to the end of the bed to rub my hand and my eyes. Mother lit another cigarette. He raised the drink with the care a scientist would take raising a test tube full of polio germs. The glass perched on his lower lip for an instant, then he took it all in one gulp. His face twisted into a grimace. He dropped the glass and fought back a heave as his body tried to reject the drink. Mother grabbed the empty shot glass off of the bed. He tried to take a quick drag on the cigarette but the heaves from his low gut were too strong and he couldn't suck smoke into his lungs. It seeped between his clamped lips and trailed out of his nose.

Mom said, "Get the slop jar over here. Hurry!"

I stuck the jar under his face without a step to spare. It came out in great gushes, his lunch, and everything ingested in the previous twelve hours. Each retch accompanied by a groan and liquid stuff coming out of each nostril. I tried to keep the vomit from getting on me by backing away, but he followed the pot like a dog on a leash. I sat on the floor with the pot and he perched over it on his hands and knees moaning and heaving. I spread my arm around the jar, not touching it, but ready in case he bumped or fell against it. His gagging made me gag and I had to fight hard to keep from throwing up on the floor. Then came the dry heaves, and then the jerks. His face turned purple, and was covered with snot and stomach contents. I thought maybe he was on the verge of a fit, like the ones I'd seen Teddy Childers have in school. My greatest fear was he would fall and knock the slop jar over, so I looped my left arm across his shoulders and curled it back so my hand had a grip on his forehead. I caught a whiff of the contents of the slop jar and gagged again. I turned my face away and sucked air hard and fast through my mouth until the urge passed. He muttered between jerks, "Christ, I'm sick, so sick."

He was on his knees, wearing nothing except underwear and shoes, his face within inches of the slop jar. I couldn't help feeling sorry for him. "It will be alright in a minute, Dad, you're rid of it now, you'll be fine." At the same time I was wondering whether I would be fine. My soul was as empty as his stomach.

After Mom and I helped him to bed, I climbed up the basement stairs on wobbly knees and on up to the second floor bathroom where I washed myself so my friends wouldn't know. But the smell, a mixture of urine, vomit, and Rose Hair Oil had scalded my brain. I still felt dirty, so I took my clothes off and got in a tub of hot water. But I would never be able to scrub it out of my memory.

When the weather warmed enough to melt the ice on the lake, usually by April, Mom would stack boxes and sacks with our gear and food by the front door on Friday afternoon. If Dad made it home from work sober, we would load the car and be on the road to the cabin within minutes of his arrival. On this Friday, when Dad pulled into the driveway, Elmer started yapping. He ran in circles, jumped up and down, and made such a racket Dad frowned.

An unhappy facial expression on Dad was an alarm button to

Mom. She hollered, “Son, make Elmer shut up.” To Sis, she said, “Shirley Jean, do your homework and if you have Tessie or Gail over, don’t be staying up all night.”

“Okay Momma,” said Shirley Jean, innocently.

Our cabin on Lobdell Lake was finished in the spring of 1941. It was a no frills structure. The basement, cut into the side of a hill, had windows and a door on the lakeside. The same level housed the wood-burning cook stove that heated the entire living area, and served as the kitchen. Upstairs, were two bedrooms and a screened-in porch. The toilet was outside. The first few months after the cabin was finished, Sis went with us. But as her sixteenth birthday approached, she became less and less interested, said she hated the outside toilet, and would rather spend weekends in Hazel Park alone. At least that’s what she told my folks.

I grabbed Elmer’s collar. “Quiet down, or you’ll get us both in trouble.” But he was too excited to be quiet and kept up the racket until it was time to go, then bound into the car and curled up on the newspaper I had spread over the floor mat.

The minute we pulled away from the house, his saliva glands went into overdrive. Fifteen minutes later, in heavy traffic I yelled, “Stop! Dad, stop the car, Elmer’s . . . oh my God, it’s too late, he puked.”

Dad said, “Jesus Christ.” The car thumped onto the shoulder, and stopped.

“Why didn’t you say something sooner?” Mom asked.

“I didn’t know he was *that* sick,” I said as I attempted to maneuver the papers to keep the mess from running under Dad’s seat. Sometimes I could warn in time for Dad to pull over so Elmer could jump out and get sick in the grass. This time, there had been no chance.

“I’m going to stop and get a drink,” Dad said.

Mom gave me a dirty look. “Now Dad, don’t start drinking. At least wait until we get to the cabin.” The car pulled into a parking slot in front of a bar. Dad got out and slammed the door.

Mom gathered up her purse. “That darned dog made him nervous.”

I rubbed Elmer's neck. "It wasn't his fault. He can't help it 'cause he gets sick. Dad was just looking for an excuse."

"You be careful what you say." She closed the car door, then reopened it. "You want a hamburger?"

"Yeah, sure, a cheeseburger. What about Elmer?"

"You'll have to get in the trunk for the dog food."

Elmer and I split a cheeseburger and fries, and stayed in the car. Every hour or so, Mom stuck her head in the door and asked if I was okay. I carped about wanting to go, but Dad was always going to have just one more, so I curled up in the back with Elmer and tried to sleep. The door slammed when they got back in the car. Mom begged Dad to let her drive. But that was never to be. The car took off weaving back and forth across the centerline, and onto the shoulder. Mom said we'd be at the cabin in just a little while. Sometimes she was right, but tonight there was another tavern. The sixty mile drive to the Lake should have taken one and a half hours, maybe two, in heavy traffic. We had left at 4:30 p.m., and would not get to the cabin until after midnight.

When we finally arrived, we were so relieved to have escaped without a wreck, it lightened the mood. Despite being stiff and cold, we laughed nervously as we helped Dad inside to bed. Just walking through the door, smelling the sap seeping from the knotty pine walls, made me feel better. I built a fire in the cook stove to take the damp chill out of the rooms. Then Elmer and I, snuggled down under a comforter. But no matter how hard I concentrated on fishing and exploring the woods, the minute I fell asleep something dark crept into my dreams.

September, 1941. Sis, started her Junior Year at Hazel Park High. I was ten and started the fifth grade at Martin Road Elementary. Less than a year after he had opened the doors to his new business, Dad sold the meat market, and went back to his old job at Ford's. Wild parties and drunken brawls were occurring with more and more frequency. It was a rare evening when Dad was not drunk or hung over. We prayed, begged, cried, and pleaded, but neither God nor Dad paid any attention.

Mom said, "I know he will quit if we all pray hard enough." Mother, not a deeply religious woman, and certainly not a practicing anything, insisted that God was going to intervene and make everything just dandy. She had attended the Calvary Baptist Church in Utica, Missouri, where she also registered me on the "Cradle Roll." In her desperation, she had convinced herself that divine intervention would wash away her domestic hell. So she taught me to pray every night, "Now I lay me down to sleep, . . . bless Mom, Dad, Elmer, and Sis; don't forget the hungry children in China, and please God, help my Dad quit drinking. Amen."

Mom joined me and prayed for God to chase the Devil, and demon rum from my father's tortured soul. I had prayed every night for as long as I could remember for God to help him quit; made it my wish on every birthday, and wished for it the day I won the speckled gum ball. But he didn't quit, and I didn't believe he ever would. As time passed, even Mom began to concede—she and her children's prayers were not going to get the job done.

In the late thirties, early forties, large numbers of citizens in the greater metropolitan area of Detroit, and across the nation, tuned in on Sunday evenings for a broadcast from the Church of the Little Flower in Royal Oak, Michigan, a neighboring suburb. Across the airwaves, Father Coughlin, a Roman Catholic Priest, castigated Protestants, Jews, Blacks, President Roosevelt, and espoused Fascism as practiced by Hitler and Mussolini. For good balance he'd throw in a few non-denominational prayers.

Protestantism had been ingrained in my Mother. She frequently made uncomplimentary remarks about Catholicism, and the Pope in particular. From her, I learned demeaning descriptions of our Catholic neighbors and their Church. That's why it seemed so bizarre when she decided the solution to our problem with Dad was to ask The Radio Priest, Father Charles Coughlin, to intervene on his behalf.

On this Sunday evening, Sis and I were herded into the living room and made to sit down in front of the radio. The green dial in the face of the cabinet lit up. After a few adjustments, the velvet-voiced priest of radio-land boomed into our home. The program was a mixture of preaching, lecturing, and scolding, interspersed with singing and praying. I tried to sneak a look at a *Donald Duck Comic Book,* but Mom kept poking me in the ribs and it's a good thing she did or I would have missed the good part. The Priest ended his political diatribe, and turned to the sins of his listeners.

At first, he spoke in general terms. There was this hell-bound alcoholic possessed by the devil, whose soul could only be salvaged by the collective prayers of his listeners. Then he said, *Join me in prayer for the tortured soul of Hiram Keith Myers, Sr., who lives in Hazel Park, and who, without the help of Jesus Christ will burn in the fires of Hell for all eternity! Now let the Holy Spirit enter his sin-stained body and cast out the demons driving him to drink.*

One of the demons Father Coughlin exorcized out of Dad must have jumped right into Sis. "Ohhh Shit!" she screeched, leaping to her feet. "My God! Mother, how could you? What will I tell my friends?" She stamped both feet so hard a picture of Grandmother Carpenter fell off the piano.

Bad dreams had started in Utica, but this night I would have my first recurring nightmare, one that would run itself over and over for the rest of my life.

It was pitch black. I was being chased, by something that had no face, no identity. Yet I knew what it intended. My hands and feet moved as though through syrup. I was suspended in slow motion, but the thing chasing me was not; I screamed, but even my voice was cut off—muted—was barely discernable. I attempted to strike back, to defend myself like Dad taught, but the blows were impotent. And then I was in its grasp, completely helpless, paralyzed. It was reaching for my genitals and I was screaming myself awake.

The next day was Saturday. I delivered my papers, and was back at the house at 10:30 a.m. Dad was eating breakfast. Mom sat across from him sipping coffee. I went into the breakfast area and took a bite or two of Dad's toast to settle my stomach. I needed to talk to somebody, but felt embarrassed. I muttered, "Had a bad dream last night."

"What about?" Mom asked.

"Something chasing me."

Dad looked up from his eggs. "What was it?"

"I don't know, it was dark. Couldn't see its face . . . actually, I'm not sure it had a face, but it was a person."

"Did it catch you?"

"Yes."

Mom had an amused expression on her face. "Did it hurt you?"

"No, but it would've if I hadn't woke up."

Dad made a fist with his left hand and jabbed from the waist like he was hitting someone. "If it ever does, give it a hard one in the gut. Maybe it'll leave you alone."

I fidgeted. I didn't think Dad's solution would do any good. It sounded stupid to think you could scare your nightmares away. Maybe they didn't understand what I was trying to say. "It seemed like my arms and legs wouldn't move. I couldn't get away or fight back."

Mom reached across the table and put her hand on mine. "There's nothing to be afraid of, nothing's going to harm you, isn't that right, Dad?"

I thought about the basement—my hand in a vice; about the boxing lessons I had come to hate; about what some of the kids at school said about my hands. "Sure, Mom."

"Everyone has bad dreams, don't they Dad?" she asked.

Dad swallowed toast, and took a gulp of coffee. "I can't remember having a dream—of any kind." He looked across at Mom. "You about ready to go?"

"Where you going?" I asked.

"To the race track."

I loved horses. "Can I go?"

Dad pushed out of the nook. I saw the look he shot Mom. She got up. "No," she said. "I want you and your sister to clean up these dishes. And no fighting."

An hour after they left, Sis's new boyfriend, Donald H. Scott, or Topper, as he was called, came over.

I was sitting at the dining room table counting the money I'd collected that morning on my paper route. I'd bought the route six months ago for twenty-five dollars. The previous carrier had neglected it, but now, after only three months, I had built it up to a hundred customers. Tomorrow, the Sunday Edition of the *Detroit News* would be so big, it would take two, maybe three wagon loads to make all the deliveries. I finished counting. My profit was four dollars and fifty cents for the week—a fortune. I put a quarter in my pocket, dumped the rest in a fruit jar, screwed the lid down, and went in the living room.

"How'd you do?" my sister asked.

"Made lots a' money," I said, sticking out my chest.

Topper was sprawled on the couch like he owned the place. Fifteen years old, a year younger than Sis, he was bigger than Dad—six foot, two inches tall, and one-hundred-ninety-five pounds. The football coach at Hazel Park's High School, Mr. Graeber, had him tabbed to play center. "Wanna flip coins?" he said.

Maybe I could impress him. "Sure. How much?"

"Dimes."

In less than an hour, my entire earnings for the week were in the pocket of my sister's new boyfriend.

CHAPTER 12

A Shocking Introduction

I was three months past my tenth birthday, and sprawled on the living room floor reading *Blondie* in the Sunday Edition of the *Detroit News*. I chuckled at Dagwood holding his toothbrush under an empty tube of paste as he ran it through the ringer of a washing machine in an attempt to get out one more squirt.

Sis, her open mouth sending high "Cs" of glass-shattering cresendo reverberating through the house, must have thought I was laughing at her practice session. She shot me a dirty look.

In retaliation, I pressed my hands over my ears and screwed my face into a mimic of a Lon Chaney werewolf. The power of my sister's voice was legendary. Whenever someone wanted me home for whatever reason, Sis was given the privilege to see to it. Ordinarily, she did not take responsibility well, griping endlessly if asked to do the dishes, straighten her room, iron her clothes for the next school day, or perform any other household task. But the chore of calling me home, she accepted with diabolical relish. Our front porch on Browning Street was perfectly suited for the task. Sis would mount one of the cement benches projecting from each side of the uppermost step, suck in a breath, and emit a caterwaul that would bounce off of buildings three blocks away. It started low, increased in both pitch and volume, and reached an ear-piercing soprano. "Broooooooooothhhhhhheeeerrrrr!"

A group of boys, including myself and a newcomer to Browning Street, were shooting marbles two blocks from our house. It was suppertime. The air was suddenly filled with my sister's shrieking call, louder than the air-raid siren the Civil Defense had been trying out. The new kid looked around as though preparing to take cover and said, "What the hell was that?"

Secretly, I loved to hear Sis sing. Her voice was the purest, most compelling soprano I would ever hear. In later years, I compared her talent to that of operatic stars, which confirmed my belief that none matched the absolute glory of her highest notes. But at age ten, I would have died rather than admit I liked anything about my sister, let alone her voice. On the floor, listening to the haunting melody of *The Indian Love Call,* I waved my arm to catch Sis's attention. When she glanced my way I held my nose to let her know how disgusting I thought her performance was this Sunday morning.

Dad was taking a shower in preparation for putting on his Sunday cloths, a ritual he had adopted since his stay at McKnight's Sanatorium where he had gone for three weeks to dry out. He refused for years to admit he had a drinking problem, let alone submit to any kind of treatment. But after screaming for two days in the basement about the rats and bugs crawling over his bed and body, he agreed to go. On this Sunday, he'd been off of alcohol for three months. There was still plenty of tension whenever he was around *(Don't say or do anything to upset him),* but our home had taken on some semblance of sanity. Mom felt secure enough to have her mother, Grandma Sherman, come to visit, and they had bought and re-upholstered an antique chair to fill a vacant spot in the living room. In the evenings, when Sis got home from school, they made her stand on a stool, and with pins stuck here and there, took measurements for a formal dress she would wear to the Junior-Senior Prom. When they finished, her gown was the most beautiful creation I had ever seen—like something from a movie—a bright red skirt with shiny squares flared below a black, tight fitting bodice, with plunging neckline. When she tried it on, she was prettier than a princess. I told her she looked like a witch.

Searching for *Snuffy Smith and Barney Google,* in the Comic Section, I turned the page. Mother hustled about in the kitchen, rattling dishes. The mouth-watering smell of bacon frying for a late Sunday breakfast filled the house.

The phone rang. Sis, exercising her undisputed monopoly, yelled she would get it, and disappeared into the entry hall. I heard her say, "Hello." It was quiet for a moment. Then she screamed, "Oh my God!" The phone banged on the receiver, and she ran back into the living room. "The Japanese bombed Pearl Harbor, we're going to war. Oh my God, we're going to war!"

For the rest of the day, we sat around the radio listening to reports interspersed with commentary. Two battleships, we were told, the Arizona and Oklahoma, had been lost in the attack. In fact, the battleships, California, Nevada, and West Virginia were also sunk, but for some reason that information was withheld. That morning, the Japanese had killed 2,344 United States servicemen. Toward evening, Sis left to go over to Topper's house. Dad went out, found a bootlegger, and got drunk. Mom and I stayed home to take care of Dad who added the Japanese to the list of people in the world he was going to whip. "I'm going downtown tomorrow and join the Navy. I'll show those sneaky sons a bitches."

"You're too old, Dad," Mom said.

"Hell you say. Forty's not old."

I wished I was old enough to go.

Soon after the war started, Dad and Mom converted the upstairs to an apartment. The bath in the basement was expanded to include a full shower. They built a master bedroom on the back of the main floor, and that's where they slept when Dad was home and sober, which after Pearl Harbor became less and less frequent.

The small room adjacent to the kitchen on the main floor, was converted into a bedroom for Sis and me. After three years of separate bedrooms, we were back to sharing a three-quarter bed, a box closet with a thin curtain to hide the contents, a chest of drawers, and a small night stand which housed a radio, our set of *Standard Encyclopedias,* and a half-dozen other books, one of which I used a razor on to cut the middle of the pages out leaving a compartment large enough for Sis to hide her cigarettes.

The screen on the one window in our new bedroom was grown over with ivy on the outside, and so well concealed that on one occasion, while outside clowning around with the hose, I turned a stream of water through the ivy into the bedroom. It was easy to forget the window existed.

On a Saturday night, in the fall of 1942, I was home alone and in bed. The weather had turned cool, but there was no breeze and the room was still hot from the heat of the day, so I opened the window and fell into a fitful sleep. I was jolted awake and sat up in bed trying to figure out what had startled me. Elmer, at the end of the bed had his head up, his ears cocked toward the window; a low growl rumbled in his throat. Maybe that's what woke me. I reached down and scratched his neck. Or maybe Mom and Dad had come home and were in the basement fighting. But no sound came from below. There was no clock in my room, but my sister, usually home by 1:00 a.m., was not yet in bed, so I figured it to be a little after midnight.

A voice came through the ivy covered window. The driveway was next to my room, and our neighbor's bedroom was just a few feet beyond the driver's side where the car was ordinarily parked. I put my ear as close to the screen as possible. The conversation, muted, as though coming from an enclosure, began to rise. Then both doors of the car slammed. Through a peep-hole in the ivy, I saw the outlines of Mom and Dad standing in front of our car. I had heard every filthy epithet ever uttered, either in my own home, or on the streets of Hazel Park, but this was different—it was my mother talking. "She's a slut! You're going to leave me for that goddamned slut?"

Dad said nothing, stood there seemingly indifferent to the tongue lashing, as though waiting for Mom to burn herself out. But his silence had the opposite effect. She reached back and slapped him hard. The crack of her palm across his face echoed off the houses. He grabbed her by the arms. She kicked him in the shins. I stopped breathing. She kicked him again.

He growled, "Stop, or I'll break your damn neck!"

I was out of bed, out the door, and on the driveway. They were stumbling around trying to get in a position to hurt the other. Dad staggered. Mom jerked one of her arms loose and tried to claw his face. I couldn't get between them, and screamed for them to stop. Dad let go of her other arm, and I grabbed her around the waist to keep her from going back for more. He stumbled through the door and down the steps into the basement. Mom followed with me hanging on, pleading for her to stop. On the bottom step, she turned and told me it was none of my business and not to get involved. Her breath was heavy with alcohol, and her words made no sense, so I stood there with my arms around her waist.

She screamed, "Go back upstairs and go to bed."

"You can't make me," I said. But she dragged me toward his bed.

Dad went to his corner, fell on the bed, swung his legs over the side, and pulled his pant legs up. His shins were covered with angry red welts. Some of the blows had broken the skin and the lesions were oozing. "See what your mother did to me." He smirked as though the injuries were proof that whatever he had done was not sufficient to warrant her reaction. "And you think she's so damned perfect."

Mom said, "Son, you don't understand what's going on here. Go upstairs. You should be sleeping."

"Sleeping? You're just as nuts as he is. Understand or not, I'm not leaving without you. Remember Betsy Sue?"

"That was just a doll. He'd never do that to me."

"When he's drunk he'll do anything."

After she realized I was not going without her, we climbed the steps together. She went in her room, and I went back to bed. As I passed the kitchen, I glanced at the clock, 2:30 am. I left my door open and laid wide-eyed waiting for something else to happen.

Sometime later, Sis came home, made Elmer get out of bed, and crawled under the covers. "Mom or Dad say anything about me not being home when they got here?"

"They don't even realize you've been gone. How come you're so late?"

"The car Topper borrowed had a flat tire and there was no spare. We had to call his parents. What are you doing awake at this hour?" she asked. She took a wad of gum out of her mouth and stuck it on the back of the head board.

For a long while, I whispered everything that had happened. Ordinarily, when my sister came home late, we fought over an imaginary line down the middle of the bed, but tonight, when she asked if she could put her cold feet on me, I thought it was swell. It didn't matter that she had slapped my face and hit me with her fists. At that moment she was there with her feet touching me, and I was thankful. We bolted upright at every creak and strange noise in the house. After Sis's feet got warm she dozed, but I was too afraid of what Mom and Dad might do to each other, so I lay wide-eyed and listened. Now and then, Dad's voice, incoherent, drifted up through the floor and I would tense waiting for Mom to go back downstairs. Morning sounds began outside my window.

The next day, both Mom and Dad were sullen and rarely spoke. Everyone was on edge. The second night, when the green Ford failed to appear, Mom fretted and paced the floor. Then she went to the kitchen and opened a can of Spam which she cut into thick slices and put in a skillet. She set the table with a loaf of bread, catsup, and mustard and told us to fix ourselves sandwiches. I gave two slices to Elmer and fixed myself a peanut butter and jelly sandwich. Sis turned up her nose and went to a friend's house. Mom sent me to bed.

Through the haze of partial sleep, I heard the front door open and steps in the hall. A screaming curse snapped my eyes open. Furniture scraped across the floor amidst loud voices. Screaming and cursing, even physical violence was commonplace when Dad didn't come home after work, but this was different. Mother was screaming at the top of her lungs, her tone choked as though she were dying. Through the bedlam there was a third, but quieter, voice.

The door to my room burst open, and Mother was quickly beside the bed. "Get up," she ordered. I hesitated, frightened by her manner. She clinched my arm, pulled me out of bed and half dragged me into the living room, where she put her hand in the middle of my back, and pushed me toward a handsome couple standing just inside the entry hall next to an overturned chair. "Meet your Daddy's girlfriend," she said. "Go ahead. Say hello to your future step-mother!"

How beautiful she was. Dressed with hat, gloves, and high heels, and snuggled intimately against my Dad, who had his arm protectively around her thin waist. For the remainder of my life, I tried to fathom why he brought his mistress into our house. Was she a trophy to be hung in the minds of his family to assuage an ego deficit? Was he showing his lover the material possessions in his life? Perhaps it was a cruel way of saying the marriage was over. Or was it an act of madness—a drunken impulse, the return of delirium tremens? Was he displaying his family like merchandise? And my mother. Why did she, in the dead of night, introduce me into such a bizarre scene, one of Wellesian madness? I never asked either of them. But whatever the reasons, Dad stood before his wife and me in the vestibule of our home, formally presenting his mistress, Eunice.

I was in front of Dad, his sublime lady slightly to the right. He directed her with his hand, and she stepped forward to within a foot of my face as though to accept the challenge and accommodate the introduction. I could smell her essence—strong and sensuous. I don't know if she said anything because I was sobbing, trying to turn around against the hand planted against the middle of my back. The last thing I remember as I broke and bolted for the bedroom was Mother saying, "I hope your satisfied, you bitch! Get out of my house, and if you ever set foot here again, so help me God, I'll kill you!"

I cried into my pillow the rest of the night. No one came to me, and the house on Browning Street, from that moment on, was empty—except for Elmer.

The next day, on the way to the kitchen, I heard a sound so wretched, it raised hackles on my neck. I stopped and listened. It came again, a high pitched wail ending in a sob. Maybe a wounded animal outside, or a soap opera on the radio. Then I realized it was coming from my room. I ran to the door and threw it open. Mother was on my bed, her face wet with tears, her glasses on the night stand. I stood paralyzed at the sight. She pressed her hands tightly over her ears, as if to keep from hearing some unwanted message, all the while emitting a soul wrenching keening. "What is it

Mother?" I cried. She wouldn't acknowledge me. The wails were interspersed with deep sobs. I threw myself on her chest and forced her to look at me. "Please answer me Mother, what is it?" But still she didn't reply, so I grabbed her arms and pulled her hands away from her ears. "Momma, tell me what's wrong so I can help you!" In my heart I knew it was the beautiful woman. Sis came into the room.

She took one look and said, "My God, what's the matter with her?"

"She's dying." I fell to my knees beside the bed and prayed, "Please God, don't let her die. You saved Elmer. Please save my mother." Then Sis was gone and in a moment I heard her on the phone telling someone to send an ambulance quickly, that her mother was dying.

As my sister's voice came through the door, mother raised her head off the pillow, and for an instant looked at me through tear-filled eyes as though trying to decide what to say. Then she whispered, "I'm okay Sonny, don't worry." Her head fell back and she emitted another mournful cry.

I lay on her breast trying to understand what it meant, and was still there when attendants lifted me aside, placed her up on a stretcher, and carried her to an ambulance. Following at their heels, I tried to ride with her, but they gently forced me out, closed the doors, and left me standing on the street. The driver told Sis we could follow them to the hospital.

Sis was sixteen, but had no driver's license. She found the car keys, and we went careening off through the streets of Detroit on the trail of the ambulance. Down Woodward Avenue we flew, my sister hunched over the wheel like a race-car driver. The ambulance, not more than four car lengths ahead, with lights flashing, and siren screeching, never slowed for red lights and stop signs. Sis, having not the slightest notion where we were going, had to keep the ambulance in sight, so she laid on the horn and ran those red traffic signals close behind.

By some quirk of fate, we arrived at Henry Ford Hospital in one piece, and were told it would be best not to disturb our Mom.

They were in the process of administering heavy sedation. We sat in the waiting room for the rest of the day. Sis was afraid to drive home. It took Dad a long time to show up. I don't know how he knew where we were or how he got there, but when he arrived, he was distant and didn't stay in Mom's room long, then drove Sis and me home.

I'll never know what had been physically wrong with my Mother on that scary day. The only explanation she attempted was vague and included the word "tension." Mom could take every hardship and indignity Dad dealt her. The one thing she could not stand was the prospect of life without him. When it seemed she was going to lose him, she almost gave up.

Dad was rarely home now, and Mom was so sedated and preoccupied it was though she wasn't there. During those nights, I walked the sidewalks looking at the lighted homes, some with the shades drawn, and wondered about the activities inside. I knew from visits in the homes of my friends who lived on the street that there was a great difference between their families and mine. The quiet, orderliness, and love manifested in other homes stirred curiosity and yearning.

On other occasions I would walk to the end of the block past the Young's house to the Little Woods. Elmer and I often sat on a rise under a giant oak and listened to night sounds, and the hum of traffic on Stephenson Highway, and sometimes we could overhear the private conversations of strollers who happened by. Crickets and night birds cried their summer songs, joined by bull frogs bellowing out from the marshy areas of the Big Woods across the highway.

On winter nights when the snow swirled in dervishes along the deserted streets and the voices from the basement rose above the howling wind, I zipped up my parka, laced my high-top boots, and quietly walked out the front door. This was one activity where I had to leave Elmer at home.

On this night, my Flyer, its runners sand papered to a silver gleam, leaned upright on the front porch. I pulled the sled past the Schmidt house to the corner of Browning and Palmer Avenue, an intersection with ditches on all four corners. I always hid in the same one. It was deep enough to conceal me, but not too steep to prevent me from coming out running. I hunched down and waited for a car to turn off of Stephenson. There were no street lights, the intersection black, so unless I got caught in a headlight, my cover was complete.

Swirling snow wet my face, encrusted my eyebrows. Sometimes the wait seemed interminable. Tonight, traffic on the side streets was sparse. The few who had ventured out in vehicles moved cautiously on the snow-packed streets. The absence of stop signs at intersections added to the hazard. Car lights cast a beam off the highway. I was on my knees at the ready. The vehicle approached, slowed, and resumed speed as it crossed the intersection, too fast to catch. I lowered myself back onto the Flyer. The next vehicle slowed, brake lights flashing. The car slid to a near stop. It was turning onto Palmer. I was up, legs pumping, boots crunching the crystalized snow. I threw myself forward and belly flopped on the Flyer. The sled hit the ice and shot forward. The car half turned, half spun, then straightened. My hand reached forward and grasped the rear bumper—perfect timing. I had a ride. I couldn't tell if this driver knew I was on. He accelerated. The tires threw ice and snow in my face. I moved hand-over-hand across the bumper, held my breath as I passed the exhaust pipe, and settled in the middle. I was flying across the ice. We came to another intersection and the car slowed. I stiff-armed the bumper to keep from sliding under the wheels. He was heading for John-R, a main street the road crews kept clear and heavily sanded. Timing the release was important. There was the danger of sliding into the middle of John-R, so a third of a block away I let go. The car slowed. For twenty feet my speed and that of the host car stayed equal. Another car turned off John-R and headed toward us in the opposite lane. I eased the flyer to the right and dropped the toes of my boots onto the ice. The car I had hitched, pulled away. I made a sharp turn into a driveway and rolled off the flyer laughing. Great ride. All I had to do now was find one that would take me back to where I had started.

I dragged the sled away from the busy street, and found another dark corner to wait for a ride. It didn't take long. I was on again. The most exciting, and dangerous hitches were those when the driver of the host vehicle tried to shake you off, and this one was trying. He fish-tailed. I held on as the sled careened crazily back and forth behind the bumper for a block. When that failed to shake me, he slammed on the brakes. I took the car bumper with both hands and hooked my toes over the back of the flyer to keep the sled from catapulting under the wheels. The driver, presumably drunk or out of his mind, and incensed I was still hanging on, slid to a stop, jammed the car in reverse, and spun the tires back toward me. My sled didn't go in reverse, so I rolled onto the curb with the Flyer on top of me. The car pulled along side. "Stay the hell off the bumper of my car, you god damned hoodlum."

"Up you," I yelled. And ran into the darkness. I chuckled about it all the way home.

The worst ride I ever had was when a driver doing about thirty miles per hour pulled me across a patch of road covered with ashes from a coal furnace. My sled stopped dead, the force almost dislocated my shoulders, and I went scooting across the ashes on my belly. But hitching was like surfing. All of the waiting, failures, and risks were worth one good ride. Over the bumps you would sail, your hand and arm cramping as the acceleration increased the pull on your muscles, the strain on your shoulders. It was the equivalent of riding under the curl of the mythical ninth wave. There was no time to think about what was happening at home. Flying across the ice and snow, fifteen, twenty, sometimes thirty miles an hour, made my heart pump wildly, made me forget for a little while who I was, and what I knew was coming tomorrow.

CHAPTER 13

A Hero By Any Other Name

Elmer acted more human than most two legged creatures in my life, which made it easy to forget he was a dog—but I was reminded every week when the Sheneyman came.

On Fridays, a rickety wagon creaked and groaned its way through the streets of Hazel Park. An old man sat atop hunched forward into the shape of a Z. His clothes, remnants from days past when the Sheneyman might have had meat on his bones were more tattered than the remnants found in my mother's rag-bag, and hung on his frame as if on a stick. The brim of his faded felt hat drooped like the pedals of a dying daisy.

Harnessed to the front of the wagon was an ancient horse whose head nearly touched the ground. It dragged its hooves as though each step would be the last before its trip to the soap vats. The bones of its front shoulders pushed against the hide, their edges almost breaking though. It was shackled with harness and blinders cracked and peeling from countless temperature changes—small difference between tack and animal. That this scrawny creature could drag the combined weight of man, wagon, and cargo was a feat of heroic proportions.

So often had the hapless horse made the trek along the appointed route that the old man didn't bother unwrapping the lines from a whip propped upright in a hole in the floor, and while the wagon moved, he sat Buddha-like, his hands in all seasons stuck up the cuffs of the opposite sleeve. The entourage of man, wagon, cargo, horse and harness creaked and rattled through the streets accompanied by the tinkle of a cluster of bells attached to the horse's collar, and the barking of a half-dozen mongrel dogs circling like Indians around a wagon train. Above it all, like the soloist in a choir, the old man in a sing-song voice intoned, "Scrap met . . . tall. I buy scrap met . . . talll. Sell me your scrape met . . . talll." The Sheneyman drove Elmer nuts!

On this day, we were in the middle of hide and seek, Elmer's favorite game. But it made no difference, he heard the wagon two blocks away, and took off at full gate, barking frantically. Only one thing caused my dog to go out of control—the Sheneyman, and nothing anyone could say or do would stop him. Around and around the wagon Elmer raced, yapping like a coyote. He snarled and snapped at the other dogs and plunged under the horse nipping at its hooves. To all of this, the creature paid no mind. It was as though the tired old hulk was fatigued beyond caring about the frivolous mayhem its presence provoked.

The price of scrap metal skyrocketed when the war started, and when it did, every kid on Browning Street became a junk dealer. We debated what we thought the Sheneyman would pay for an old metal tub or a piece of iron bed rail. What price for a discarded stove or car fender? It was a disappointing day when the Sheneyman came and I didn't have at least a dollar's worth of goods to trade.

I grabbed Elmer by the collar. He was panting hard from running around and under the wagon. The old trader climbed down from his perch to look over my trove of goods. He began shaking his head before his feet touched the ground. "This is no good. Look at the rust! I can't give you more than a penny for that wash tub. You have to bring me better metal. This iron gate is not worth lifting up on the wagon. Don't try to cheat a poor old man. The most I can give for the whole lot is 35 cents. Well, if your not interested it's alright with me. I can't waste my time here. I have to go. There's always good merchandise to buy over on Garfield Street. If the alarm clock works it will fetch a nickel. Now this roll of copper wire might be worth a quarter. Scrap met . . . talll! I buy scrap met . . . alll!"

I turned Elmer loose while I collected the agreed price. The heft of a fifty cent piece in my pocket felt good. While I was completing my sale, Elmer, found the fresh manure left in the street by the old horse and promptly rolled in it. He was covered. "Elmer! What's the matter with you? Why do you always have to roll in horse shit? God! You're just like the rest of the common dogs on our street. Shame on you. I ought to give you to the Sheneyman!"

I scolded him all the way home, holding his collar at arm's length until I could get him to the garden hose for a preliminary rinse. In the basement, I took him to Mom's wringer style Maytag. Shaking and shivering from his encounter with the hose, he whined and begged not to be put to more misery. But in he went. I lathered him with Fletcher's brown laundry soap, strong enough to kill every flea that had taken up residence since his last bath. He stood belly deep in the water, hang-dog, but obedient. When I lifted him from the tub, dead fleas were thick on the surface of the water. If he hated the bath, he loved the towel treatment with the same ardor. I rubbed him until the skin under his white and brown coat was pink. He licked my face, his behind wiggling with energy and anticipation. His ears perked with the tips bent forward. "Come Boy!" I said, "Let's go buy a tootsie roll."

By the summer of 1943, I had the best collections of War Cards, comic books and marbles of any kid in the neighborhood. Every spring there were marathon marble contests on the vacant lots up and down Browning Street. My knees and knuckles developed thick calluses from kneeling, as did the tip of my forefinger and the cuticle area on the thumb of my right hand from gripping the shooter. Mom complained about having to sew patches on top of patches onto the knees of my jeans.

I won most of the time. Some of the kids wouldn't play when I was in the game; said the growth on the side of my hand gave me an unfair advantage, made me a strong shooter, or raised my hand up off the dirt like the tee under a golf ball. My hands were small, but powerful. Maybe it had to do with the extra knuckle, or because my dad was always busting my knuckles with his hand shake. But with one shot, I could knock a marble from the center clear out of the circle. So I didn't have to buy marbles. I saved my money for other things. Like cheap packages of bubble gum containing War Cards, the gruesome pictures of death and dying that held such morbid fascination for the not-quite-old-enough-to-go generation of Americans. And there was a Schwinn bike my Mom said was too fancy, and if I wanted it, I had to earn enough to pay for it.

Money was easy. I had my paper route. Mom was always lecturing me on how I should invest in War Bonds, and I bought a few, but she didn't know how much the route paid, nor the amounts I made selling the Extras that came out every time there was a dramatic development in the war. Sometimes I made twice the regular weekly income by selling a sensational headline.

There was also poker money. When Dad wasn't in Toledo at the speakeasies, or at the Detroit Race Track, he was playing poker with his buddies. When the poker games were held at our house, as it had been last night, Mom served a buffet snack for the players at about midnight. The games started early and this one was still in progress when I got up to deliver my papers. When I finished my route, the players were gone and the house quiet. Mom, Dad, and Sis were still in bed, and would be until sometime after noon. I had the house to myself.

The dining room table had been fitted with a custom-made, felt cover its green surface now peppered with cigarette burns. Both the table and buffet were littered with overflowing ashtrays and cigarette butts. Whiskey glasses, beer bottles, and mugs—some half full of stale liquid and cigarette butts—were everywhere.

On this morning I helped myself to a package of Camels from an open carton on the buffet. No one knew or cared how many packages were left. I couldn't understand how we continued to have a seemingly unlimited supply of rationed commodities. I'd been hooked within a year after I caught my sister smoking and blackmailed her—cigarettes for silence. That had been two years ago, when I was nine.

In addition to cigarettes, we had an abundance of whiskey,

sugar, steak, gasoline, cheese and butter, all were rationed, scarce and expensive, but never in short supply at our house. Mother cautioned me not to go around the neighborhood talking about the hundred-pound sack of sugar hidden in the back of her closet.

I stashed my cigarette supply, got on my hands and knees, and crawled under the table. Dad's poker group never used chips, it was currency and coin only. All night sessions meant more drinks, and usually produced a bonanza of fallen coins. It was like an Easter egg hunt. I spotted another quarter under the buffet. My take this morning was $1.25, no record, but nothing to sneeze at either.

Starting in 1943, I caddied at the Red Run Gulf Course. That summer, during the Buick Open, I carried a bag thirty-six holes for two consecutive days, and made eighteen dollars. At the end of the second day, I shot craps in the locker room and lost it all in fifteen minutes. But the easiest money came when Dad was drunk and in a maudlin mood. It didn't happen often, but when it did he'd put his arm around the three of us, if Sis was around, and repeat over and over, "Just you and me and the kids. Together we can whip the whole goddamned world! We have to stick together, just you and me, and the kids."

Mom loved it. When he talked like that she could pretend he didn't have a girlfriend. And deep down, I yearned for him to mean those words, and secretly I believed they were true—if he would have quit drinking and stayed home, our family could have whipped the world. But then I remembered the nights he didn't come home, the long nights searching for him, his girl friends, his meanness, and the damnable handshake. Taking on the world was fantasy borne on alcoholic wind. And why, if we stuck together, would we even have to fight the world? Why was he always concerned with fighting? His private war was one I never understood.

When he was drunk and melancholy, Sis and I would ask for money. He'd pull a wad of crumpled bills from his pocket, peal off one, and give it to us without looking at the denomination. Once he handed me a ten dollar bill in front of Mom, who promptly snatched it out of my hand. That taught me to be a little more covert in my solicitations.

I also sold magazines, Christmas Cards, garden seeds, homemade peanut butter fudge, and other items door to door all over Hazel Park. Magazine sponsors offered, in addition to cash income, a variety of prizes for selling more than the required minimum. I won a pair of roller skates, a headlight for my bike, an Australian boomerang, a Red Ryder BB Gun, with a thousand rounds of ammunition, a book sized radio for my night stand, a fishing reel that back-lashed, a gyro-top, and dozens of cardboard put-together items that lasted five minutes out of the box.

When the Browning Street Gang ran out of tailor mades and needed emergency money for tobacco, or the Saturday matinee, or to buy dirty pictures sold from under the counter at the candy store, we'd make the rounds of the houses that partied every weekend and steal empty bottles left in sacks by the back door. The refund on twenty bottles would buy eight sacks of Bull Durham, or forty pieces of bubble gum with War Cards, or eight frozen Baby Ruth's, or four comic books, or three pictures of naked girls and boys trying to do it.

I handed Princeton Bush one of the *Big Daddy Suckers,* I had bought on the way home from school. "Where'd you get so much money?" he asked.

"From the deposits on the bottles Mackey and I stole yesterday."

"Who'd you steal them from?"

"Burl's place."

Prince scowled. "Dicky finds out we're stealing from his mom he'll quit The Gang."

"They never cash 'em in. We only took half, and it was all we could carry. Some of those bottles must have been from parties she threw a year ago." I picked at the paper on my sucker which had fused into the dark caramel. "I'll bet this sucker is older than my Dad." I tore enough paper off to get a lick.

Elmer came racing through the Little Woods, and jumped as high as my chin. "Hey Boy. You been waiting for me?" I dropped my hand with the sucker to my side. After Elmer licked the rest of the paper off, I stuck it in my mouth.

Elmer sat down and cleaned his privates.

"Yuk!" said Prince. "You let Elmer lick your sucker?"

"Sure, why not?"

"Good God Myers, look. He's licking his butt. You gonna eat after him? My mom says dogs have lots of germs."

"An article in the *News* said a dog's mouth's cleaner than ours. It's safer to kiss Elmer than your mother."

"Yeah. Well if the guy who wrote that article would have seen what Elmer just did, he wouldn't have wrote it. I ain't putting no sucker in my mouth after a dog's been licking it."

With money easy to come by, I could afford the Saturday Matinee at the Hazel Park Theater where the serial saga of *The Perils of Pauline* ran every week. I especially wanted to attend when the feature film was a cowboy movie starring Lash LaRue with his long black whip. Sis hated Hopalong Cassidy, Gene Autry, Roy Rogers, and the rest of the cowboys, but those were the only movies the Hazel Park Theater showed on Saturdays.

On occasion, Mom would punish me by saying I couldn't go to the movies unless I went with Sis. There would be a big fight over where we would go, and what movie we would see, but Sis always got her way. Off we'd go to The Kashmir Grand, on Woodward Ave near Six Mile Road, where the seats were cushy and the place refrigerated like a meat locker. She took me to see gushy stuff like *How Green Was My Valley.* Could anything be more boring than watching Roddy McDowell and Donald Crisp? Thought I'd go nuts. And worse yet, the movie, *Love Affair,* with the stuck-up Frenchman, Charles Boyer, and beagle-faced, Irene Dunn. Both were as boring as Missus Parrish's Sunday School Class, and about as believable.

I went to the Hazel Park Theater to see the good stuff, and always went into the candy store next door. If I had lots of money, I'd buy dirty pictures, but always saved some to play the gum ball machine. Every week I put money in, sometimes five pennies one right after the other, and never did get another speckled ball. But

I always made the same wish, just in case. The sound of each penny clinking into the lock box was hollow, empty, like it had traveled into a dark space where it would remain a symbol of my soul forever. Somehow I knew, as in other aspects of my life, I was being cheated. The guy behind the counter with the unlit match in his mouth, smirked every time the box captured more of my money. So I never bought any of his candy. As Sis said, there was fly shit on it, and I was beginning to believe she was also right about wishes.

My collection of comic books contained a copy of every issue of Superman and Batman published. I read them over and over, and decided it was time for me to also become a super-hero. It took a month to make my costume, but it hung unused in the back of my closet except for one brief escapade when I scared Dick Mackey by jumping out of a tree in front of him after dark.

The opportunity to solve a real crime came when my best friend, Wayne Schmidt, told the Browning Street Gang, his father suspected one of us of stealing kerosene from their home heating oil tank. Mr. Schmidt knew he was being robbed because recently a tank of oil had been lasting only half as long as it should.

The crime would have gone unsolved if I'd been able to sleep, but on this night, I was thinking about what would happen to me after Mom and Dad divorced. Who would I live with? Probably Mom. Dad was drunk all the time. Would we sell the house and go back to Vassar Street, or Missouri? And, I had the jim-jams. That's when you can't hold your legs still. The regular name is Restless Leg Syndrome, but back then we referred to the affliction as Mister J. Sometimes, Dad and Sis had them too. We kidded around about it. Mister J. asks you to dance, you dance, period. He pays you a visit in the middle of the night you get up, no questions asked.

I sat on the edge of the bed wondering what school I'd be going to when Mom and Dad separated. At the side of the bed, I did a little dance for Mister J., and thought about who might be stealing Mr. Schmidt's kerosene. If I couldn't sleep, I might as well be doing something fun. At midnight I donned the costume of The Red X.

I had watched the movie, *The Mark of Zorro,* at least ten times. Tyrone Power, in the role of a Spanish Robin Hood, clad in his black cape and mask, had sliced the top off a candle with his rapier without causing so much as a ripple in the flame.

The Red X's disguise was modeled after Zorro's. A black hood covered the head and face, leaving openings for only the mouth and eyes. Attached to the hood was a black, silk cape upon which was sewn a large, magenta X. Black pants, shirt, and a pair of black leather gloves completed the disguise. It was hidden in the back of my closet, and had been used only one other time—the night I dropped out of a tree in the Little Woods and scared the pants off Mackey. The only weapon the Red X carried was a three-cell flashlight hung around his neck on a halyard.

In full regalia, the super hero crept from the house. In the backyard, a clothesline post with cross-bar was set in the ground within a foot of the back wall of the house. I climbed the pole and hoisted myself to our roof. Below, on the east side, was a clear view of the Schmidt's kerosene tank. I laid on my back, my body slanted down, feet braced in the eve-trough.

There were no street lights on Browning Street. All was dark, save for an isolated porch light here and there, left on for those men and women who worked the graveyard shift. Without trees or bushes to obstruct the view, the night sky was spectacular. Stars, clustered so tight they appeared as sparkling clouds, bejeweled the moonless night. A comet blazed briefly, and died on the other side of Detroit. I tried to concentrate on my mission, but the spectacle of the Milky Way and its deep mysteries coaxed despairing thoughts, and made it hard to think about missing kerosene.

I knew I was supposed to love my Dad. Mom had said it a million times. When we first moved to Browning Street, he let me sit on his lap and told me stories of his past, and warned me against the dangers on the streets of Hazel Park. I was never, ever to accept any pill or strange substance from anyone. He cautioned me to never drink alcohol, and to go to college and use my brain instead of my back to get by in life. And I loved it when he told me to be honest in all my dealings, even though I knew when he was saying it, he was cheating on my mother, and then later started buying rationed materials on the black market. At least he wanted me to believe he was honest.

I wondered what it would be like to have a father who took an interest in whether his son was doing good or bad in school, participated in his activities, took him to the library, the Y.M.C.A., or to watch Bo Bo Newsome pitch for the Detroit Tigers, or to play basketball, or swim, or help with home work, or help repair toys, or make a rubber-gun, or work in the garden or yard. I knew boys who had fathers like that. He did none of those things, so when he stayed out all night, and hit mother, and brought his girlfriend into our house, it made it easy to hate him. When I wasn't hating him, I felt sorry for him and guilty for not loving him, like when, after a particularly wild binge, he would cry and swear he'd never do again the things he always did when drunk. And he'd hug and kiss me and say he was sorry for hurting my hand. We would cry together, and I'd lie and tell him it was okay, knowing well he would do it again.

I thought a lot about running away. I would change my name, have my hands fixed, assume a new identity, I didn't like having the same name as his anyway. Maybe that's why I became The Red X. I didn't want to be the son of Hiram Keith and Helena Mae Myers. But when I went over the possibilities, I knew I was doomed to stay with them at least until I was old enough to quit school and get a job or join the military. If I went to Missouri, Uncle Vern would send me back.

My friend Henry had already said I couldn't live with him. He also said I would never be trash. Odds were he'd been wrong. I really was trash, or felt like it at times, and for sure would be if Grandmother hadn't died and left us some money.

The crime fighter was crying. What the hell was the matter? What difference did anything make? The whole world was sick, including me. I wiped my nose on my silk cape.

A twig snapped near the side of the Schmidt house. The Red X came to attention. He pulled himself to the edge of the roof. Below, a figure tip-toed around the edge of the house. A man carried something, but the night was too black to make out details. I slipped the flashlight from around my neck. The figure was fooling with the kerosene tank. I aimed the light and flipped it on. "Gotcha!" I said in my deepest, gruffest voice.

In the beam of the light, a pair of glasses glinted. There stood Kenneth, the oldest of the Schmidt children, the one whose glasses Sis had smashed with a right hay-maker the first month after we moved to Browning Street. In one hand he held a syphon tube, in the other a five-gallon gas can. He squawked like a chicken, dropped his equipment, and took off running.

The next day, Wayne Schmidt, found a note in the handlebar of his bike that said Kenneth, his brother, was the culprit stealing Mister Schmidt's fuel, and unless he had a change of his larcenous heart, the Red X would strike again, and the next note would go directly to the Hazel Park Police Department. By noon the next day, the identity of the masked, nocturnal sleuth was a matter of speculation by the kids, not only on our street, but Garfield and Moorehouse Streets as well.

Princeton Bush and I were in my bedroom exchanging comic books when he asked, "Did you hear about Mackey having the crap scared out of him on the way home from the store night before last?"

"No," I said. And it was true, no one had told me about it.

Prince flipped the page of a *Superman Comic*. "Mackey said he was going through the Little Woods on his way to Berger's to get some bread for his mother. Someone with a mask and cape, dropped out of a tree in front of him and shined a flashlight right in his face. Mackey ran home and told his mom he'd been attacked by a German spy."

I laughed so hard, I fell off the edge of the bed.

Princeton gave me a look and continued, "Later, Wayne told Mackey it was The Red X who caught his brother stealing kerosene to burn in that old junker car of his 'cause he couldn't get any gas rationing stamps. Mackey says it must have been The Red X, because of the mask and cape, even though he didn't see no red X on the cape. Mackey thinks it's Larry Estes from the Garfield Gang."

I jumped up. "Estes doesn't have the balls to be the Red X."

Princeton said, "He's as good a possibility as anyone I know. It's probably him."

I told him I knew damned well Estes was not the masked hero. But despite my best arguments, Prince was going to go home believing an imposter on the next street was the super hero I had created. I'd have none of that. I walked to the closet, and with a dramatic flourish, threw back the curtain, slid the clothes aside, and revealed to Prince's eyes the mask and cape of the masked marauder.

He glanced at the costume, sniffed, looked at me with a smirk, and said, "I knew all the time it was you."

I'd been had.

The next day, everyone on the street bragged how they knew all along it was me. Wayne Schmidt told me his brother Kenneth was going to kick my snooping ass for getting him in dutch with his dad. He'd have done it, except for one thing—my sister.

CHAPTER 14

A Home Remedy

The longer we lived on Browning Street, the more often Mom, Sis, and I waited in vain at the front window for Dad's car to round the curve on Stephenson Highway.

Bad traffic had, on occasion, accounted for a fifteen or twenty minute delay. But on this night we were into the second hour. Mother had fixed supper in her dogged delusion that Dad was going to walk through the door cold sober, and everything would be domestic bliss. All the while, tension was building like static electricity on a winter day.

Mother ran through the usual litany of dos and don'ts: *Be nice to him when he comes in and for heaven's sake Sonny, don't argue or fight with your sister.*

Sis gave me a smug smirk, and a taunt. Her version of our frequent arguments and violent fights had, as usual, been accepted as the gospel.

Mom continued: *You understand? Keep the radio down. You know how tired he is after he's worked all day; he needs peace and quiet. Sister, don't mention Miss McCrory sending you to the office.* Miss McCrory was Sis's High School history teacher with whom she waged daily warfare.

We held our vigil at the window, watching the cars come around the curve on Stephenson. Mother wrung her hands, paced, and hurriedly moved back and forth tending an overcooked dinner incinerating in the oven.

At six o'clock, we moved to the nook and picked at a dry pork roast and shriveled potatoes. It was hard to fault Mom for being anxious. There was the specter of him sitting in one of his favorite haunts with his lover or a lonely war widow. If, by some miracle, he made it home at this late hour, he would be a wild man, and we'd be all night getting him in bed—a lose, lose situation. She hurried back and forth stacking dishes in the sink, and storing the ruined supper in the refrigerator. At seven o'clock, she said, "Shirley Jean, go call a cab."

The taxi driver's arm was on the back of the passenger seat, his fingers drumming a staccato, as if to say he'd sure like to know what we were going to do. The blinking neon light from Eddie's Half-Moon Bar, kept lighting one side of Mother's face. Dark, then light. Green, then red. It flashed through a torrential rain pounding the roof and refracting neon through the windshield of the cab. Rainbow, black, rainbow, black, while the wipers slapped like a metronome. I was suspended in some goofy psychedelic world where I would never see anything normal again.

Sis argued loudly with Mom about whether she should go into Eddie's. If Sis talked long and hard enough while the cab's meter was running, it would be me going. Maybe for once my sister would lose one of these discussions. *Make her do it Mom, I don't want to go in that place. People will stare and mutter things when I walk by their tables.*

Mom's voice interrupted my pipe-dream. "She's right. It's not proper for a young girl to be walking through a bar alone so . . ." I reached for the door handle, and was out in the rain before she finished the sentence.

Inside on the left, a bar started at the door and disappeared into a dark, smoke-filled tunnel. It might have been a block long—or a mile—I couldn't see where it ended. People lined the bar, some sitting, some standing, and others dancing around in the aisle. Music blared over the cacophony of mixed voices and loud laughter. The only lights were from the jukebox and the back-bar where Eddie and his bartender were busy rinsing glasses. The place was so dim, I had to feel my way to keep from stumbling over chairs and feet.

Twice before, I had gone into this bar and out again without anyone knowing I had been there. This time, as I walked toward the far end checking faces, someone behind the bar yelled, "Hey kid! What the hell you doing in here?"

I was too embarrassed to tell him I was looking for my Dad, so I turned and ran out the door. At the cab, Mom wanted to know if he was there. I said he wasn't, without really knowing.

The next stop was The Rainbow Club, on John-R Street. There he was. I knew it was him the minute I walked in the door. He was the guy at the bar with a cluster of people hanging around. He was the big spender. It was nothing for him to order a round or two for everyone in the place. Mom, whose nature was to pinch pennies, argued with Dad about it all the time. She kept tab on the finances, and it's a good thing she did, or Dad's inheritance would have been long gone, and we'd have been back on Vassar Street. Anytime I spotted a circle of people around one guy, odds were I had found Dad. I got close enough to be sure, then high-tailed it out the door. "He's there."

"You're sure?"

"No doubt about it. He's buying drinks."

She sent Sis and I home in the cab.

Sometime near dawn, they came in fighting. I crept down the basement stairs and hid behind the furnace to listen. Dad's voice: *Yeah, in a pig's ass. Next time you walk in on me like that, I'm going to backhand you. I'm sick of you following me around like I'm some goddamned kid. Just 'cuz we're married doesn't mean you own me, and you'd better remember it.*

Threats and physical violence didn't deter Mom from following him around the Detroit metro area, but as quick as she discovered his current haunt he'd move to a new one. There were hundreds of legitimate bars and nightclubs in the Greater Metropolitan Detroit area, and an equal number of speakeasies during the war. Apparently, Dad intended to try them all. Numerous nights were spent searching in vain—a game Mom was destined to lose.

When he was home, and Sis wasn't out with Topper, we'd lay in bed listening to the screams and curses coming from below, and nothing could shut out the hellish sounds. Fingers in the ears, head under the covers, humming a tune, nothing worked. It seeped through the floor and into our bed like a cold fog.

Dad's shift at Ford's was from 7:00 a.m., until 3:30 p.m. Mom got up at five o'clock, fixed Dad's breakfast, packed his lunch-pail, and saw him off to work. The morning after one of our bar searches, I got up with her. She was cutting the crusts off Dad's sandwiches. "Give me something to eat quick," I said. "I'm sick at my stomach."

"What are you doing up?" she asked, handing me a piece of crust.

With my mouth still full, I blurted, "Give me another—quick."

"What in the world's the matter with you?"

"I'm sick at my stomach; . . . feel like I'm going to throw up."

"I don't see how you could be sick. We had a decent supper last night."

The bread made the urge to throw up go away, so I went back to bed and laid there until I heard our car pull out of the driveway. The start of another day.

The doorway between the kitchen and dining room was filled with his bulk. His right arm, braced against the sill, prevented the door from swinging closed. His tank-top undershirt accentuated the strength of his upper torso and arms. "The dirty son-of-a-bitch pulled a knife on me—you unerstan—a goddamned knife. Put it on my neck, told me if I ever came near her again he'd cut my fucking throat." He was reciting an episode he had repeated ten thousand times. He looked in my direction. "You didn't know old man Sherman did that to me, did you?"

I tried to reply as I had done countless times before. "Please Dad, you've already told me. Let's not talk about it."

Mom fidgeted and picked at her cuticles. She was always tense when he replayed the incident. In a pleasant voice she said, "Come on, Honey, he's been dead all these years, what difference does it make now?"

He continued as though she hadn't spoken, "The son-of-a-bitch tried to kill me." He started grinding his teeth; the muscles in his jaw knotted. "And you defend the dirty bastard. You always stick up for him, don't you? Well, that suits me just fine. Jeeesus Christ! What a gawd damned family I've got." Then he looked at me. "You always stick up for old man Sherman, don't you?"

"Please Dad, leave it alone." I said, with a touch too much irritation in my voice.

"That's what I thought you'd do. Go ahead, defend the sombitch." He started clenching and unclenching his fist. The skin in his palms squeaked and snapped. Then he looked off into space and talked to Grandpa Sherman as though the dead man were standing in front of him. "You gawd damned bastard. Pull that knife on me again, why don't you? I'll break yer chicken neck."

Dad and Mom started dating in high school. Will Sherman, Mother's hot-headed father, had prospered enough from his farm to send mom's sister, Florence, to Steven's College, the girl's finishing school at Columbia, Missouri. He had had the same thing in mind for Mom and was extremely unhappy about the prospect of having Dad as a son-in-law. One night when Dad walked Mother home from a date, Will was waiting. Twenty years later, Dad was still raving about what had happened.

The muscles in his right arm bulged as he steadied himself against the doorsill. His drink of preference was cheap bourbon, but on this night his left hand held a shot glass filled with gin. His eyes were completely out of focus and his jet black hair hung in greasy strands over his forehead.

I looked at him, then the doorway. I wanted to go to my room, but I would have to get past his one-hundred ninety pound frame. No way I was going to try that. I would change the subject. "Don't spill your drink, Dad."

"Shiiit, I never spilled a drink in my life." He held the shot glass brim full of gin straight out in front of him. "See this hand, steady as a gawddamned rock."

No casual boast. The man was blind drunk, but the hand holding the drink never wavered. He had been cursing a dead man, but now his focus changed to the shot glass. Not a drop of the liquid ran down the side. Even when his body lurched or swayed, the arm and hand, like a gyro, compensated. The glass, steady and level, was brought to his mouth; he threw the drink back, stifled a gag, and wiped his lips with the back of his hand. Another wave of nausea took him. I wondered what demons this fresh intake of alcohol would conjure when it reached his bloodstream. Mother was on her feet. She took the shot glass from his hand and replaced it with a lit cigarette. He took a long drag and talked through the smoke pouring from his nose and mouth, slurring every word, "You bastard . . . tried to cut my throat."

Mom went to the refrigerator, took out a beer and said, "Split a beer with me, Honey?"

"Pour me another shot of gin," he said.

Mom ignored the order, went to the cupboard, and poured the beer into two glasses, and set them on the kitchen table. She reached into her pocket, came out with a small vial, removed the cap, and put it to her lips. Back at the table she put one of the glasses of beer to her mouth, turned to Dad and handed him the same glass.

"Jesus Christ! Do I hafta go to a bar to get a drink of gin?" he said pointing at the half empty bottle on the table. Then added, "Give me the keys to the car." The words, like a shock from a 240 volt outlet, stood Mom straight as a ruler. He may have been embalmed, but he understood perfectly the power in those words.

Mom grabbed the untouched beer out of his hand, set it on the kitchen table, and in her most appeasing voice said, "Now, Honey, you don't want to get out in the car. I'll get you another drink of gin, but first, help me drink this beer."

"I tol' you no beer. Do I get a drink of gin or not?"

Mom reached for the gin, knocked it over, and scrambled to set the bottle back upright. "Just a minute, I'm getting it." She hurriedly poured gin into the empty shot glass.

"Fill the gawd damned thing up for Christ's sake—fill it up!"

"That's all there is."

"Yeah. If you'd of done what I told you in the first place, you wouldn't of spilled it."

She handed him the glass which he turned up and then started grimacing. She grabbed the beer glass, took the empty gin glass, and thrust the beer into his hand. "There you go, Dear, use that as a chaser."

After a few moments the urge to heave passed and he said, "Now give me the keys to the car." He looked at the beer in his hand, put it to his mouth, and downed it. "I want those keys and I want them now." He lurched as though to grab me, but stopped at the breakfast nook table; the movement startled me and I jumped up and ran to the other side. He grabbed the back of a chair and leaned into it for support.

Mother whispered, "Don't let him go."

I had no clue how I was supposed to keep him from going, but mother's command scared me. I knew he couldn't drive, and now felt responsible for keeping him from harming himself or others. I begged him not to go.

"You always stick up for that dirty somfa-bitch, don't you?" He said, looking at me with his vacant eyes.

"Aw Dad, nobody is sticking up for anyone," I pleaded, "please don't leave, stay home with us and we'll do whatever you want, right Mom?"

Suddenly he was taken with violent retching. He tried to stifle the gags, but his need to purge his body was strong. He clamped his mouth shut but the waves of nausea started waist high and moved with increasing force through the esophagus, throat and mouth.

Mom grabbed him on one side and I the other. "Hurry Sonny! Help your dad to the bedroom." She cleared furniture out of the way. He leaned heavily on my skinny frame, and I was barely able to keep him on his feet as we lurched crazily through the dining room toward his room. He muttered about how sick he was between heaves.

"Hurry Son, get him to the slop jar." Mom came along side

and helped direct him toward the bedroom door. Dad stumbled and staggered the rest of the way to the pot. Then went to his knees with his head in the jar, disgorging everything.

Later that night, Mom and I were back in the kitchen trying to get our breath, thankful Dad was in bed and the possibility of his leaving no longer a threat.

"What'd you put in Dad's beer?" I asked.

Mother looked sheepishly at the top of the table for a moment. "I guess your old enough to keep a secret."

"What're you talking about?"

"Swear that you will never repeat what I'm about to tell you. Dad must never know, and you have to promise, or I won't tell you. Understand?" Convinced I understood the sacredness of the oath, she said, "Remember Ruth and Joe Harper? Joe was an alcoholic, and stayed drunk for twenty years. Then someone told Ruth about a medicine called syrup of ipecac. Ordinarily it's used to induce vomiting in people, mostly children, who have swallowed something harmful. They give them this medicine and it makes them throw up so they can get better. Ruth started slipping it into Joe's drinks. It made him so sick he quit drinking. That's what I put in your father's beer tonight."

Until the day Dad died, Mom kept a bottle of the purgative in her purse. But it was the color that defeated her. Syrup of ipecac's brown shade blended perfectly with whiskey or beer, so as long as he was drinking something brown she could doctor his drinks. But after she induced violent illness and vomiting in Dad several dozen times, he began experimenting with other drinks. Several gin and vodka binges without nausea convinced him that whiskey and beer didn't agree with him anymore. The older he got, the less he could be tempted to take a drink of any brown beverage, and eliminated her opportunity to make him sick. His tenacity won out. He continued drinking gin and vodka—outsmarted himself.

The oak had been down for many seasons before Elmer and I claimed it as our own. When it fell, its great weight pulled giant roots out of the ground and left them protruding into the sky like the petrified legs of a monstrous spider. The woods, where the tree lay, were swampy after the snow melt and following heavy rains. The first time Elmer and I had gone there, we worked our way across a patchwork of dry tundra and climbed into the maze of roots. Grass and moss grew from soil still held in the grasp of tendrils tightly grouped, and in hollow places and other depressions on the trunk. Wind and bird borne seeds sprouted and grew into a profusion of plants and trees projecting upward—an aerial garden floating above the forest floor.

We climbed high into the roots and then toward the trunk. Among the tangle, and discernable only when deep inside, was a cavity in the belly of the giant tree—a wooden cave. I had spent enough time in the Big Wood at home to know better than to barge into a potential lair without making sure it was not occupied. I broke off a piece of limb and rapped it on the trunk like a wooden drum. All around clouds of butterflies floated skyward. Tips of wings caressed my face and whispered in my ears. They spiraled up, up through the maize of roots, into the dappled shadows, through the canopy of the forest and into the clear sky. We had discovered a butterfly house.

The den was large enough for Elmer and me to be sheltered from weather and hidden from sight. A ledge in the gnarled wood was suited for stashing cigarettes and other private things, like my favorite dirty picture from the Hazel Park Candy Store. The items were so well hidden that I was confident they would remain undiscovered until my next visit. While huddled shivering within the bowels of the old tree, a monarch butterfly floated down through the labyrinth, made a sharp turn into our haven and landed on a twisted perch only inches from my face—as though to remind me of who had priority here. Its wings moved in slow motion, then, as abruptly as it had entered, it rose through the tangle of roots. I was still pondering the mystery of its visit and the magnetism of this tree to butterflies, when a white-tail deer, stepped out of the underbrush, followed a few moments later by her spotted fawn. Together, they fed on the tender spring shoots of grass growing by the water's edge. My heart raced at the closeness of the pair. Elmer shook with excitement. Despite my whispered command and a hand over his muzzle, he let out a muffled yelp. In an instant, the deer were gone, and a blue heron, standing on one leg nearby, unnoticed until that moment, swirled the shallow water and lifted heavily out of the marsh.

After we were alone for a moment, I said, "What should I do?" Elmer cocked his head and looked at me with watery brown eyes. I hugged his neck. "I wish you could tell me." Sensitive to my moods, or perhaps to share warmth, he wiggled up close and licked my face.

The question had to do with Mom and Dad. I lost track of the number of times we had stopped on the way to the cabin the night before. The last time we'd been here, I forgot to split enough kindling and logs for a fire, so I crawled into bed sometime after midnight and shivered while listening to them fight. Elmer curled across the foot of the bed and warmed my feet.

When I got up, no one was stirring, so I gave Elmer a scoop of Purina, took two slices of bread for myself, went outside and down the hill to the lake.

"Go get it, boy," I said, and threw a golf-ball-sized rock into two feet of water. Elmer was in the frigid water in a flash. It didn't matter if he had to dive, or had only half his teeth to pick it up, he swam to the spot where the rock had hit the water and went down. Only his hind legs and short tail were visible above the surface. He soon deposited the rock at my feet and yapped for me to throw it again. After awhile I felt guilty and substituted a stick so he wouldn't drown diving. When Elmer tired, we walked along the edge of the lake. After a short distance, my pants were soaked from the wet grasses and weeds, and I took a chill. Elmer was shivering from the cold waters of the lake.

When we returned to the cottage Mom was cooking breakfast and preoccupied. The night before they had talked again about a divorce before I fell asleep. Nothing had meaning to my mother without Dad, and she had no time for anything except that shattering prospect. The only source of heat in the cabin was the small cook stove that Mom was bent over. "Heat feels good," I said. "Where'd you find wood for the fire?"

She didn't look up. "I didn't find it. I cut it, which is what you were supposed to do."

"Sorry," I said, and I huddled up next to the stove drying my pant legs. Elmer was laying between the stove and the wall, steam rising from his coat. Dad was nowhere to be seen. "Mom, can I go fishing?"

"No."

"Why not?"

"You know why. The boat's not in the water. I'm not going to wake your dad to fool with that boat. He worked hard all week and is resting."

She chose to ignore the fact that I was with them the previous evening while he drank himself into oblivion. I tried to deal with the nonsense of her statement, but couldn't, so I tried another approach. "We could all go fishing." I said.

"Your father's *not* going to feel like fishing."

There was a statement I could believe. "I don't have anything to do if I can't go fishing."

"You and Elmer can go shore fishing."

"But it's too weedy, my line gets tangled and hung up. I never catch anything. That's not fishing."

She wheeled away from the stove and slapped me hard across the face. "Don't argue with me. Your father's trying to sleep. I don't want to hear another whine out of you. Now get out of here before you wake him up!"

The blow shocked me. There was something trashy in the slap, something that caused rage to boil up into my throat. "Don't do that again."

She acted like I'd not spoken. "Go," she said. "I have to fix Dad's breakfast."

I put my hand on her arm. "Did you hear me? Don't do that anymore." It wasn't the first time she'd slapped me, but this was worse, it was for nothing. The rage became uncontrollable. My fingers bit into her flesh.

She looked down at my hand, then at my face. "Take your hand off me."

"No, by God. Not until you listen. You and Sis have been slapping me in the face, and beating around on me for years. But no more. What you just did was the last time. From this day on, I'm defending myself. The next time you slap me I'm going to slap you back. Understand? And if Sis so much as touches me, I'm going to hit her right in her new set of tits."

That got her attention. "Don't you dare hit your sister in the breasts!"

"Then you best tell her to keep her hands off me. Dad rants and raves about defending myself, taught me to be a fighter. Guess he didn't figure I'd be defending myself against my own family—but I will." I headed to the door.

"Get out of here," she said. "I don't care what you do as long as you do it outside. Now go."

"Come on Elmer." I turned back again. With hate in my voice I said, "Remember what I said."

I couldn't figure out what to do. My outburst confused me. Should I wake Dad up? What for? He didn't care about anything except that woman he had brought home. Paraded her right into the house! A trophy to show to his family. Maybe Elmer and I should walk into the small town two miles north of the cottage. But what would we do after we got there?

Shadows outside the cave, told me it was getting close to noon. My pant legs were still wet, and my soul as cold as my feet. The loneliness, more profound, had become a familiar part of my life—at times unbearable. Sis, almost seventeen, wasn't around much any more. She didn't even come to the cottage with us on the weekends.

"Come on Elmer, we're going home." I meant Hazel Park, and had no idea why I thought going there would help. I knew I couldn't stay around my parents. I took my cigarettes out of the hiding place and left the butterfly house.

The first ride we caught took us out on the main highway going southeast toward the city. I told Elmer to sit. On the edge of the road, he went up into a posture that would have made any military man proud—except for the one ear cocked a bit more than the other, and one paw bent downward. He looked like he was hitch-hiking—irresistible—the next car picked us up.

No one questioned why a boy of eleven and his dog were hitch-hiking alone. We made the trip in record time. I was amazed at how fast one could travel without tavern stops. And none of the thousands of miles I thumbed in later years were as easy as those when Elmer was my companion.

The front door of the house on Browning Street was locked. I rang the door bell, but no one answered. It was mid-afternoon on Saturday, so Sis must have gone to the movies. I went around to the side door. Locked. Not a problem. The coal chute was never locked. I crawled through the opening and dropped into the bin. In the basement bath, I stood in front of the mirror washing the coal smudges off my arms when suddenly another face appeared. "Sis! You scared me to death."

Her face was flushed. "What're you doing home?" she said. "Where's Mom and Dad?"

"How come you didn't answer the door?"

I took the stairs two at a time with Sis right behind me. Before I could make it through the door into the dining room she grabbed the back of my shirt. "Don't go in there."

"Take your hands off me," I said. Her fist wrapped in my shirt. I pulled her with me through the door. Out the front window I saw Topper going down the steps. "You were here all the time. And you saw me out on the porch. I guess you didn't give a damn whether I ever got in or not. Well you'd better get yourself together. I ran away from the cabin, and maybe that will cause Dad and Mom to come home. Ha. I doubt they'll even know I'm gone."

"You little sneak. You always spoil everything." She set her jaw and drew back like she was going to slap me.

I doubled my fists. "Don't do it. I've taken all the shit off this family I'm ever going to take. And get your hand off my shirt. I'm not your punching bag. From now on every time you hit me, I'm going to show you how Dad taught me to fight.

CHAPTER 15

An Unwelcome Addition

They walked into the living room on Sunday evening in the early spring of 1943. Sis had been gone since Friday after school. Mom and Dad were frantic. Sis was seventeen; the tall, heavy-set kid standing next to her, sixteen.

Mom had her feet planted squarely in their path, arms folded, and was firing questions like a trial lawyer. "Where've you been?" Her voice rose to a near scream. "And don't lie to me!" She directed the question to Sis, contemptuously ignoring the awkward kid fidgeting nervously at Sis's side. Dad, standing behind Mom, hadn't said anything yet, but from the ashen color of his face, it was obvious, he was mad as hell. I was at the dining room table doing homework and thinking, Daddy's little Darling had finally done something serious enough to get her butt in trouble, and how lucky she was that Dad was sober.

Sis moved forward tentatively and said, "We're married."

"Jesus Christ," Dad said and slammed his fist into the palm of his hand.

The boy with Sis flinched.

The pencil dropped from my hand. The significance of the announcement nullified the satisfaction I'd been feeling over her predicament. How could my protector, the only person I could depend on, the one whom I idolized, betray me and marry Donald H. Scott, the big, fat ugly football player called Topper? True, we fought and she hit around on me, but it had been better since I started fighting back. There had to be a law against her marrying a sixteen year old slob.

Mother, visibly shaken, recovered quickly and yelled, "Married! What do you mean your married? You're both babies," She looked at Topper with loathing, while speaking to Sis. "He's not even dry behind the ears for God's sake. How could you be married?" She paused for just a second. "We'll get it annulled. You're both too young to get married." She relaxed her stance slightly as though she felt she had stumbled onto a solution to an impossible situation.

Sis lowered her chin and quietly said, "Mom, I'm pregnant."

It was like jabbing an inflated balloon with a knife point. All the fight went out of Mom in one long moan. "Oh my God," she said, and began to cry.

From the dining room I yelled, "What did you expect? She's home alone two or three days at a time." I ran to the basement. My head pounded; thoughts spun crazily. Elmer followed me down the steps and barked. Maybe he sensed my pain. At the foot of Dad's bed, I stared upward where my sister and her new husband stood. With clenched fist I screamed. "I hate you, Topper Scott, you miserable bastard. I will always hate you." The tears flowed. "You pretended to be my friend, and all the while you only wanted to steal my money and my sister away from me." How could she, after all we'd been through, leave me? Who would take care of me, stick up for me when in trouble? She had shown me how to stand up for myself, gave me my first cigarette, cuddled me in bed when I was afraid. There was no one to take her place. Dad and Mom hated each other and were talking of divorce. Now she belonged to that pig. She didn't even have the decency to confide in me what she was going to do.

The days following were filled with melancholy. I yearned incessantly for someone to hold me, someone to touch. My sleep dreams were bloody nightmares, some faceless thing chasing, sometimes catching me, always intending to rip out my genitals, and kill me.

That spring, Sis graduated from high school, and I finished the sixth grade at Martin Road. In the fall I would transfer to Lacy Junior High, in downtown Hazel Park. I hung out every night with The Gang. Fought more. All that sustained me was Elmer, and the girl of my dreams.

Dorine didn't know me from scat. She was the Burl children's babysitter. Dickie told me her name and that she was fifteen years old. I was too shy to introduce myself, so I waited for her to show up on Browning Street and followed her, day-dreaming about something I could never have. She was who I wanted to hold me at night, but her age and aloofness scared me, so when I knew she was at the Burl's house, I'd hide in the ditch out in front hoping to catch a glimpse of her. In later years, I might have been arrested for stalking. I couldn't explain the powerful attraction. Her face was ordinary, except for one thing: a soft sprinkling of freckles across her cheeks and nose which were absolutely beguiling. To top it off, she had a body that made me sweat in private places and drew me—no, pulled me along like a powerful magnet.

On a hot July day in 1943, Dorine left the Burl home early in the afternoon, and I followed. I would find out where she lived, and then figure out some excuse to speak, maybe I'd leave a note with my name and telephone number. But why would such a gorgeous creature want to call me?

The details of her bra-less breasts were sharply defined against the damp material of her t-shirt, as she walked out of the Burl yard, turned west on Browning Street, crossed Stevenson Highway, and entered the Big Woods—my territory. I knew those woods better than anyone on Browning Street.

The path she chose, was one I had traveled everyday while attending Martin Road Elementary. It wound serpent-like through the woods, completely canopied. As I fell in behind staying out of sight, I regretted that in the fall I'd be entering Lacy Junior High, and never walk this path again on a school day.

She moved quickly in and out of the twilight like an mirage. I crept between clumps of foliage keeping always to the side of the trail. Then, like the shadow cast by a moving cloud, she simply vanished. I hurried to where I last saw her, but the wood was silent, the trail ahead deserted. I ran on in the general direction she'd been traveling, fearing she'd taken a sudden turn off the main trail, and I'd never find her. Suddenly she stepped from behind a tree three feet from my face, and said, "Why are you following me?"

It scared the wits out of me. My face felt fiery. I stammered some lie about wanting to make sure she got home safely. For a long moment, she stood, hands on her hips, eyes level with mine, staring as though trying to decide whether I was telling the truth. "You're the kid that's been hiding in the ditch outside the Burl house. Dickie said you're a friend of his, and that sometimes you tie a cape around your neck and jump out of trees in the middle of the night to scare people."

Another one of my stupid escapades. "That was last year, before I grew up." I was mortified that she knew about the Red X, and how dumb I had acted.

Casually, as though we'd known one another our entire lives, she took my hand, smiled, and said, "Come on, if you really want to know, I'll show you where I live." She stopped again and peered down at the hand she was holding. Her voice was soft. "What happened?"

I waited for her to pull away, but she held on. "Don't know," I stammered. "My mother says I was born with it."

"Doesn't matter." With a feather touch she massaged the extra knuckle. "My dad has a strange looking thing on his neck. He doesn't know where it came from, just showed up one day. I tried to get him to go to the doctor, but he says we don't have the money for stuff like that." She walked fast, her bare feet making puffs of dust in the summer dirt. I felt self-conscious in my almost-new shoes and wished my feet were bare and dirty like hers.

I'd never seen a trailer house. This one looked like a wet cardboard box. The ceiling swagged low enough in places to touch. Orange crates, broken furniture, and packing boxes were scattered about, and there was a smell of mustiness and stale air—Vassar Street! Shock must have registered on my face.

She started raising windows and said, "We're moving tomorrow. The finance company's coming to get the trailer—what's left of it." She pulled me through a living area into a tiny compartment with bunk beds. A line of perspiration traced the back of her shirt. "This is where Angie and I sleep. She's my sister. Cleans house for a crippled lady in Ferndale." She sat on the edge of the bunk bed, crossed her arms at the waist and pulled the wet t-shirt up to her shoulders.

I sucked air between my teeth.

She stopped with the garment around her neck, her nipples inches from my waist, and laughed. "You poor thing. Don't you go to fainting on me. I'd guess these are about the prettiest pair you ever saw—maybe the only pair."

My heart was pounding so hard, I couldn't breathe, let alone answer.

She loosened the buckle on my belt.

I wanted to tell her I'd seen several girl's breasts, but was afraid she'd think I was bragging. Besides, she was right. If I lived to be a hundred, I'd never see anything more beautiful—white as snow, they were lined with delicate blue veins, and capped with bright red nipples over pink circles.

She unbuttoned my jeans and pulled them to my ankles. I glanced around nervously. She said, "Don't worry, Angie won't be home for at least a couple hours, and Dad never gets here til around midnight."

I was standing stark naked in front of where she sat. Dreamy-like, she laid her cheek on my chest. "We don't dare do what you want 'cause I can't take no chances you'll make me pregnant; Lord knows this family's got enough trouble." Her voice was so low and husky I could barely understand her. "But I'll show you some other stuff that'll make us both forget everything for a little while."

I put my hand in her hair. She slipped her shorts and panties out from under her. Then she closed her eyes and held her mouth up. I bent over her and brushed my lips over her freckled cheeks, then kissed her lightly on the mouth. I wanted my life to end at that precise instant, with my mouth on hers, so I would forever know the taste of her. Our chests were heaving when we broke, and with both hands on my loins, she pulled me forward and pressed my aching hardness against her breasts. With feather strokes she brought me to a climax, then asked me to stand over her and do it to myself, while she watched. My knees buckled and I went to the floor. With her hand on mine, she guided me between her legs and led my finger to the place where she said all girls liked to be touched. For more than an hour she gently coached. But I was not sated, and told her I wanted to be deep inside her. She whispered she wanted me too, but the words must have frightened her for suddenly it was over. As she pushed me out the door, I said, "I'll be back to tomorrow. I want to see you every day, forever."

She smiled. "You'd better come early, 'cause the trailer people are supposed to be here first thing in the morning. And we won't be able to . . . you know, 'cause my sister will be home."

"I don't care, I'll be here."

The next morning, I hurried through my paper route, returned home, and was on my way out the door when the phone rang. The Assistant Distribution Manager at the *Detroit News*, my boss, told me Allied forces had landed in Sicily, and the paper had printed an Extra. How many bundles did I think I could sell? *Only one*. Surely you can do three, you've done it in the past. *Only one*. I'll drop two in about an hour.

I pulled my wagon to the corner of Browning and Stephenson and waited. An hour passed, and still no truck. I was on the verge of saying to hell with it when the truck pulled up to the corner. A boy riding the load, threw me two bundles. I pitched them on my wagon and ran back to the house. The clock in the kitchen showed 9:45. I opened the can where I hid my paper-route money. Four dollars in change. The truck had thrown one-hundred Extras. At three cents each, I'd owe three dollars. I pulled the wagon around to the side of the house, opened the coal-chute, and pitched in the bundles. Good to light winter fires.

I ran back through the woods, and along the block where Dorine had lived. Her trailer was setting on the bed of a truck. My knees started shaking. The lot where it had been was an empty space with old cans, a headless doll, a car hood, and beer bottles scattered about. The truck was turning around in a driveway across the street.

I ran and jumped on the running board. "Where's the family that lived there?"

"Hey kid, you nuts?" the driver said, "get off this truck before you get me fired."

"Not until you answer my question."

"The place was empty when we got here, now get lost." He pushed me off the truck.

What a fool I'd been! She'd think I was lying, that I didn't care. I should've told the circulation man I wasn't going to sell any damn Extras. Should've let him fire me. Last night I had slept better, and without nightmares for the first time since I could remember. The thought of never seeing her again was unacceptable. I wanted her to hold me at night like she had held my hand. I wanted to touch her, taste her. She and only she could fill the void, take my loneliness away.

I ran as hard as I could back to the Burl house. Had she told them anything? Dickie said she was moving to Ohio, where her grandparents lived. Where in Ohio? I would run away and go to her. Dickie didn't know the name of the town. I ran back through the woods to the street where the trailer had been. The truck was gone. Half a block away there was another trailer house. I ran to the door and knocked. I heard the floor creak and the door opened a crack. "Yeah?" a woman's voice said.

"Excuse me Ma'am for bothering you, but do you know where Dorine and her family moved to?"

"Dorine who?"

It dawned on me I didn't even know her last name. Why in blazes didn't I ask Dickie, he'd have known. How stupid! "I don't know her last name, but she lived in the trailer that was parked down the block."

"Never spoke to them. The old man was a queer duck. Had a strange thing growing on his neck. They only lived here about six months. That's all I can tell you Sonny." She closed the door.

I never saw Dorine again, but the memory of her feather-like touch burned me like a fresh brand every night. I hugged the pillow pretending it was her. And I masturbated like she taught me, not from lust, but from loneliness. Relief came in fleeting bursts of orgastic spasm. But after each episode, I lay exhausted, mentally empty, more alone than before. The less satisfaction I derived, the more I indulged. And it didn't matter that Dad told me he once knew a boy my age who abused himself. "The boy," he said, "went nuts."

I didn't care what happened. Sis was gone, and it seemed certain Mom and Dad would also go. Self-sex became a substitute for love—an attempt to satisfy a craving for something I couldn't define, a form of self-flagellation, punishment for something I must have done wrong.

Dad was right, I was either crazy, or soon would be.

CHAPTER 16

A Musical Interlude

The dreaded day. Mom and I were in the car on the way to Lacy Junior High School for pre-enrollment. Situated on the main corner of downtown Hazel Park, it was a big, ugly two story brick building which served only seventh graders. All elementary schools in Hazel Park funneled their students into Lacy for one year.

Dad was working the afternoon shift from 3:30 p.m., until midnight, so Mom had the car. She drove up John-R to Nine Mile Road, and parked near the school. I picked nervously at a pimple on my chin. Before I could get out of the car, it gushed blood, not a little, a geyser. Great. Just what I needed.

I was scared witless. Lacy was overrun with gangs and drugs—real gangs, real drugs. Not like the Browning Street gang whose drugs consisted of cigarettes and whose weapons were fists. We smoked, stayed out late, played dirty tricks, had street fights, but we were tame compared to what we were about to get into. The Lacy gangs smoked pot, shot heroin, carried switch blades, chains, and guns.

It wasn't enough to be skinny with strange looking hands, one of my many pimples was squirting blood in cadence with my pulse into a sodden handkerchief. My changing voice jumped around in three separate octaves. "Can I go home, at least until I stop bleeding."

"Nope," said Mom. "Not going to do this again tomorrow." She would find someone to take care of the bleeding pimple.

The school nurse dabbed something on my chin, pasted on a Band-aid, and sent me to register. The next day classes would start.

On the first full day of school, I wandered up and down the

halls until I found the room where my art class was to meet. I hated the strange surroundings and the unfamiliar faces. It seemed like all the other kids had friends. Graduation from Martin Road School, had been more like an eviction. After six years, I knew the teachers and Mr. Clark, the principal, the class-rooms, the halls and the stairwells. I was friends with Mr. Parsons, the janitor, who on Sundays put on a shirt and tie, and conducted the services of the Calvary Baptist Church in one of the rooms of the school. It had smelled of dirty socks, pencil shavings, unwashed bodies, and disinfectant, but it was comfortable and familiar, and I knew every kid in our class. I didn't want to go anywhere else, especially not to this creepy school, where I was waiting for the bell to ring.

I located the room and leaned against the wall outside the door, trying, without much success, to look like one of the unruffled. A mixture of whistles, catcalls and obscene remarks, came from down the hall, and a slinky figure approached from the same direction. The person stirring up all the boys looked about the same age as my friend Barbara Kite. She made a sharp right and entered the room where my class was to meet. I followed her in. If this was the teacher, I wanted a desk as close to the front as possible, so I fell in behind her, and walked lock-step to the accompaniment of giggles and hoots.

She whirled and said, "Okay fun's over. Find yourself a seat or go to the office." Then she turned back and wrote her name in big letters across the blackboard: MISS CRANSTON.

I was dumbfounded. This sex-pot couldn't actually be my art teacher. She turned back toward me, feet apart, hands on hips, and a challenge in her eyes. The heat climbed into my face. I backed away and slid into the first available chair.

She wore skin-tight, black skirts and satin blouses. Her hair, jet black and shiny, was pulled straight back and tied with a white satin ribbon, accentuating almond eyes. Oriental. Her lips were full and always wildly red. To me she was a panther, not only in her black sleekness, but in the smoothness of her movement—a cat.

Art had always been my favorite subject. For years I begged

Mom and Dad to let me take the correspondence course offered on the matchbook covers that said if you could draw a circle, you could have a career in art. But they laughed. I had no talent, and besides, artists were a dime a dozen.

The kid that sat in front of me was known as, Major. Every boy feared him, and most of the girls, including the art teacher, lusted for him. He was the trend-prototype of TV's Fonz, and the Elvis Presley look, down to the duck tail and the leather jacket. Five feet eleven inches in his Wellington motorcycle boots, he had been in the seventh grade for three years, waiting for birthday number sixteen so he could quit. He was interested in two things: art and Miss Cranston.

From the first minute of class to the ending bell, Major and the art teacher had their heads together. Today she was at his desk, less than four feet from me. I had a question about shading a half finished charcoal. I cleared my throat, and raised my hand. No response. I waved my hand like a flag in windstorm. Nothing. I'd have to wing it, so I bent over my charcoal, trying to be creative, but couldn't concentrate on art with her provocative rear-end wiggling in my face and reminding me of Dorine. She was leaning across Major's shoulder making a big fuss about his beautiful drawings. Sixty seconds later, she turned, bent forward and cocked her head to study his work from a different angle. I was going to raise my hand again, but didn't want to risk losing the spectacular view down her satin blouse. What little was left of my short attention span vaporized.

Major swaggered around the halls of Lacy for two months in the fall of '43, and then on his sixteenth birthday stopped coming to school. What made his absence intensely interesting to the sex charged lads of the seventh grade, was that Miss Cranston submitted her resignation shortly after Major dropped out. Coincidence or not, gossip ricocheted through the halls of Lacy like a ball slammed off the wall of a racquetball court. The guys were envious and sexually aroused by the rumor that the art teacher and Major had run off together. A seventh grader making it with a teacher! That's all we talked about for the remainder of the semester.

The girls were green with jealousy. No way their dream boy, Major, would run off with that slut. "Yeah," countered the guys, "and Hirohito wouldn't eat rice." And so the debate went for weeks.

The furor concerning the duel departure of the student and teacher had almost faded, when one of Major's friends said the former student had falsified his birth certificate to show age seventeen, enlisted in the Marines, and that Miss Cranston had followed him to Cherry Point, North Carolina, while he went through basic training. New fantasies were born and the debate continued.

Lacy's coach, Mister Mackey, taught hygiene. A tall, gaunt fellow with only a fringe of brown hair outlining a shiny pate, the Coach spent the class period looking straight at me, and talking about the dangers of running with Hazel Park gangs; said one bad apple would spoil the whole barrel. And he meant me. But there was something about Mister Mackey that reminded me of my dad. Maybe his height. Or the way he looked at me, like Dad staring at me when he was drunk. Or maybe it was just because he was a male authority figure throwing his weight around, the likes of which I would not be able to tolerate for the next twenty years. So I paid no attention to anything the Coach said, and barely eked out a "D" in what everyone else said was a pushover class.

I had taken up with Red McCauley, the tough my sister shot with a BB gun five years earlier. He had quit school and hung out on the street across from the junior high, looking for drugs and girls. I hated his guts and he hated me, but I feared him and he feared the wrath of my sister, so we entered into an uneasy truce. I didn't seem to have many choices about friends. My attitude was becoming more and more caustic. I became further isolated from my grade-school friends, and Red, as vile as he was, was better than no friend at all.

I stayed out too late, had bouts of insomnia, and listened to the fights in the basement. I came to class exhausted and slept through most lectures. Mechanical Drawing was an introduction to drafting. I loved to draw, but I must have slept through the teacher's lectures on three dimensional, and she had neither the time nor inclination to tutor me at the expense of other class members. I flunked.

At the end of the first semester I had failed one course, barely passed the others, made no friends, and was lonelier than I'd ever been. The only light in an otherwise dismal fall had been the birth of my niece, Dona Mae Scott, September 30, 1943. When I wasn't hanging out with Red, I'd hurry to Browning Street, find Elmer, and together we'd race up the stairs to see the new baby. I thought it would be neat to teach her to call me, "Uncle Brother."

Barbara Kite's father worked in the defense industry, and as the demand for more tanks, planes and other war materials accelerated, he and most everyone else not in uniform worked seven days a week, this included Barbara's mother, a telephone operator. Barbara was home alone most of the time.

Carol Young was the youngest of five children. Her father, a building contractor, was gone most of the time and his wife was ill, so the parents had neither time nor energy to devote to Carol.

The three of us had started and finished at Martin Road Elementary. Carol lived across the street, and Barbara was just two doors down, so we became buddies and spent much time together. Both were several months older than me, and frequently claimed they knew all about sex and life. We had played, *I'll show you mine if you'll show me yours,* for five years.

Shortly after we had started to Lacy, and before either of them had made any new friends, I was in the living room of the Kite house. Barbara and Carol were in the hall changing the bag on the vacuum cleaner. My eyes bugged as I thumbed through a deck of cards that Barbara had found in her father's underwear drawer next to a six-pack of Trojan rubbers. The playing cards were embossed with color photos of adults in various positions of copulation. I stared dumbfounded at the seemingly endless and ingenious ways of doing it. My penis, always at a state of readiness, throbbed.

"Come and look at these fucking pictures," I hollered, my voice cracking like an AM station in an electric storm.

"We've seen them at least a dozen times," Carol replied with a hint of boredom. "And besides, we've got to get this house cleaned up before Barbara's folks get home tonight."

I started to protest, but the motor of the vacuum sweeper roared into action. Over the rumble, came the peal of laughter. The machine rolled into the living room. Carol was on one side of the handle, Barbara on the other, their skirts draped over the neck of the sweeper, and naked from the waist down. I had seen their pubic triangles on several other occasions, but not in conjunction with fifty-two pictorials on how to do it. "Holy mackerel," I whooped, and fanned the deck. "Come over here. Pick a card, any card." I jumped off the arm of the chair and unbuttoned my jeans. When I got my underwear down around my ankles, the girls jerked their skirts down, covered their bare bottoms, turned off the sweeper, and ran down the hall screaming. I followed with my clothes in one hand and the cards in the other. The door at the end of the hall, slammed and the lock clicked. They laughed hysterically.

"Come on girls," I said. "Open up. We'll try every position twice!"

There was a long pause. "We can't do that," Barbara said.

"Why not," I demanded.

"'Cause that's how you get pregnant," Carol said in a matter-of-fact tone.

"Jesus, I know all about that," I said with too much emphasis, afraid they'd figure out how dumb I was about sex stuff. I actually knew nothing other than what Dorine had shown me. A brilliant idea flashed. "We can use the rubbers," I said, referring to the supply in Mr. Kite's underwear drawer.

"No, we can't, he'll know they're missing, and I'll get in a lot of trouble," Barbara said. "Besides, you don't know how to do it anyway."

"Just because I haven't done it, doesn't mean I can't. Besides, I'm a fast learner. Any fool can follow the instructions on these cards. Come on gals, don't be chickens."

They whispered on the other side of the door. I could hear my chance slipping away. I would try another approach. "Carol, come on, why shouldn't we do it? Everyone else does. And besides, I know you want to."

There was another long silence. "Sometimes, I do. But, other times, like now, when I get right down to it, I'm afraid. If I got pregnant, my mother'd kill me."

I knew they were right. But, as they say on the street, a stiff dick has no conscience. The animal heat of the moment was fading, so I capitulated. "Okay. Come on out. I promise I won't try anything funny."

"Not 'til you put your pants back on," one of them said.

"Oh, sure, it's fine for you to run around showing me your fun-place, but I've got to put my pants back on. What am I supposed to do with this hard thing I've had for the last two hours?"

Carol opened the door a crack and said with a grin, "Surely you can figure something out. There's more ways than one to skin a cat."

"Yeah. Someone else taught me how to skin a cat. I don't want c-a-t, I want P-U-S-S-Y."

That had been my last intimate encounter with Barbara and Carol. Even though they had been my friends on Browning Street for six years, in the halls of Lacy they acted different. Maybe they were embarrassed about our last get-together. Sometimes, they would speak, but only in a casual way. One day I passed Carol kneeling in front of her locker digging around as though she had lost something. I stopped and asked if she needed help. She hardly looked at me and mumbled something about she was just fine.

Barbara, eyes shadowed, lips and cheeks rouged, dressed hooker style. She was always hanging on some stud's arm, and when we passed, she'd look away. Our friendships had ended.

Second semester at Lacy required all students to take a course in music appreciation. I ranted and raved about how stupid it was for the school to make me take such a "nothing" course. The requirement was a joke. When Red and his gang found out they fell on the sidewalk laughing. I said I intended to do zero in that class.

There had been little music in my life until that time. I was gone most of the evenings when Sis practiced her voice lessons. There had been the brief period when Mom and Dad bought me an accordion and employed a Hungarian émigré to come to our house once a week to teach me to play. It might have been a lack of musical ability, or that my teacher couldn't speak English, or my self-consciousness about my hands, but whatever the reason, the accordion lessons were a disaster.

The word accordion always reminded me of the "Brown Recital." I was eight years old when my parents selected the accordion as my musical instrument. I was eager to be good at something, but it completely confounded me, and the Hungarian teacher's broken English didn't help. Despite my complete inaptitude, and after half a dozen failed lessons, I bragged around the neighborhood how well I could play.

The Brown Family lived in the last house on the street. All three of the children were older than me and attended St. Mary's Catholic School. Why Mister Brown asked me to come to their house and play for them, I'll never know. I suppose it was because I had lied and bragged all over the block about how great I was. My big mouth had gotten me into an impossible situation, and I didn't know how to get out. So, at the appointed time, I took my accordion to the Brown residence. What happened there could not be called a recital. It's impossible to recite anything with a frozen brain. The sounds that came out of that box were scary. Mister Brown flashed a haughty smirk, as if to say he had exposed a frightful fraud. I figured they must have invited me there to look at my hands.

The other exposure I had to music came as a by-produce of Mom buying a piano to help Sis with her voice lessons. Mom had taken lessons as a young girl in Missouri, could read music, and played most of the old standards. We had a collection of the old-time Gospel hymns, and another with the favorite songs of the early part of the century. When liquor turned Dad maudlin instead of mean, he'd gather the family around the piano to sing his favorites. The first was *The Old Rugged Cross,* and the last song of the evening was always *Beautiful Dreamer*. He'd be crying before the first stanza was completed. We'd all be gathered around the piano singing at the top of our voices with Dad singing and bawling. It had been Grandmother Carpenter's favorite song.

The day I walked into the music room at Lacy Junior High, I was downright surly. I didn't like myself or anyone else at the rotten school. And then the teacher walked in. One look at the diminutive red-head, carrying an arm load of sheet music, and I was head over heals in love. Miss Porter, according to the Administration, had come to Lacy to teach music appreciation. But I knew the true reason. She was there because destiny had finally smiled and fulfilled my wildest fantasy.

A light sprinkling of copper-colored freckles dotted her cheeks and reminded me of Dorine, but her ankles were smaller and more feminine, her breasts more perfectly shaped. All other females were little or nothing by comparison. I became faint-of-heart, hyperventilated, and dizzy every time she walked into the room or came anywhere near me. And the smell of her! With my eyes closed, I could tell whether she was within twenty feet of the class room door. She was the most sensuous female ever born. Whatever interest I had in other girls evaporated. Miss Porter made Dorine look absolutely boring. She erased that girl right out of my mind. I would be her slave, and to prove the depth of my devotion, I would learn to like classical music.

The incident involving Major and Miss Cranston was only a few months old. I had not been totally taken in by the stories concerning their amorous adventures, but when I met Miss Porter, I began to pray they were true. Such things do happen I told myself, and better yet, it could happen again.

I was the perfect Mister Cool. No one would have suspected that I was twisted inside-out over my music teacher. The first time she asked if I would mind staying after class to help her straighten up and wipe the blackboard, I almost fainted. She had asked *me* to wipe her blackboard. Jesus. I never dreamed there could be anything erotic in wiping someone's blackboard. Music was the last class of the day, and everyone would be gone home except us. We'd be alone. But when she asked if I'd stay, I couldn't answer. She stood three feet in front of me, hands on her hips, feet spread, and her perfume filling me with something that paralyzed my vocal cords, and asked me to help her after school. The sound that came out of my throat sounded like the croak of a dying bull frog.

She said, "I knew you wouldn't mind."

While I choked and blushed, she politely turned away and went about some other task. There are three thousand six-hundred seconds in one hour. That's how many ticks there would be on the clock before class let out. I started counting. I would never last. Just as I was on the verge of hyperventilating myself unconscious, the bell rang and I was alone with Miss Porter.

I worked like a janitor. There was enough adrenalin and testosterone pumping through my veins to power a locomotive. When I finished, the room was spotless. I fidgeted around not wanting to leave, but having no reason to stay I made a half-hearted gesture of gathering up my books. She looked up from her desk and said, "Please stay a few more minutes. There's something I'd like to talk to you about." She gestured toward the desk closest to hers.

I had died. I had never expected to go to heaven, but this was it. She wanted me to sit close to her for a chat. My head swam. What could this goddess possibly have to say to me in private? My heart pounded, blood rushed to my face. I crossed my eyes and looked at my cheeks—two overripe tomatoes. My God! She was going to suggest we run away together.

Her voice was very gentle. She told me she knew it was difficult for some students to make the transition from grade school to Lacy. I was mesmerized. Her lips, without a trace of makeup, were like lovely red flowers moving in a soft summer breeze. The look in her eyes could have been love—who was I to say otherwise? "I've heard you're hanging out with a tough street gang at noon and sometimes after school."

"Yes, Ma'am," I responded meekly.

"You're a nice young man, and I'm afraid you'll end up in trouble if you don't start keeping respectable company. You could be using that time to study."

It isn't exactly a proposal of elopement, but she cares for me and referred to me as a "nice young man."

When I could breath, I told her she needn't worry ever again about the company I was keeping, and I was going to become her best student. She locked the door to the music room behind us, and we walked down the deserted hall together, my knees shaking like a sapling in a California earthquake. At her car, she said goodbye. She would see me tomorrow.

I ran as fast as I could the nine blocks home. Nothing in the world could have made me happier than the conversation I'd just had. The loneliness was gone. This goddess actually cared about my well-being, and more important, had taken the time to tell me. Maybe she was in love with me and too bashful to say so. What greater expectation could a pimple-faced juvenile have in this life?

I lived for the last class of the day and once it arrived watched her every move, every gesture, waiting for her to ask me to stay after school again to confirm that she cared. A week passed, then a month. I was jealous every time she called on another boy in the class. I was irritable at home. I studied and I put together a symphonic musical instrument notebook—the most homework I had ever done in my life. It was the semester project, and if she wanted it, I was going to do it come hell or high water, and regardless of what was going on down in the basement.

The semester was almost over the day we turned in our notebooks. I was seated near her desk on the front row. She pulled my note book out of the pile, put it on top of the stack, and opened it. It was clear, she was telling me I was still her favorite, and she really cared for me more than just as a student. Toward the end of the class, she asked if I might stay for a few extra minutes to discuss my homework.

I fidgeted nervously while the rest of the students filed out of the room. At last, we were alone. She walked over to her desk and perched provocatively on the edge. When she looked at me, I could see true affection in her eyes.

Her words would be as clear to me a half century later, as they were the day she spoke them. "I have some wonderful news and want to share it with you."

I had sacrificed and worked all semester waiting for her to utter those words. She was going to share some important, and I hoped intimate, information with me. Me! Mister Nobody. She was taking me into her confidence. Her face became very solemn. I edged forward in anticipation. Maybe she would suggest we run away together.

"I have met a very wonderful man, and he has asked me to marry him." There was a long pause. "I have said yes. I wanted to share that with you."

I was gasping. She stepped away from the desk and stood in front of me. I thought I was going to die. She put her hand on my shoulder and said, "I knew you would be happy for me."

"Yes, Ma'am," I stammered. "Congratulations." She had said I was a man, so I couldn't let her see me cry. I walked out, and for the second time that semester ran all the way home.

Many years later, I wrote:

Dear Miss Porter:

I just listened to Grieg's First Piano Concerto and, as always, it reminded me of you and of the gift you gave me. I was in the Seventh grade, failing most subjects, and in the Principal's office for discipline almost everyday, and still, you taught me to love music. What an accomplishment. What a blessing. Your method is what I think about most. You knew how I felt and treated me special, not out of pity, nor as a favorite, but simply as an equal, and showed me you truly cared about my well-being, and my future. You gave me love and music—the perfect combination. And your influence? Everlasting. Thank you.

Your devoted student,
H. K. Myers

I never mailed it.

CHAPTER 17

The Rise And Fall Of Heroes

It didn't matter that Topper was the father of their first grandchild. My parents, particularly Mom, hated him. He had destroyed their plans for Sis's future. If not for him, she would have been a world famous opera star, or pop singer. Shirley Jean had unlimited potential as an actress, especially in musicals, and Topper had destroyed all those dreams.

Not that Mom didn't love her first grandchild, to the contrary, she loved baby Dona with the same intensity with which she despised the child's father, and watched over her like a guardian angel.

The early months of 1944, had been bitterly cold. The weather hovered near zero for weeks, then meekly climbed into the mid-twenties where it stayed another month. By early March there had been over eighty inches of snowfall, most of it still on the ground, or heaped into giant gray piles along the curbs. Every nose on Browning Street was snotty, including baby Dona's.

On this night, neither Dad nor Topper were home. The rest of us were in the living room. Mom was helping Grandmother Sherman, who had come to visit for a week, finish a quilt for her first great-grandchild. Elmer was under the striped chair watching Sis and me as we sang, *The March wind doth blow, whoooo; and where does the Robin go then? Poor thing! She sits in the barn to keep herself warm, and hides herself under her wing—poor thing!* Dona Mae, the center of all this attention, was lying in the middle of the floor filling her pants.

Grandmother lifted her head, looked over the rim of her glasses, sniffed and said, "Shirley Jean, don't you think you ought to change that baby's diaper?"

Sis took the baby into my room, peeked inside her britches and said, "Peeeee youuu!" Dona blew a bubble of phlegm out of her nose. Propping a pillow on each side to keep the baby from rolling onto the floor, Sis said, "I've got to get a clean diaper." She took the stairs two at a time. Dona Mae, unhappy at being left alone, let out a prolonged wail, drew a rattlely breath, and abruptly stopped.

Mom cocked her head toward the bedroom. Sis was on her way back down the steps when Mom jumped up, ran out of the room, and screamed, "The baby's choking."

Everyone rushed into the bedroom.

Mom stuck her finger down Dona's throat. Nothing happened. The baby's pink cheeks had already turned purple. "My God, she's dying," Mom said. Then she covered Dona's mouth with her own and blew in a breath. With her mouth partly connected to the baby's, she said, "Someone—no you Shirley—call the fire department."

Sis was standing in the door with her hands over her ears, screaming. Grandmother and I went back to the living room and began to pray. Sis ran to the phone. "Operator! This is an emergency. My baby's dying. Send an ambulance to 428 West . . ."

Mother sucked a mouthful of phlegm from Dona's lungs, spit it on the floor and yelled, "Dammit, Shirley Jean, I said *the fire department!*"

Sis, the phone at her chest, said, "Momma, my baby needs a doctor!"

Mom, with desperation, said, "No! Listen to me. She needs a *respirator*. Now call the fire department, or she's gonna die."

Sis stood motionless for a moment, then screamed the message into the phone, and slammed it back in the cradle.

Mom lifted Dona by the heels and pounded her on the back. The baby's eyes bulged. Mom blew another breath into her—hit her again. She repeated the routine. Dona coughed feebly, then whimpered. Momma kept blowing air into her lungs until the firemen arrived and attached a respirator. Her color changed from purple, to blue, and finally back to pale white. Everyone started crying, and thanking God. But if there was a God in the room that night, She was disguised as my mother.

At the same time she was caring for Dona, Mom was also contriving to get Topper out of Sis's life. There had to be a way to separate the newlyweds. Both Topper and Sis were still in high school when they married. Neither had income and had no means to set up a household. My folks let them move into the apartment upstairs and paid their bills, including food.

Sis graduated from high school in June of '43, but Topper still had a year to go. He tried to work part time, play football, and keep his homework current, but it was too much. He missed work, lost his job, and continued to hang out with his friends at night. Arguments and fights were now coming from both upstairs and down.

Topper laid in bed until noon everyday, got up and loafed around the house until dark, then left and stayed out half the night with his high school friends. My parents seethed and talked incessantly about what a lazy, no-good scoundrel they had for a son-in-law. Neither saw any parallel between Topper's situation and Dad's dependence on his stepfather's charity for six years in the previous decade. I took great satisfaction in their hatred and joined in the daily diatribes. This was the guy who had stolen my sister away. In the winter of 1944, with his grades failing, Topper dropped out of school and registered for the draft.

Our cousin, Weldon, had already been drafted, completed basic training, and was with Patton's Third Army in Europe. Fern, his wife, read aloud his letters about the harsh winter, and the hellish conditions of soldiers living in fox-holes and trenches. Dad and Mom persuaded Topper that his chances of surviving the war were much greater in the Navy than on the battlefields of Europe, and urged him to enlist rather than waiting to be drafted. In the spring of 1944, Topper joined the Navy.

My sister was fine featured, her face delicate and perfectly proportioned. Her wide, hazel eyes were dazzling against unblemished, burnished skin. Hair, thick and black as ebony, was shoulder length. Males looked upon her with longing, females with envy.

If Shirley Jean Scott's physical appearance was striking, her voice, a combination of Maria Callas and Jeanette MacDonald's was even more so. She had studied for three years at the Detroit Conservatory of Music, where her recitals earned rave reviews. In her senior year of high school, she played the leading role in a production called *The Trail of the Lonesome Pine,* which led my parents to believe she could also act. Their faith provided the impetus for the next phase of the plan to end her marriage to the loathsome Topper. While the son-in-law was sweating out boot camp in San Diego, California, Mom finalized her scheme.

Peaks Island, off of the coast of Maine, boasted a summer stock theater with a reputation for enhancing the discovery of new theatrical talent. Mom sent for an application.

In the meantime, a letter from Topper said that when he finished basic training, his company would probably join Admiral Hulsey's Fleet in the South Pacific. I got all excited and combed the *Detroit News* for stories of battles being fought on the Pacific Front. At first, most of the news was from Europe. Allied Forces had stormed ashore at Anzio, Italy, in January, and we all wondered whether Weldon had been in that invasion.

In February, 1944, Allied forces took Kwajalein Island in the Pacific, and launched an attack on the main Japanese Central Pacific Base at Truk. Mid-February, Marines landed on Eniwetok in the Marshall Islands.

March, 1944. Topper completed basic training at San Diego, and was shipped out to a censored location.

June 6, 1944. One-hundred-seventy-six thousand troops, landed at Omaha Beach, Utah Beach, and other beaches on the Normandy coast. D-Day. That week, I sold Extras on the streets, and in the bars and bowling allies of Hazel Park. With tips, I made eight dollars profit.

June 15, 1944. B-29 Bombers attacked Japan's home island, Kyushu.

July, 1944. A letter from Topper. He had been assigned as

boatswain aboard an LCT, a landing craft, which transported troops and tanks to shore during an invasion.

August, 1944. Allied forces took Guam.

September 30, 1944. Dona Mae had her first birthday.

October 20, 1944. Allied forces invaded the Philippines. Topper's LCT landed troops and tanks in the invasions of Leyte and Luzon.

November, 1944. Letter from Topper. He was okay. Things not easy. Had a tropical disease called, "jungle rot" which caused running sores on his chest. "Tell your pesky little brother I miss him. Have something for him when I get back."

I began to realize what a great brother-in-law I had.

December 22, 1944. Germany demanded surrender of General McAuliffe's 101st Airborne Division at Bastogne, Belgium. McAuliffe's reply: "Nuts."

December 26, 1944. General Patton's Third Army relieved McAuliffe's Bastards of Bastogne. Our cousin, Weldon, was one of Patton's infantrymen.

December 31, 1944. The Browning Street Gang met in the loft over the garage at Sunny Pearl's house for a New Year's Eve smoke. I was telling Dicky Burl, Wayne Schmidt, Princeton Bush, Sunny Pearl, and Billy Mackey about all the battles being fought in Europe and the Pacific, then said in a bravado tone, "The war's going to be over before I'm old enough to join."

Everyone got quiet and looked at Dickie. He said, "We haven't heard from my dad in a month. I want it to end tomorrow, so he can come home."

I felt stupid. "Sure," I said. "I didn't mean I wanted your dad to have to fight longer. That was a dumb thing to say. The quicker it's over the less of our guys will be hurt or killed. Where's your dad?"

"Don't know. He was somewhere in North Africa. Now maybe Italy."

I lit another cigarette from the homemade candle burning in the holder.

Mackey said, "Where'd you get those tailor mades?"

"Out of my dad's pack." I was ashamed of the black-market rationed stuff we had at our house. Like the hundred-pound sack of sugar setting in the back of Mom and Dad's closet, the liquor, cigarettes, steak, butter, and extra gasoline rationing coupons we always had. I was beginning to understand. During war, families with money didn't suffer or sacrifice the same as those who were poor.

Dicky was saying, "All I want is for my dad to make it through this alive."

I started bragging and telling everyone about Topper being my hero. "Me too. All I want is for my brother-in-law to make it back in one piece. He's fighting Japs in the Pacific." When he mentioned me in one of his letters, and said he missed me, I forgot how much I hated him. "He's got the jungle rot," I added, like I knew all about it.

"Wow!" Several exclaimed.

I swelled up a little.

Weldon Sherman was Mother's favorite nephew and a fun guy. He was Uncle Vern's son, and lived in Missouri on the farm until after high school. He excelled in math and attended a business college for a year before quitting to follow my dad to Detroit.

When Weldon arrived in the Motor City, the war had started, and, with the manpower shortage, he had no problem getting a job at Chrysler's. He brought his Missouri sweetheart, Fern, with him and they were married. Pictures of them on their wedding day in front of our house on Browning Street show a handsome, happy couple. They moved into an efficiency apartment on John-R Street near his work. Then came his draft notice. He was twenty years old, married, with no children, and in good health. His job at Chrysler's was not priority, so he was classified 1-A, and by late 1943, was in uniform.

Fern, his wife, was a tall, lithe blond, with wide-set blue eyes, and a perky, turned up nose that made her cute, if not beautiful, and she loved to party. She couldn't live on the army allotment sent to her each month, and had neither the skill nor desire to work. Mom and Dad invited her to move in with my sister in the apartment upstairs. She fit into our household like a stripper at a bachelor's party. Happy-go-lucky to a fault, she was always ready for a good time—laughed easily, loved risque jokes, men, and drank like a sailor.

When Fern came to live with us, I was in the throes of puberty. Hormones ruled my life. I went to bed with an erection, got up with one, and thought of nothing but girls and sex all day. Every time Fern walked through the room jiggling her cute little bottom, it drove me crazy—and she knew it.

The apartment upstairs had a kitchen with a small stove, but no refrigerator, so both households used the one in our kitchen. Mom told Fern to make herself at home, and she did, moving about with ease between the apartment and our house.

Late one night, I heard footfalls on the stairs followed by the squeak of the swinging door between the kitchen and dining room. I crept out of bed and quietly cracked the door. Fern, bent to the waist, was taking something out of the refrigerator. The filmy thing she wore was so transparent I thought at first she was naked. Her breasts were outlined by the interior light as she leaned forward. She hummed a Latin tune, wiggling her behind in time with the melody. Her breasts were doing the Tango. My imagination went wild; my erection jumped out of my pajamas and froze like a pointer on a covey of quail. In the heat of the moment and my anxiety to cover myself, I bumped the bedroom door with my elbow. As it swung open, I dropped my hand in front of my pajamas and leaned nonchalant-like against the door frame.

"Hi," she said coyly, a sexy smile on her heart-shaped mouth. She'd known I was there all the time. "What's a little bitty boy like you doing up this time of night?" The words came out sticky with an exaggerated southern drawl. She continued humming her tune, and all the while her bottom and breasts were jiggling with the rhythm.

"Can't sleep," I replied. My voice cracked, jumped an octave—

a hybrid between a croak and yodel—and ricocheted around the room. Sweat ran down the back of my legs. "What're you doing?"

She had a glass of milk in one hand and two bananas in the other, turned away from the refrigerator, and started toward me with a slow undulating walk. The frontal view was almost too much for a twelve year-old. She hesitated for a stutter step three inches from my raging penis, looked down at my hand covering my crotch, then right into my eyes, and said, "I got a couple of bananas, and I'm going to eat one of them." She winked, grinned mischievously, bumped her hip against the swinging door, and was gone.

Buzz bombs fell on Londoners nightly killing thousands; our government said it could happen here, and the sinking of ships by enemy subs within a few miles of our coasts was proof. The nation was reminded of the uncertainties of tomorrow by twenty-one gun salutes, American flags folded and stored in moth proof boxes, and windows forlornly decorated with silver and gold stars. Women filled multiple roles.

The Honorable Harry S. Truman headed a U. S. Senate Committee which exposed how American corporations were engaged in war profiteering while the youth of the nation were dying on foreign fields and seas. But the whole nation had gone hedonistic, its rational compass destroyed, and war was the excuse.

In our house the moral compass had long ago lost its pole. No one thought of anything except the next good time, so I shouldn't have been shocked when Sis and Fern, aged eighteen and twenty, both married to men fighting overseas, were encouraged by my parents to participate in the war-madness as though they were single. If the girls wanted to go out, Mother would make herself available to babysit. If they needed transportation, Dad would let them use our car. Mom hoped Sis would find someone else and divorce Topper. But why encourage Fern, whose husband, Weldon, was a favorite nephew of both Mom and Dad? Never mind that Sis had a baby just a little over a year old, they encouraged the girls to go to the nightclubs. On one particular night, that turned out to be a bad decision.

Dad, at great expense, had spent another month in McKnight's Sanitorium, his second attempt to dry out. After he got home, he stayed sober and had, at least for the time being, dropped his girlfriend. Mom, her great fear alleviated for the moment, stopped worrying me about who I was going to live with when they divorced. The household gave a hint of becoming stable. True, we still had to tip-toe to avoid upsetting Dad, but it was an improvement over what we were used to.

Sis and Fern took the car to the Rainbow Bar on John-R Street, one of the hot spots in the suburbs, and one of the places I'd been in looking for Dad. At 2:30 a.m., the phone outside my bedroom door jangled. Mother's voice: "Hello," A pause. "Oh my God! Where are you?" Pause. "Have you called the police?" Pause. "Get in a taxi and come home." Another pause. "I'll be waiting at the front door with the money to pay him, just do as I say." Long pause. "Shirley Jean, settle down. You can tell me about it when you get here. Be quiet when you come in. Dad's asleep and I don't dare tell him 'til in the morning."

When she hung the phone up, I stuck my head around the corner, and asked what was wrong. Mom told me to mind my own business and to get back in bed. In a few minutes a car door slammed.

Sis, Fern, and Mom huddled in the living room on the couch. I crept through the door. Sis was talking excitedly. "We locked the doors before we went in, didn't we Fern?" There was no discernible reply.

"What did the police say?" Mother asked.

"They would do what they could, but most stolen cars are never recovered."

"Oh my God," said Mom.

The stolen car, a forest green, 1941, Ford sedan was in new condition. It was one of the last new cars manufactured by Ford Motor Company before conversion to war-time production. A car of this vintage and quality would bring a fortune on the black market.

The next day, Dad went nuts. He ranted and raved, first at Sister, then at the goddamned thieves that took his car, then at the idiot Hazel Park Police Department for not finding it. That night, he got drunk.

Monday morning they found our car. It had been stripped. After that, Sis and Fern had to be a little more innovative. Mom would take them to the night spot of their choice and drop them off. Transportation home was strictly up to them.

A week later, I was on the couch in the living room with a sore throat. Late in the morning, Sis, Fern, and two Marines came in the front door. Fern was giggling like a school girl about something one of the Marines had said. The four of them acted like they were on a prom date. Sis grudgingly introduced me to the servicemen as her little brother.

Shortly after they arrived, the marine corporal, who appeared to be with my sister, began to shake. Then sweat ran in streams down his face. He hugged himself as though on the verge of freezing. He gulped a handful of pills. Sis ran and got him a wet washcloth for his face, then threw a blanket over his shoulders. When the violent shudders began to calm, she said, "Stay right there, Fern and I are fixing us breakfast."

I watched the marine hunched over in Dad's chair with our blanket draped over his shoulders and hoped he would die. But as I watched, it was hard not to feel sorry for someone as sick as he appeared to be. For awhile I was afraid he'd have a convulsion like Ted Childers. Then he looked over the edge of the blanket and said through chattering teeth, "What's the matter with you, kid?"

"Nothing. What's wrong with you?" I asked, barely able to disguise my hostility.

"Malaria," he said. "If nothing's wrong, how come you're laying down?"

I wasn't about to tell him anything. "What's Malaria?"

"Something you get from mosquitos—got mine on Guadalcanal last year."

Ha. Injured by a mosquito. I'd been bitten by about a million of them and it didn't hurt me none. "Where's that?"

"In the Solomon Islands." He threw more pills in his mouth.

"What're you taking?"

"Quinine, it's supposed to make you stop shaking."

"Where are the Solomon's"

"The South Pacific. Why?"

"'Cause that's where my brother-in-law's fighting. He's in the Philippines right now."

Suddenly my sister was through the swinging door, her arms crossed over an apron she had put on over her good clothes. I'd never seen her look so domestic. She'd never cooked anything in our house, and certainly didn't fix breakfast for Topper. She glared at me. "Calvin," she said to the marine, "can you come to the kitchen, we've got bacon, eggs, and toast."

The marine, staggered to his feet. "I think I'd just as soon have a Bloody Mary."

Fern's voice from the kitchen chirped: "We can take care of that too."

Papers the past week had been full of news about U. S. Forces invading the Philippines. Topper operated one of the landing crafts that put troops ashore. He and Weldon were our families only contribution to the war effort, and I idolized them for it.

Until that Saturday morning, I had persuaded myself that what my sister and Fern had been doing over the past several months was innocent fun. But the Marine setting in my dad's chair, in our living room, covered with one of our blankets, and eating our food, ended the rationalizations. All the forgiveness and excuses for Sis were used up. I saw it all in a new light. Nothing was right. My parents hoarded rationed goods, and encouraged irresponsible behavior by my sister and Fern, who, by appearances, felt no compunction about partying while their husbands were risking their lives.

CHAPTER 18

Mistaken Identity

I was bare to the waist, surrounded by beautiful girls. My sister circled me with her hands on her hips giving orders. "Pin the straps up at the shoulders," she said to Gail Palmer who was fitting a brassiere across my scrawny chest. Gail pinched cloth between two fingers and inserted a pin. "You need more hair here," she said to Tessie Wrisorowski.

Tessie worked bobby pins into my hair to hold the rat and wig she was styling. Finished, she backed off a step, put her hands under her chin, fluttered her eyelashes, and said, "Doesn't he make about the cutest girl you've ever seen?" Everyone chorused, "Un Huh."

Audrey Young rifled through a stack of dresses on the bed. "This is it! Oh my God, this has to be the one," she said, displaying a pink and black slip-on. "Perfect!"

My Sis and friends who had graduated from high school in her class had been drinking cokes at the house and were gossiping about Eloise Burl. Mrs B. as she was called, lived five houses away in the direction of John R. Street, and was the favorite topic of conversation in the neighborhood since her husband Stan had shocked the neighborhood by joining the army.

It had happened in the spring of 1944. The nation was saving tin foil out of cigarette packages, and ransacking basements and attics for scrap iron. Every week the Sheneyman drove his horse-drawn wagon through the neighborhood buying anything made of metal. Newspapers were scoured for details of the war, then bundled and sold. Everyone was buying War Bonds, and singing *Let's Remember Pearl Harbor*.

Stanley Burl, draft exempt due to marital status and children, and married to Eloise Burl, easily the most beautiful woman in Detroit, joined the Army. Unbelievable! Princeton Bush, who lived just two houses from the Burl's told me about it. "I'm not lying," Prince said, as we carried sacks of stolen bottles toward the grocery store to cash in for cigarettes. "Dicky's old man joined the Army."

"That's got to be *bove excretia*," I said, snorting at the prospect. "Nobody in their right mind would voluntarily leave Eloise Burl."

"What the hell did you say?" asked the Prince.

"Bullshit," I said.

Eloise Burl was the sexiest lady on the street, maybe in the whole universe. Every kid in the Browning Street Gang fantasized about running away with her. She dressed like a catalog model. When she strolled down the street we all stopped to leer, even if we were in a game of fire-tag. Her legs made Betty Grable's look like an elephant's.

It was well known that Eloise and Stanley fought like Louis and Conn. The Gang spent weeks arguing about why he left, but after Dicky dropped a few remarks about the intensity of the fights in their house, we agreed that for Stanley Burl it must have been a choice between fighting Eloise or fighting the Germans. He chose the Germans. And he wasn't gone long before rumors began to fly about Mrs B. not missing him much. That was why my sister and her friends were dressing me up like a girl. They decided it was their patriotic duty to find out if Missus B. was entertaining a certain draft dodger who lived in the neighborhood.

Three of my sister's sexy friends were making a huge fuss over me. Not quite thirteen years old, being surrounded by good-looking girls was almost too much to ask. The only draw back was the possibility that one of the Browning Street Gang might see me in drag. A casual breast against my arm sent a charge of testosterone straight to the groin. *So who cares who sees me.*

Audrey and Gail pulled a skin tight dress over the bra, which was now stuffed with falsies. They adjusted the wig to hide my Clark Gable ears (Sis said they reminded her of Dumbo). Audrey dropped a safety pin, bent over to pick it up, and gave me another cheap thrill. Off came my scruffy tennis shoes. I pulled my jeans off under the dress, and blushed when they hooted and cat-called. Then more boob adjustment. Tessie and Sis pulled nylon hose over my bony knees and fitted me with spike heels. Someone applied a heavy layer of pancake makeup to cover pimples. A slash of magenta lip gloss, and voila! The transition was complete.

Elmer came up from the basement to check out the ruckus, took one look at me, and ran in circles snapping and barking. I had to call his name three times to settle him.

The mirror on the dresser caught me about waist high and what I saw was remarkable. The girls were oohing and awwwing and making crazy remarks like, "Stay away from my boyfriend," and, "Where do you get your hair done, Sweetie?"

"Brother, you make a lot better looking girl than boy," Sis said, never missing a chance to get in a little dig. There was more hooting and laughter and a lot of good natured teasing. No getting around it, the mirror was reflecting one good looking lady! I was well rehearsed and the costume looked great. My one concern was about balancing myself on high heels. My feet were flat and legs bowed. With every step there was danger of an ankle turning.

"Keep Elmer in the house or he'll follow me," I said.

The girls cheered and pushed me toward the door. Something slipped down my leg.

"My God," Tessie yelled, "His nylons are falling down."

"Can't have that," said Sis, and rummaged around in a drawer of her dresser. "Here we go." She dangled a weird looking strap in the air.

"What's that?"

"A garter belt. It holds your hose up." Sis grabbed the hem of my dress and started pulling.

I pushed my dress down with both hands to keep from showing her friends my underwear. "Whoa. I ain't putting that thing on."

"Well you can't go to the Burl house with your stockings around your ankles. And would you please stop saying 'ain't'?"

"Then you'd better figure out how to hold them up some other way."

I turned my back to the other girls while Sis lifted my skirt, took a wad of hose and twisted it in a knot. "There," she said, "Now let me do the other one."

Arms outstretched for stability, I wobbled down the street to the Burl home, made my way gingerly along the front walk, climbed two steps, punched the door bell, and stood there teetering like Charlie Chaplin in one of his drunk scenes.

The ring sounded from the bowels of the house. It was 10:00 p.m. A dim light was on in the living area. No sound came from within. I waited. Without encouragement from my cheering section, I began to feel a bit lonely. The possibility of rewards from the girls who sent me on this mission helped me overcome the urge to urinate. I reached up and punched the door bell again. This time I heard footsteps. I went into rehearsal: *Missus Burl, my name's Peggy McNeil. I have tuberculosis and cannot work. That's the God's truth. I have four small children and we rely on the meager wage that Mister McNeil brings to us each week. I can see why he favors your company, but he's bringing home less and less of his paycheck. If you could find it in your heart to send him home we would be eternally grateful and I know the Lord would bless you.*

The door opened. The platinum Missus B. peeked through the crack and said in a soft tone, almost a whisper, "Who is it?"

The sound of her voice coupled with what I could see through the crack in the door took my breath away. There were big Betty Boop eyes in an oval face, and a body wearing nothing except a filmy thing clinging to her like skin. I stood there swaying on my spikes like a hula dancer at a luau.

She glanced over my shoulder as though to see if I was alone. Apparently satisfied there was no one but a lone female standing on her porch, she opened the door and turned on the porch light. Her voice lost some of the soft quality. "Who are you? What do you want?"

Not a single word of my canned speech came to mind. But I had to say something because Missus B.'s expression suggested agitation. I opened my mouth. The sound that came out was like a gargle. The knot at the top of my right hose sprung loose, and the nylon started a slow wiggle down my leg.

Missus B., mystified by this mute standing on her steps, came out the door for a better look. Light was behind her, and I was looking through her transparent garment at less than naval high. She leaned forward, her hands on her hips, face so close I smelled her lipstick. "What do you want?" she said.

I looked into the open top of her negligee. Sweat popped on my upper lip. My bra was absorbing moisture at an unsustainable rate, and the maverick nylon had reached my calf. *I had to say something.* "Leave my husband alone," I croaked.

Missus B. gasped, grabbed me by both shoulders, and shook me like a rag. Between clinched teeth she said, "Who the hell are you? What are you talking about?"

My head was jerking back and forth. The hair piece moved down on my forehead, and the stocking fell around my ankle encasing my high heel like a womb.

"What are you trying to pull," she said, and relaxed her grip. She was staring at the wig perched an inch above my eyebrows. Mascara and pancake makeup ran down my face.

When her fingers relaxed, I jumped off the steps. The high heels collapsed. The skin-tight dress the girls had taken so much joy in squeezing me into, had me short stepping like a hobbled penguin.

Missus B. gathered her wits and flew off the porch. I kicked the heels, including the wayward hose into the ditch, hiked the skirt over my ass, and ran like an ostrich. Faster and faster I flew, praying that Dicky was in bed because he could outrun me. After sprinting half a block, I glanced over my shoulder and got my second big thrill of the night. She was right behind me—and gaining. Dickey's thirty year old mother was a fine athletic specimen. Visions of being collared and hauled in by this near-naked beauty swirled through my head. I'd be killed by the Browning Street Gang, but tortured first if they found out I was in drag.

Just when I felt the game was up, my wig flew off and landed at her feet. She broke stride, turned around, and picked up the hair piece.

I rounded the corner feeling lucky, and took one last look. The near naked Missus B. was standing in the reflection of someone's porch light with something hairy in her hand.

It was pure bedlam at my house. Sis and her friends were laughing and jumping up and down like they were going crazy. Tessie Wrisorowski, on the floor pounding her fists into the rug, screamed, "Oh, Jesus, if only I could've seen her face when the hose fell down."

Audrey and Gail grilled me for every detail. "What happened after you told her to leave your husband alone? You could *not* see her, you-know-what," they screamed.

"I could so," I said.

"She wasn't actually naked?"

"Yes she was—well about as close to it as you can get. I can promise you she is not a true blonde." My fans erupted in laughter.

The questioning had gone on for fifteen minutes or more when it occurred to me that my sister was no longer in on the fun. She was across the room by herself looking serious. I hollered, "Hey Sis, that was the neatest idea you've ever had."

A smile flashed. She sauntered across the room, pulled the ottoman up, and sat down. "You're sure she didn't see you come to our house?" she asked, slowly.

"Naw, she didn't see me, 'cause I ran right past our house and went around the block. By the time I got back the coast was clear."

"But she has the wig, shoes, and one nylon, right?"

I wasn't sure I liked the tone of her voice. I was, after all, a hero in the eyes of her sexy friends. I felt good, so I tried to humor her, "She has the wig alright, but there's no way of telling whether she found the shoes and I sure ain't going down there to find out." This drew a giggle from Audrey, and a cold stare from my Sis who said, "I told you to stop saying ain't."

"If you're curious, you can just walk down that way and see if you can find those shoes. They're near the ditch in front of her house, and one's wrapped in a stocking; shouldn't be too hard to spot."

She was looking at the floor and shaking her head as she stood up and started pacing around the room. "I don't think we have any choice but to tell her it was you, and that it was all a joke."

"Your kidding! I said, jumping out of the chair. "You wouldn't tell Missus Burl." But in my gut I knew she would. Dickie would never speak to me again. The party spirit evaporated, and within a few minutes her friends had all said goodnight. I begged my sister not to tell what we had done. Dicky Burl was a member of the Browning Street Gang. We went swimming in the summer, hitched cars in the winter. He'd quit the gang. "Jees Sis, it was your idea."

"I'm going to call her first thing tomorrow," she said, and marched upstairs.

The next morning, Elmer prodded me with his cold nose. I crawled from under the sheet and let him out the front door. I looked down the street toward the Burl house. *Shit, what am I going to tell Dicky and The Gang?*

I poked around the kitchen looking for grape jelly and found an empty jar in the trash. *This is going to be a wonderful day,* I thought. Feeling sorry for myself, I piled marmalade that I hated on a piece of bread trying to figure some way of convincing my sister to keep her mouth shut.

Elmer yapped at the door and I ran to let him in. "Shhhh," I said, not wanting to wake Sis, but she came flopping down the stairs and went straight to the frig.

"Who ate all of the grape jelly?" she asked, giving me an accusatory look.

"How would I know. I thought you did. Maybe it was Fern." The door bell clattered.

"My God, whose ringing the doorbell at this time of day?" Sis said. "I can't go to the door like this." She continued to peer into the frig. Ordinarily I would have argued about whose turn it was, but on this morning I wanted to build some points so I headed for the front door. The bell sounded again. Whoever it was would wake Mom and Dad and the baby. I pulled the door open.

Missus B., feet spread wide, stood posed like a gunfighter, both arms bent at the elbow—Tex Ritter pointing six-shooters. Dangling on the end of her right index finger was a pair of spike heels wrapped in a nylon hose, on her left, an auburn hairpiece. "I'd like a word with your sister," she said.

"Yes, Ma'am," I sputtered, backing away from the door.

"Jesus Christ, I'm in for it now," I said on the way to the kitchen.

"Who was that at the door," Sis asked, with a mouth full of leftover chicken.

"It's Missus Burl, and she wants to see you."

She looked up from her breakfast, smiled, and said, "Well, let's get it over with." She grabbed a comb on the way to the front door and pulled at the tangles. I followed like a whipped puppy and hid behind the door frame.

"Good morning Eloise," Sis said, in her sweetie-pie voice.

"Where's your mother?" The question was no nonsense. Missus B. was dangling her trophies.

"You want me to get her up?" Sis, asked.

Dicky's mother hesitated for a second and said, "Never mind." She dropped the shoes and wig at Sis's feet. "Seems like juvenile conduct coming from a married woman with a baby. Don't you ever pull anything like that again Shirley Jean Scott, or I'll snatch your real hair out." She did a one-eighty and marched down the steps.

"Wait a minute," Sis said, flabbergasted. "That was my brother."

"Yeah," Missus B. said over her shoulder, "and I'm Eleanor Roosevelt."

That summer, I became the leader of the Browning Street Gang. I didn't know why, but suspected it was because the boys were afraid of my sister. It sure didn't have anything to do with the size of my biceps, or any other body part. The only thing I could figure, was that nobody, except me, knew how to fight like Joe Louis.

This was 1944, and the Champ hadn't fought since he beat Billy Conn, June 18, 1941, a fight broadcast by every radio in

America. Sportcasters had picked Conn, Ireland's Middleweight Champion, as the boxer who would finally end Louis' phenomenal career. Dad said the experts didn't know licorice from shoe polish. There was no one, including this Irishman, capable of beating Lewis, and he didn't give a damn how fast Conn was. That night, Dad and I huddled in front of the radio. Starting with the opening bell, and through Round Eleven, it looked like Dad had been wrong. The Irishman pounded The Brown Bomber relentlessly with lefts and rights while dancing away unscathed. But Louis kept advancing, left up, head tucked behind his shoulder, and right hand poised. By the end of Round Eleven, Conn had begun to slow, but he continued to outscore Louis through the Twelfth.

The bell signaled the opening of Round Thirteen. The challenger was not quite as fast coming into the center of the ring. Louis, who had taken every punch the Irishman was capable of throwing, came out of his corner on the hunt. During the break his handlers had told him he had to put Conn away or lose the bout on points.

Louis stalked the Middleweight, and finally maneuvered him into a corner. There, he slammed the Irishman with a powerful left cross buckling his knees, then followed with a right cross to the chin. Conn went to the canvas for the full count.

Dad jumped up and clasped his hands over his head, then pounded me on the back. "I knew Louis was too tough for that damned *mick*."

"What's a mick?" I asked.

Dad looked at me and shook his head. "How should I know. It's what everybody calls the Irish. Look at the measurements. Louis's biceps are two inches bigger, his reach three inches longer. Conn didn't have a chance."

"Don't we have some Irish blood in us?"

"That's different."

"If the Irish guy didn't have a chance, why'd he fight?"

Dad threw back a shot of gin and chased it with a drink of water. "He thought he did. But he's just a piker compared to our Champ. You have to be strong *and* fast to win fights. Fast alone is not enough. Power. It takes power. Look." He made a fist and bent his arm at the elbow to exhibit his muscle. After the Conn fight, Louis joined the Army. That had been three years ago—seemed like a life-time.

I had fair hand-eye coordination, and while I didn't have much in a left jab, I learned to put every ounce of my one-hundred ten pounds into my right hand, and that had a lot to do with the fight between me and Robert Peevy, the leader of the Moorehouse Gang.

It had been prearranged. Peevy and I would meet at the corner of Palmer and Browning, in the vacant lot the City Fire Department flooded in the winter for an ice-rink. It was to be bare knuckles, a fight till one gave up, no gouging or biting. I had already fought two of his gang and won. This fight would decide whether members of Peevy's gang could come to Browning Street and hang around at Carol Young and Barbara Kite's houses.

I looked at Peevy, a kid I hardly knew, trying to figure out why I was about to take part in something I hated, then remembered Dad's words. *When you know you have to fight, don't hesitate, or you'll look scared. The first punch is the most important. Never, ever, let the other guy hit you first. And when you throw that first one, put every goddamned thing you've got into it. Understood?*

I jabbed with a left. The punch was weak and only grazed Peevy's chin. He turned to profile and leaned back like he was going to throw a round-house. As he came forward, my right hand, with all my weight behind it, hit him on the temple. A confused look came on his face. A film slipped over his eyes, they rolled upward, the lids fluttering like a wounded bird. He dropped in a heap at my feet. It wouldn't have happened if it had been just my fist, but it was the stump, the remnant of that sixth knuckle that had put him down. I ran like I was chased by old Beelzebub himself, through the field, across Palmer Street, down Browning, and into the side door of our house. I stood with my back to the door, panting, shaking.

Mother's voice from the kitchen: "That you, Son?" I didn't say anything. The door to the kitchen opened. "What's the matter?" she asked.

"Nothing."

She must have heard me gasping for breath. "Don't lie to me. Tell me what's the matter."

"I hurt somebody. Hurt 'em bad."

"Come up here and tell me what happened while I fix Dad's supper."

"I hit Robert Peevy with my fist, and he went down."

"If it was a fair fight, don't worry about it." She turned and started back into the kitchen.

"I didn't mean to hurt him that bad. A black knot jumped out on the side of his head."

She stopped. "I thought you said you hit him with your fist."

"Mother. Look here!" She came down the steps. "You ever seen this before? I hit him with this." I held up my right hand and stuck the boney growth under her nose. "Ever wonder what the kids at school say about this thing?"

She put her arms around me. "You can't help it if those growths are on the side of your hand. You tell those kids, you're just as good as they are. Now listen. If it was a fair fight, forget it. Dad will be home after awhile, and you can tell him about how you whipped that kid."

"They say I'm a damned freak. You hear? A freak. Me saying I'm as good as anyone else doesn't make it so. You think I'm proud of hitting him with this thing? What if it killed him?"

She pulled me up the stairs. "Don't pay any attention to kids that say stuff like that; stay away from them."

"I don't *want* to stay away from them. Can't you see? I don't want to be different."

She turned and walked away. "You always over dramatize. Tell Dad. He'll be proud you knocked that kid out, you'll see."

I followed her to the sink. "You think I over dramatize? Remember last winter when our class went to Palmer Park for a skating party?" We all gathered in the middle of the rink to hold hands and skate in a circle, then form a line and do a whiplash. Want to know who was not included?" Mom filled the sink with water and poured in soap. "Me. Not even the goddamned teacher would hold my hand—and I had gloves on. How's that for over dramatizing?"

Her hand came out of the dishwater, but she must have remembered what I told her about keeping her hands off, and put it back in quick. "Watch your mouth. You're not going to talk to me like that."

"Really. You've never heard any swear words?" I sat on the edge of one of the breakfast nook benchs. "Mom, isn't there anything a doctor could do to make my hands look normal?"

"You don't need anything done. Doctor Carpenter told me those things would go away."

"Momma, he was wrong. These things, especially the one on my right hand, are getting *bigger* every year. Are you blind? Or maybe you don't give a damn."

"Don't be such a baby about it. Besides, it would cost a lot of money."

"I have forty-three dollars saved from my paper route."

"That's just a fraction of what it would cost." She dried a pan, draped the dishtowel over her shoulder, and sat opposite me. "Son, I want you to forget it. Everything will work out just fine."

"Sure," I said. "Like everything else around here—and by the way, don't call me a baby."

CHAPTER 19

Fat Lips And A Short Fuse

September, 1944. Compared to the previous schools I had attended, the building I entered looked like a palace. The exterior was beige cement block with clean white cornices. There were lawns on all sides, crisscrossed with foot paths. Behind the main building was a manicured football field with stadium seats on two sides. Inside, the halls were wide, well lighted, and lined with lockers, one for each of the eighteen-hundred students, grades eight through twelve, who attended. This was where my sister graduated, where my brother-in-law would be a senior now if he weren't off on the business of fighting a war, and where I intended to finish high school.

It had been Miss Porter's encouragement that enabled me to squeak through the seventh grade. She believed in me, and I promised to get my life straightened out. Dropping out of Red McCauley's gang was the first step. And there was my friend, old Henry Crain, in Utica, Missouri, whom I yearned to see, and who had said I would never be trash. For the love of him and Miss Porter, I would make it though high school come hell or high water.

My eighth grade would be a new beginning, in a new school, a new chance. No more Cs and Ds on my report card. I would make good grades, like I did back in Miss Beasley and Miss Tinder's rooms at Martin Road. I knew I could. I would force myself to shut out the sounds from the basement, do my homework faithfully, to concentrate on learning, and not worry about Dad and Sis. I'd do it!

Sis had warned me about Miss McCrory, the American History teacher, and how "the old bitch," had sent her to the office several times. I would have to be on my best behavior, especially if she found out I was Shirley Jean Myers's brother.

Miss McCrory's class was held in the last room on the ground floor of the building, adjacent to an emergency exit. She lectured standing with her hands clasped behind her and always dressed in a tweed skirt, a wool sweater buttoned to the neck; never mind that heat and humidity in the fall and spring often climbed into the nineties. Her steel gray hair was tied in a large bun behind her head. Thick glasses were either on the end of her nose or hanging on a thin black ribbon across her bosom. She wore no wedding band or other jewelry—austere to a fault.

Miss McCrory had an unerring eye. No miscue or shenanigan escaped her, and she conducted her class with an iron fist. When the last bell rang, everyone was to be in their seats. One tap of her ruler on the desk and a silence, funereal in its completeness, fell upon the room. If you coughed or sneezed without a handkerchief over your nose and mouth, you went to the nurse's office for tissue, and maybe a hypodermic needle. If you chewed gum or whispered, you went to the principal's office, and if you went twice in one grading period, you were suspended for one week—no exceptions.

It was late September, Indian Summer. Miss McCrory's classroom was hot and humid, causing heads to nod. But a student did not sleep in her class, regardless of how boring the lecture, so people bit their thumbs to stay awake and avoid a trip to the office. In the minutes before the dismissal bell, the tantalizing jingle of an ice cream wagon came through the open window. When class broke, I bolted and ran out of her room and through the emergency exit. By the time I got outside, the wagon had rounded the corner of the school. I sprinted after it, waving at the driver until he stopped. I bought creamscicles, and, with ice cream in hand, hurried back.

Miss McCrory was half in, half out of the door, tapping her foot on the sill. She lowered her head and peered over the top of her glasses. "This sign clearly states that this exit is for emergency use only." She gave me a withering look. "I presume, Mr. Myers, that having made it to the eighth grade, you can read."

"Yes, Ma'am," I said. "And I won't do it again, but it was hot in your room and I wanted to buy you something." I handed her a creamscicle. "If I'd of gone out the front, I'd of never caught the ice cream wagon."

The color in her cheeks changed from wax to peach. She pushed the door open. "Get in here. Your English is atrocious. Don't let me catch you using this door again." The faintest of smiles broke the straight plane of her mouth. "And if I would have made you go all the way around to the front to get back in the building, the ice cream you bought would have melted." The smile disappeared like a wisp of smoke in a high wind. "Don't think this confection on a stick is going to buy you any special privileges in my class."

"No, Ma'am, I won't." I unwrapped mine and took a bite. The orange coating was sweet and tangy. "Don't let it melt."

She gave me a suspicious stare while she peeled the wrapping away and put it to her lips. I turned. "Mr. Myers," she said, pointing the ice cream at me. "You've been doing well on your homework. Keep it up."

At the beginning of the semester, I tried to prepare for Miss McCrory's American History class, a subject I didn't need to spend too much time on. When I raised my hand in class and answered some hard questions, it impressed Doris Griffith and Mary Marino, both serious students. They started speaking to me between classes. Mary Marino invited me to her Halloween party. Things had taken a decided change for the better.

I tried out for football that semester. I let Coach Graeble know I was Topper's brother-in-law, but it didn't do any good, he said I'd have to put on a lot of weight before I could play on his team. With a pat on the back he said being skinny might be an asset to the track team. But the track coach shook his head. I was flat footed, bow-legged, and smoked a pack a day. No hope there. The only reason I even tried out for sports was because of Topper, and the Roberts twins.

Jeffery and Jake Roberts had started coming by my house in

the mornings to walk to school with me. They had both made the football and track teams, and I was hoping to impress them. Deep down it didn't matter whether I made it in sports, I just wanted to be good at something, and really wished it was music so I could make Miss Porter proud.

That weekend, I raided my money cache, got on the bus to Royal Oak, and went to a used musical instrument store. I looked at all the great instruments I had studied in Miss Porter's class: the oboe, French horn, clarinet, bass cello; all of the strings, brass, and winds. And inside a glass case, shining like a giant nugget in Sutter's Mill, was a gold-plated cornet, with mother of pearl on the plungers, snuggled down in a carrying case lined with purple velvet. It had been made for me alone, and cost the equivalent of five months earnings on my paper route.

Monday morning on the way to school, the Roberts twins wanted to see what I had in the black case. At the corner of Palmer and Browning, after I made Elmer go back home, I showed them the gleaming horn. With a bit of pride, I told them how I'd bought it with my own money so I could go out for band. They thought it was a great idea.

At noon I gulped my lunch, took my cornet out of my locker, and went to the band director's office. The plate on his door said, "R. P. Gelliston, Director of Music" I tapped on the door. A voice invited me to come in.

"Mister Gelliston?" I said to a flabby man sitting behind a desk. Half of a foot-long Cony covered with chili and onions was poised in his hand.

Without looking up, he said, "Its Gel-*LIS*-ton, not *Jellystone*."

"Sorry. Mister Gel-LIS-ton, I'd like to go out for band."

He looked up. His eyes were so close together, there wasn't room between them for his nose—two eyes under one eyebrow. Weird.

"That's just dandy," he took half the remaining Cony in one bite and said with his mouth full. "I'm short a couple of positions. Do you know where the band room is? I suppose not. It's the small building on the east side of the football field. Be there at four o'clock, and we'll get you started on a practice schedule. My band marches. If you can't keep cadence and play an instrument at the same time, I can't use you. We placed third in state last year, and I expect to win it all this time around. We'll try you out. If you make band, its worth a credit. I grade on ability, faithful practice, and marching." He squinted at my case. "What've you got there?"

I set the case on his desk and unsnapped the latches. They popped smartly. I turned the case so he could see the treasure. "My cornet," I said proudly.

The eyebrow wrinkled. He shook his head. "You can't play that instrument."

"I know, but that's 'cause I've never had lessons. But I'll practice hard."

His head was jerking. "I mean you'll *never* be able to play that instrument."

"Why not?"

"Your lips are too fat." However, I have two positions that your lips won't interfere with. One is third clarinet, the other, third saxophone."

At first, I thought he was kidding. Then I remembered. A couple of years ago Sis started calling me, "nigger lips." So he was probably right, my lips were too fat for the cornet or trumpet. How stupid of me. My face got hot. I spun the case back around and snapped the lid into place. What a waste of money. Jesus, was there anything I could do right? And what would I tell the Roberts twins, and my mom and dad, when they found out I'd spent a fortune on something I could never use?

Mister Gelliston said, "I have both instruments at the band room. We'll try you out and see which one you're best suited for."

As I went out the door, he called, "You didn't tell me your name."

I let the door slam. I had heard Louis "Satchmo" Armstrong's magic trumpet on the radio many times, and had read that when he was seventeen years old, he replaced a cornetist in the Kid Orly

Band in New Orleans. But I didn't see Satchmo's face on television until fifteen years after my encounter with Mr. Gelliston.

I gave up on music.

Christmas Eve, 1944. Mom put the six foot spruce tree in front of the living room windows. Sis and Fern came downstairs and helped Mom and me load it with ornaments, blue lights, icicles, and something called angel hair. Dona, my fifteen-month-old niece, was pulling icicles and bulbs off the tree faster than Sis could put them back. Elmer and I ran out the front door for the third time, and from the sidewalk looked back at the house. It was like a fairy tale. The light spread through the angel hair like tiny, blue moonbeams on water. I ran back in the house, Elmer barking furiously at my heels.

Mom came out of the kitchen with a plate covered with her homemade fudge and divinity. "Everyone can have two pieces, but no more until Dad gets here."

I grabbed the biggest piece of divinity. We only got Mom's white fluffy candy at Christmas, and there was nothing in the world better. She always added handfuls of chopped, fresh black walnuts gathered from under trees on trips to and from the cottage. For those who loved the flavor of black walnuts as I did, the chore of retrieving the meat, while onerous, was worth the time and effort. That fall we had picked up two gunny sacks full. At home we spread them on the concrete at the back of the driveway. Within a week, the hulls were crawling with maggots. After they rotted and dried, I peeled the skins. My fingers and hands were stained black for days. I threw the walnuts in a bushel basket and buried the hulls in the garden. Mom said they'd make the soil loose and fertile. A black walnut shell is too hard to break with a regular nut cracker, so I laid each nut on the driveway and whacked it with the flat side of a ball peen hammer. Mom and I, and sometimes Sis, would use nut-picks to dig out the small meat. Lots of effort for little return, but the flavor the walnuts added made it all worth while.

Elmer yapped and sat up begging. I broke off a piece of fudge and gave it to him, but ate all of the divinity myself. We watched for Dad to round the curve on Stephenson. When it got too dark to recognize the car, I read a Superman Comic Book, while Mom mixed batter and put a spice cake in the oven. At eight o'clock, Sis and Fern took a plate of Mom's roast beef and boiled potatoes upstairs. Mom fixed me a sandwich. I took it into my room and turned on the radio and listened to Christmas music. I was nervous 'cause Dad wasn't home, and excited about opening presents in the morning.

My stomach started burning. I tiptoed into the kitchen, ate a piece of plain bread, cut the fatty end of the roast off and gave it to Elmer. Mom wasn't around so I snuck another piece of divinity, and went back into my bedroom. This time I gave Elmer a taste. The announcer on WKY radio said Santa had left the North Pole and was headed for Detroit. I thought about when Sis had told me the truth about Santa years ago in Utica, opened the window a crack, and lit a Lucky Strike. When I turned the radio off I heard a board in the floor of the dining room creak. Mom was pacing. I fanned smoke out of the room, and closed the window. Elmer whined in his sleep. I reached down and petted him. He quieted. Humans weren't the only ones who had bad dreams.

I had just dozed when Elmer jumped off the bed and started barking madly. There was a loud crash from the direction of the living room. Two doors opened into my room, one into the kitchen, the other into the front hall. I raced through the one into the hall and on into the living room.

Dad was laying in the corner flailing his arms and legs, the Christmas tree on top of him. Tinsel and angel hair hung from his ears. Mom stood knee deep in packages and broken ornaments, her hands on her hips. She screamed, "You bastard! You've been with her again. I can smell her perfume and sex all over you." She ran in their bedroom and slammed the door.

I backed up and out of sight. The real Santa Claus had just arrived at 428 W. Browning Street.

The day after Christmas, 1944. Colonel Wendell Blanchard of Patton's Third Army, led his column of tanks one-hundred-fifty miles, in nineteen hours, to relieve General McAuliffe, whose 101st Airborne Division, known as the Bastards of Bastogne, had been under siege taking heavy losses since December 16. Our cousin, Weldon, was among the infantrymen supporting Blanchard's tanks.

First semester grades came in. I didn't do much better than at Lacy. Miss McCrory had seen through my attempt to soft soap her and gave me a D in history. The best surprise was the D plus Miss Salinsky had given me in English Literature. She was one of my favorite teachers, her class the most interesting. I'd quit hanging out with the McCauley Gang, but that hadn't solved the problem of not being able to concentrate on my studies. My resolution to make good grades had failed, but somehow I'd made it through another semester.

I came out of the office strutting. The report card was stuck in the pocket of my new rayon shirt. Mary Marino stopped me in the hall. "Neat shirt," she said and put her hand on my arm. "Feels good too."

The shirt was pale yellow, with a thin maroon plaid—my favorite Christmas present. The label on the gaily wrapped package said it was from Santa, which meant, Mom. It was the first grown-up shirt I'd ever had, and it felt soothing against my skin. I sauntered into the first meeting of Miss Salinsky's English Literature class of the second semester. I was ready.

Students at Hazel Park High were given two bells between classes. The first signaled the end of class break. The second indicated you were to be in your seat ready for instruction.

Miss Salinsky was delicate of build, her complexion fair, wearing a pair of thin, gold rimmed glasses. She was striding back and forth in front of the blackboard, chalk in hand, waiting for final bell. I was standing, talking to Mary Marino. The warning bell went off. The teacher said we should take our seats. But seat assignments hadn't been made, so I started toward the chair I used the previous semester. Another student beat me to it. While I looked around the room for a place to sit, the final bell sounded. Everyone was seated except me.

I didn't see her coming. Suddenly Miss Salinsky was twisting the cloth of my new shirt in her fist and pulling me toward an empty seat; dragging me across the room, like a dog on a leash in front of Mary Marino, Doris Griffith, and the Roberts twins. Something snapped. I jerked my arm away from her. The shirt tore from elbow to shoulder. There was a ripple of nervous laughter through the room. She lunged toward me. In one motion, I knocked her arm away with my forearm and let it swing around like a scythe. It caught her just above the breast and swept her across the room. She flew backward, tripped over a student's feet, and landed on her rear, exposing her legs all the way to her garter belt. Her glasses hit the floor and splintered. The room became deathly quiet. Then she looked at her legs, jerked her skirt down, scrambled to her feet, and screamed, "Get out of my room!" I started for the door. She gathered the rim of her glasses and ran after me. "To the office you hoodlum," she said. "March!"

At the Principal's Office, I couldn't think of anyway to defend myself. There was no getting around the fact I should have been in my seat when the final bell sounded, but I couldn't understand why Miss Salinsky had grabbed my shirt, nor why I had reacted with such ferocity. All I could think of was how she had put her hands on me, humiliated me in front of my new friends. Intentional or not, I had struck a teacher, the ultimate sin. I was immediately expelled. It was ironic, Miss Salinsky had been my favorite eighth grade teacher.

February 4, 1945. U. S forces, under the command of General Douglas MacArthur captured the city of Manilla, in the Philippines.

The month I was suspended I tried to keep up with the assignments, but without benefit of classroom lectures it was impossible. I apologized to Miss Salinsky, and was re-admitted on probation. My grades hovered on the brink of disaster. The friends I had made first semester became cool. The Roberts twins stopped walking to school with me. And my stomach hurt.

Mom let me take fifty cents a day to school, so I could eat lunch at Clara Mae's, a restaurant that advertised home cooked meals. I went there alone, poked around in a nasty meat loaf and mushy green beans, paid my bill, and walked over to Santana's Drug Store and drank chocolate Cokes. I preferred Cherry Cokes, but they always gave me gas which caused a lot of coughing and groaning in my afternoon classes. I put a nickel in the jukebox and punched, *I Had The Craziest Dream Last Night.* It was a Harry James creation, and he blew the insides out of his trumpet—fabulous. I wondered about his lips.

February 13, 1945. British planes fire-bombed Dresden, Germany, killing 135,000 civilians.

March 9, 1945. U.S. B-24 Bombers rained incendiaries on Tokyo, Japan, killing 124,000 civilians.

March 16, 1945. After a thirty-five day battle, U.S. Marines took Iwo Jima, with loss of 6,000 Marines.

April 12, 1945. President Roosevelt died of a brain hemorrhage at age 63, and Harry S. Truman became Commander-In-Chief.

May 7, 1945. Germany surrendered unconditionally. President Truman declared the next day V-E Day. I sold two-hundred Extras. A man in the Cast-Away Bar, at the corner of John-R and Ten Mile Road, started crying and tipped me ten dollars; said his son would now be able to come home. A few days later, I read where a G. I. in Germany had been killed moments before the surrender. I hoped it wasn't the son of the man at the Cast-Away.

June, 1945. Mom's plan was put into motion. Shirley Jean went to Peaks Island, Maine, enrolled in the summer stock theater group called The Peaks Island Actors. Their brochure said scouts from Hollywood studios and Broadway casting agents were sometimes present during performances. After Peaks Island, Sis would move on to New York, with the hope of landing a role in a Broadway Musical. Her tuition, room and board, and expenses in New York were more than I could earn on my paper route in ten years.

Preparations had been elaborate. If one were to be "discovered" by the talent scouts, one had to be appropriately dressed. It was quite an event at 428 W. Browning Street. Measurements were taken, a new wardrobe acquired. Voice lessons and practice sessions accelerated. All expenses paid by Donald H. Scott's in-laws. Mom and I would take care of Dona Mae, who, at the time of her mother's departure, was twenty-one months old.

June 3, 1945. School let out for the summer. It had been another squeaker. My report card showed Cs and Ds in everything except two subjects. I got a B in music theory because of what I had learned from Miss Porter, and a B in gym because they offered boxing, which I'd been practicing on the streets. My grade in Miss McCrory's class dropped to a D minus. I'd be a freshman in high school in the fall, and resolved to benefit from the incident with Miss Salinsky by learning to control my temper.

June 21, 1945. One half million U.S. Forces battled one-hundred-ten thousand Japanese for three months before taking the island of Okinawa. 49,151 American servicemen were killed.

I was at Princeton's house. His dad answered the phone, and handed it to me. Mom said I should come home right away. Something was about to happen, she wouldn't tell me what. I burst through the door, and there, in the middle of the living room, with a foot propped up on a duffle bag, was a soldier. Fern and Mom were hanging on his shoulders. He looked sharp in his envelope hat, Eisenhower jacket, and chest covered with an array of medals. He looked at me and said, "Hey, H. K. Damn boy, you've grown up on me."

"Weldon!" I shouted.

"I told Aunt Mae to call you, so you could be here when I open my duffle bag. He bent and fooled with a lock, pulled the cords wide, and turned the bag upside down. There fell upon our living room floor an eye-popping array of Nazi symbols, weapons, and civilian plunder: two, six by four foot flags, one black with a white German Cross, the other a black Nazi Swastika on a red field, like the ones I'd seen in war movies and newsreels; an assembly of bayonets and knives, two German Lugers; and a gold pocket watch with a chain.

Weldon picked up the watch and popped the lid. "Listen to this." From inside the miniature works came an enchanting tinkle, an ensemble playing the *Blue Danube Waltz.*

From the bottom of the bag, he lifted out a large object wrapped in several pair of his underwear and tied with a cord. He set it on the dining room table and removed the layers of cloth one at a time. When the last cloth came off there was a collective intake of breath. Setting on our dining room table was a Belgian mantle clock, its ivory case intricately carved with figurines, each carrying a bouquet of flowers, the blossoms inset with sparkling gems. The face of the clock was mother of pearl with gold numbers and hands.

I was more interested in the items associated with war and death. "Where'd you get all this stuff?" I asked, picking up a scabbard and unsheathing a wicked looking knife. It was either rusted or blood-stained.

"Off dead Krauts. 'Cept the clock. I found that in a bombed out house."

"Were the people who owned it dead?"

"How should I know? And what difference does it make? Look here what I brought you."

He stirred the array of items, and held up a silver chain and medal that sparkled as it turned in the light. My eyes widened. "What is it?" I asked.

He hung it around my neck. "It's called a Saint Christopher Medal—and it's solid silver. Supposed to keep you safe on your travels."

"Where'd you get it?"

"Off a Kraut I killed."

As soon as Weldon went upstairs with Fern, I took the medal from around my neck and put it in my pocket. I showed it off to all the kids on Browning Street, and told the story of how Weldon got it, but I never put in on again. I didn't want it to keep me as safe as it had the German that Weldon took it from.

CHAPTER 20

Alone

August 6 & 9, 1945. The United States dropped atomic bombs on Hiroshima and Nagasaki, killing 350,000 civilians.

August 10, 1945. Japan surrendered. President Truman declared August 14, 1945, V-J Day. The war to end all wars was over.

Sis had been gone to Peaks Island, Maine and New York city for almost three months. Her mail was still coming to our house and I checked it every day. There had been no letters from Topper for weeks. I could hardly wait for him to get home. I thought about the G. I. killed in Germany minutes before the war was over.

Things were getting steadily worse at the house. Since Christmas Mom had asked me at least a dozen times who I wanted to live with when she and Dad divorced.

Mother's dream of Shirley Jean becoming a star was not to be. In mid-September, at the end of the summer theatrical season in New York, she returned home. She had played in the same troupe at Peaks Island with Steve Cochran, the dark, handsome actor who went on to win supporting roles in numerous movies, but she returned home without a new love, or a career, and as my mother feared, with an ill-defined intent to stay married to Topper.

The day I enrolled as a freshman at Hazel Park High School, Elmer didn't meet me at his usual place at the corner of Palmer and Browning. I called and whistled for him the rest of the way home. I climbed the steps, opened the front door. "Elmer, come here boy. Where are you?" Maybe he was asleep in the basement.

I pushed through the swinging door into the kitchen. Mom and Dad were sitting in the nook.

Mom said, "Son, come sit for a minute, there's some things we have to talk to you about."

I put my hands over my ears. "No! I don't want to hear." They were going to tell me about their divorce again.

Dad said, "We feel as bad about this as you, so come over and talk to us."

"No. You don't feel bad about anything. You're going to get a divorce, and I have to choose which one to live with. I don't want to hear it. Leave me be." I went to the basement stairs and called to Elmer.

Mom said, "He's not down there."

"Shut up. I hate you both. You never tell me anything good, it's always bad. I don't want to live with either of you." Then the implication of what she had just said sunk in. "How do you know he's not in the basement?"

Dad stood up. "Don't you talk to us like that. We're your parents and you're going to show some respect."

"Respect? Ha. You make me sick." I went into my bedroom, slammed the door, and threw myself on the bed. "Please don't be dead Elmer. Please. I need you. You're all I have left. Come home boy. Who's going to play ball with me and keep my feet warm at night?"

Mom opened the door. "Can I come in?"

I started crying.

She stood by the bed. "Let me sit with you for a minute."

"Momma," I said. "Please, don't tell me something bad about Elmer."

Dad must have been standing in the door. He sounded stern. "Son, you're going to have your fourteenth birthday in less than a week. You have to take bad news like a man."

"I don't want to be a man! I want Elmer. And you're telling me how to handle bad news? That's a joke."

"Shit," he said. "I've never been able to talk to him. You tell him." The door closed.

Mom put her hand on my back. "Elmer's dead—was run over by a car right after you left this morning."

"Nooooo," I wailed. "You're lying—get your hands off me. You've done something to my Elmer. Where is he? What have you done?"

"Son, your father's right. You're old enough to be able to take this like a man. We buried Elmer this morning."

"Where?"

"That doesn't matter. Just forget about him, he's gone."

"Doesn't matter? Forget him! Jesus. What kind of mother are you anyway? Sick, you're both sick. Leave me alone. Elmer's not dead. He'll come home."

That night, I sat in the little woods so I could see up and down Stephenson Highway. Every few minutes I called, then whistled. In the distance I heard a jingle. Elmer's collar! I jumped up and ran in the direction of the sound. But it was a bell on a bicycle across the highway. The night air was damp, and I shivered. It didn't matter. If Elmer was hurt or sick, he'd hear me and know I would take care of him, like the time he was hit by the car. There was a rustle in the underbrush. "Elmer," I said. "Here Boy, here I am."

It was mother. She said, "Son?" Is that you?" I didn't answer. She walked to my side and put her hand on my shoulder.

I jerked away. "Don't touch me."

"Please come home. You can't sit in this woods all night. You'll catch pneumonia."

"I don't care. And neither do you."

She knelt with one knee on the ground. "Don't say things like that."

"Leave me alone. I'm waiting for Elmer."

She got up. "You know I love you Son. I'll be waiting for you." She walked away. Elmer didn't come home, not that night nor the next. I moped around, then took a package of Camels out of Dad's carton, and walked to Mackey's house. His mother let us smoke inside. I told Mackey, Elmer might be dead. For a minute it looked like he was going to cry. Every kid on Browning Street treated Elmer like their own. He went with us everywhere, did everything we did, shared in all our candy, sandwiches, and cupcakes.

I stayed out late again that night, hoping everyone would be in bed, but when I got home, all the lights were on, even the ones in Sis's apartment upstairs. I went in and climbed the stairs. Everyone was in Sis's living room laughing and talking. She was back from New York, surrounded by luggage, holding Dona in her lap, and telling about her experiences. No one paid much attention to me, so I listened for awhile, then butted in. "Did they tell you about Elmer?"

Sis looked at Mom, then at Dad. "Tell me what?"

"That's what I thought," I said, and went back downstairs. No one cared about Elmer except me. Well screw them all. Sis didn't bring me anything from New York, and acted like she couldn't have cared less whether she saw me, didn't even say thanks for helping with Dona while she was gone.

The next day, I got up, dressed and went into the kitchen. Mom was frying eggs. Dad was at the table drinking coffee. "Hey son," he said. "Come over here with your Dad."

I crawled into the booth beside him.

"Feeling any better?"

"Maybe. But I don't believe what Mom said about Elmer." Dad didn't say anything, so I asked, "How come you got the day off? It's Wednesday."

"I don't work at Ford's anymore. Friday was my last day. Can't take the paint in the lungs."

I'd seen him cough up large hunks of the stuff he sprayed on new cars. And there was always paint in the corners of his eyes, when he got home, and in his handkerchief after he blew his nose. "What 'cha gonna do?"

"Your mother and I have bought a business."

"What kind? Another butcher shop?"

"No, no. Nothing like that. It's a tavern."

"You mean like Eddie's Half Moon, or The Cast-Away?"

"Yes and no. It's a lot smaller and sells only beer and wine."

"Is it in Hazel Park?"

He twisted in the seat and looked at Mom. She brought a plate of eggs, set them in front of Dad, and said to me, "How 'bout some breakfast."

"I'd take a piece of toast. My stomach doesn't feel so good."

"Let me fix you some eggs."

"Maybe later. Where's the new business you bought?"

Toast popped up in the toaster. I jumped. Mom buttered the pieces and put two more in. Then gave one to me and the other to Dad. I tore off a corner for Elmer and held it under the table for a second before I realized what I was doing. I choked up, then stuck Elmer's piece in my mouth and ate the rest quickly to quell the nausea.

Mom buttered the other pieces of toast as she talked. "How'd you like to live in a small town where there are lots of lakes and streams and the fishing's great?"

I pretended like I didn't hear. "I enrolled in school Monday. I have to buy supplies today. Classes start tomorrow."

Mom filled Dad's coffee cup. He swiped at the bottom of his plate with the last piece of toast, and with his mouth full asked if anyone at school had mentioned what happened in Missus Salinsky's class last semester.

"I didn't see Missus Salinsky. Maybe she won't hold it against me when she sees how hard I'm going to study. Even Miss McCrory smiled at me when I went to sign up for her class. I'm going to do good this year."

Dad pushed his plate back. "You don't have to worry about Missus Salinsky anymore. You're not going to that school."

"I *want* to go to Hazel Park High. That's where all my friends from Browning Street are going, and I . . . . I'm not leaving. I'll live with Sis until Topper gets home, and maybe he'll let me stay until I finish high school."

Mother scoffed. "Topper can't support himself, let alone you."

"Don't you say anything bad about Topper. He's been fighting, and he's a hero whether you like him or not, while you were hoarding rationed goods and buying liquor on the black market."

Dad said, "You think you're so damned smart. It's no wonder you can't get along in school."

"You're moving away from Browning Street aren't you?"

Mom scooted in beside me. "Son, stop talking so crazy. Sometimes a family can't stay in one place. Circumstances require changes. People do it all the time—children have to go where their parents go."

"That's what my friend Henry told me, but he was wrong. I wish I'd never left Missouri. And I don't care about lakes and streams. We never go fishing anyway."

Dad said, "That's about the most ungrateful remark I've ever heard. You've got everything that a boy your age could possibly want."

"That's how much you know. This place we're going to. It's far away, isn't it?"

"Yes. Takes about six or seven hours to drive."

"And that's why Elmer's not around. You didn't want to be bothered with him getting car sick on a long trip. What'd you do with him? Take him out in the country and dump him? Give him away? Kill him? What?"

Mother took her glasses off, laid them on the table, and put the heels of her hands in her eyes. She didn't say anything for a long moment. "What must you think of us? Do you really believe we would take Elmer away from you?"

"I don't know what to believe. I know what you did to Drumstick. Last week I was supposed to choose which one of you I wanted to live with. Today you tell me we're all going away together. I want to be with both of you, but I don't want to leave Browning Street. And I want Elmer to be with us."

Dad put his arm around me. "You have to go with us. Things will be better for you."

Mom started happy talk. "You'll make new friends before you know it."

"I'm not going anywhere without Elmer."

Dad said, "Son, you have to accept the fact that your dog is dead."

"Then tell me where he's buried. I walked every inch of this property, and there's no grave."

Dad sighed. "Mom, tell him."

Mother took my hand. I pulled it away. "Monday," she said, "a Missus Tarrington from over on Garfield called. Said you were friends with one of her kids, and you'd been over to their house several times with Elmer; that a dog that looked like him was laying in a ditch by Stephenson Highway. Dad and I took the shovel and drove over there. Sure enough, it was Elmer. We buried him right there."

"How did you know if he was dead? Elmer was strong. Remember, you said he was going to die once before when he got hit by a car. And he lived. Why didn't you take him to one of those animal doctors?"

Dad messed with the leftover eggs on his plate. "Believe me Son, he was dead. Had been for quite awhile."

"He couldn't have been dead a long time. He walked me to Palmer Street the morning you say he was killed. And besides Elmer didn't go near Stephenson Highway without me."

Mom laid her hand on top of mine and said, "Maybe he followed another dog—a female in heat, or the Sheneyman."

"Sheneyman doesn't come 'cept on Fridays." I wiped my eyes on the back of my hands. "I want to go see."

Mom squeezed my hand. "No. It won't do anything other than make you feel bad."

"I already feel bad. Besides, I want to say goodbye to him. Don't you understand? I don't know what I'll do without him. Nothing's right without Elmer."

Dad said, "I think this has gone far enough. Now listen to me. We are moving in two weeks . . ."

Mom interrupted. "And we're all going to make a fresh start, aren't we Dad?"

There was a slight hesitation before Dad reached around me

and put his hand on Mom's shoulder, and said, "Sure—a fresh start. But between now and when the moving van comes to take our stuff, we've got a lot of work to do around here."

"Where's Elmer's collar and tags?"

"We left them on him."

I braced my hands on the table to get up. "I want them back, something to remember him by."

Mom hugged me. "Your not digging around for a dead dog. Besides, his collar would just make you feel worse. I'm going to get boxes to pack our things in. Son, get together everything you want to take and I'll give you boxes. And oh yes, you'd better start looking for someone to buy your paper route."

"I'm not taking nothing."

"What do you mean?" they asked in unison.

"I mean, I don't want anything. I'm going out on Stephenson and find his tags."

"Son, you don't mean your model planes? Your comic books, your marbles. Those are wonderful collections."

"Nothing's wonderful in this house." I had built a balsa wood model of every U.S., German, and Japanese Plane that fought in the war. After Sis moved upstairs, I hung them on the ceiling of my bedroom. I had over a thousand War Cards, three Quaker Oats boxes full of the best marbles in Hazel Park, piles of comic books. "If I can't have Elmer's collar, I don't want any of it. I'll give it all to my friends. And I'll give my route to Wayne Schmidt. He's asked me about it several times"

Mom slide out of the booth. "Okay, if that's the way you feel about it. You paid for most of that stuff yourself, so if you want to give it away, it's your business. I've got to start packing or we'll never get ready."

"What about Sis?" I asked.

Mom stacked the dishes on the table. "She's staying here."

"Then why can't I stay with her?"

"She has her life to live. She can't be looking after you."

"Looking after me? Who's been looking after me? Do either of you know what I got on my last report card? Or give a damn?"

"Mom came back over to the table. You'd better start realizing how much other people do for you, Mister. Dad pays all your bills, buys your food. I cook all your meals, do your laundry, change your bed. Besides, Sis has Dona to look out for."

"I could do those things and help her with Dona until Topper gets home."

Dad pushed up against me. "Let me out." I got up. He slid out of the booth. "You're going with us, and that's final."

For two days, I scoured the ditches and the median between the lanes of Stephenson in the area of Garfield Street. I never found the grave.

PART III

Maple City and Leland, Michigan

1945-1949

CHAPTER 21

A Fresh Start

When the Browning Street Gang wanted to know where in Michigan I was moving, I held my left hand out in front with the back facing me and pointed to the nail on my little finger. That's where you'd find Leelanau County and the village of Maple City, if for some nutty reason someone wanted to locate it in an atlas.

It was two-hundred and seventy miles northwest of Detroit, a hard six hour drive. In terms of latitude, the village of Maple City was near the 45th parallel, occupying the same relative position as Halifax, Nova Scotia; Lyons, France; Belgrade, in the former Yugoslavia; Portland, Oregon; and Minneapolis, Minnesota. It was four miles inland from the eastern shoreline of Lake Michigan.

We were going there, or so my parents had said, to allow Dad to escape the leaded paint he was inhaling every day on his job at Ford's. I figured there were other reasons. Mom had loved her home in Hazel Park. While not lavish, it was comfortable beyond the expectations of a girl who had been raised on a remote farm in Missouri and who had been taught to ask for and expect nothing. Our next door neighbor, Missus O'Donnell, had been her closest friend for eight years. Income from Dad's job, together with his inheritance, was more than enough to provide a high standard of living. Only one thing would cause Mom to leave Hazel Park for the backwoods of Maple City—the other woman.

As for myself, I had lost everything. My sister had started another life with no place in it for me, and Elmer had disappeared. To make matters worse, Mom and Dad talked of divorce constantly. My grades in school were near failing, and I had few friends. The situation couldn't conceivably get any worse in the town where we were going, and I had spent most of my youth outdoors, so the prospect of moving to the north woods had an adventurous ring to it. Maybe Mom and Dad were right. Perhaps this would be a new beginning.

The day of the move, we traveled almost three-hundred miles, stopping twice for gas and once for lunch. Conversation in the car became strained or ceased every time we passed one of the numerous taverns along the way, but Dad never mentioned a drink. It seemed promising, and a bit strange.

The last sixteen miles of the trip were breathtaking. The narrow road wound its way through hills, deep woods, and through the tiny village of Cedar, three miles east of our destination. Then we thumped and bumped along a mile stretch of blacktop known as the Cedar Swamp Road. In the winter the water under the road-bed froze. Spring thaws left pot holes deep enough to den a pair of wolverines. Then the road climbed up out of the swamp, topped what was known as Fire Tower Hill, and swept downward through a tunnel of brazen scarlet and yellow maples, around an "S" curve past a Catholic Church, and into the Village of Maple City. Nothing could have been more suggestive of peace and tranquility than this sleepy Alpine-appearing settlement of less than one-hundred fifty souls.

Every house in town was occupied except the one known as the Davis place, named for its ancient owner, who lived across the highway with his retarded wife and son. It was a dilapidated two-story frame structure, built around the turn of the century, its weary exterior patched with blue asphalt over tar-paper. The windows, loose in the frames, rattled with the slightest motion of the wind, and its sole occupants for several seasons had been mice and spiders.

The plumbing consisted of a water well situated in the kitchen and a drain pipe from the sink through the outside wall, its end was covered with wire mesh to keep the rats and mice out. Primitive by Hazel Park standards, it was still better than having to hand-carry buckets of water from outside. The privy, a duplicate of our Vassar Street facility, was located ten steps from the back door.

Central heating in the Davis place was a potbellied coal stove in the middle of the living area. My room was directly above and was warmed by the stove pipe poking through the floor next to the bed. With no insulation or storm windows, only a roaring fire in the winters could make it comfortable enough to remove one's coat. When the fire died at night, the water in the glass next to my bed froze, sometimes so solid it cracked the glass. Thick ice accumulated on the inside of the windows.

In the harshest months it took a pot of boiling water to unthaw the frozen well before we could pump fresh water.

On school days, my alarm went off at 5:45 a.m. In the spring and fall, getting around in the morning was not a big chore, but in the middle of winter it was a challenge. Downstairs, I started a fire in the kitchen stove, thawed the pump, and put another pan of water on to heat. Bundled like an Eskimo, I went out the back door, stopped at the privy on the way to the coal shed, filled the coal bucket, and returned to the house. A hot fire in the living room stove signaled time to wake Mom. Back in the kitchen, I used part of the boiling water to wash up while Mom cooked my breakfast and fixed a pot of coffee. On all mornings except Tuesdays (the tavern was closed on Mondays in the winter) she didn't get home until 3:00 a.m., and had no appetite for food. So while I ate, she packed my lunch.

Maple City's school had closed the year before we arrived. Its windows were boarded, the bell hung in the weather worn tower at a skewed angle, as though its motion and sound had suddenly been frozen during the act of summoning the children to class. I have wondered what difference it might have made in my life had the bell still been ringing when I moved there. But all children from the Maple City School District, grades nine through twelve were bused to Leland Schools, fourteen miles north of the village. The students were from widely disbursed farms throughout the district, which required the bus to take a circuitous route and backtrack several times on remote stretches of road. The trip took an hour.

School at Leland had been in session four weeks the day I climbed aboard the bus for the first time. It was October, the weather cold and blustery, almost wintry. The bus wound its way through the countryside stopping frequently at cross roads and farm houses. As we rumbled along the road, often through thick forests, one might have imagined passing through an art gallery. Clusters of oak and maple trees, drenched in the brightest colors of the artist's pallet, arched their branches over the road like protective arms. Leaves were caught in the wind eddies of the bus and thrown high creating a wake of crimson, orange, and gold. After we left the back roads the highway hugged the shoreline of Lake Michigan, with deep wood on one side and frothy, cobalt waves on the other.

The other students stared out the windows or straight ahead, casting an occasional furtive glance toward where I sat. The few words spoken between those who shared seats were in an undertone, almost a whisper, no frivolity or gaiety. Other than the sound of the engine, the bus was eerily quiet as though it were empty. The hushed atmosphere inside, and the cold wind from across the lake, sent chills down my neck, a portent of what was to follow.

Two miles from our destination, the highway bent slightly east and wound its way along a sprite of land between Lake Michigan and Lake Leelanau, the narrow peninsula upon which the village of Leland was situated. The bodies of water on each side were connected by the Leland River which ran through the village and emptied into the big lake. A small fishing fleet bobbed between its banks. This was Fish Town, a cluster of weather-grayed shacks perched askew along rickety docks on both sides of the river. The small harbor provided shelter for the fishing fleet and a place where the daily catch could be cleaned and sold.

The town itself was quaint and quiet. Well kept houses lined streets canopied by magnificent hardwoods. In this season, the beachfront homes owned by wealthy summer residents from down state were closed, their windows shuttered against the coming winter storms. The village was isolated and breathtakingly beautiful. Fishing, fruit orchards, in the nearby countryside, and tourism provided Leland with a prosperous and stable economy.

The wealth of Leland contrasted sharply with that of Maple City, where poverty was pervasive, and the war economy had done little to raise the standard of living. Its residents depended entirely on agriculture and logging. The village, once known as "Peg Town," was named for the shoe-pegs made from the surrounding hardwood forests. The ethnic composition of its citizens was Polish and Bohemian. The people were kind, earthy, and poor. Their children attended Leland Public Schools.

I was scared when I got off the bus. The other students were not hostile, but reserved. They offered no advise or encouragement, and I had no way of knowing that their silence was reserve, a trait I would come to admire. But on this day, I wished my mother had come with me to enroll. I had no idea what classes would be required, or what material had already been covered in the first four weeks. I followed the other ninth-graders into freshman Engish.

Noon came and still no one had talked to me. These kids were entirely different from my outgoing friends in Hazel Park. I didn't want to sit in the lunchroom alone, so I took my sack with the sandwiches Mom had packed, and walked out the door.

The school, perched on the highest hill in town, afforded a visage of white caps on Lake Michigan stretching to the western horizon. Dark gray clouds scudded across the sky, forerunners of winter blizzards. I leaned into the October wind, and headed for the gathering of boats and shanties known as Fish Town.

I crossed main street, passed the general mercantile store, and down a gentle slop to the docks. Smoke poured flat from the chimneys of shacks, their sides bleached silver by age and weather. A dozen or so boats rocked fretfully on their moorings. The gale off of the big lake caused even the safe haven of the Leland River to become choppy. Three or four smokehouses emitted the pungent smell of maple smoke and drying fish. Sea gulls hung motionless above the harbor, their sorrowful cries carried away eastward.

On the lee side of a shanty, I sat on a splintered bench and ate the contents of my sack. With the time left before I would have to return, I wandered along the shoreline. It was a beach unlike any I had ever seen. Occasional pockets of sand were surrounded by long stretches of multi-colored stones of every conceivable size and shape. No craggy rocks, just beautiful round, flat stones—perfect for skipping. I threw several, but the waves were too turbulent. The stones splashed and disappeared.

Refreshed, and with the wind at my back, I climbed the hill to school.

Inside the main entrance, one could turn left, descend three steps and enter the gymnasium, or go right down a long hall to classrooms. The steps had handrails on each side and another in the middle. Leaning against the center rail was Mr.William Wall, Superintendent of Leland Public Schools.

Six feet tall, and three-hundred pounds, he presented a formidable figure dressed in a dark suit and vest, complete with gold watch chain and fob. His hair was thin and gray, combed straight back in a pompadour. Glasses perched above a large nose, which hooked over his upper lip. He had a ponderous mid-drift, jowls, and a triple chin that bobbed in a distracting way when he spoke angrily, as he was doing now. "Come over here Myers!" His tone was threatening, and he jabbed his finger at a spot on the floor in front of his feet. Something was awry. It was apparent I was in trouble, but couldn't fathom the reason. I stepped into the spot he was pointing to on the floor. He said, "I got a call from one of the town folks who tell me that you spent your lunch period throwing stones at the sea gulls."

I was flabbergasted. The charge was completely false. "No, Sir," I sputtered, "I didn't throw any rocks at the sea gulls."

"Don't lie to me!" He thundered, his face red, chin flapping, he bent over me, his nose within inches of my own. "You're a Detroit hoodlum. I have your record and I know what you've done. Don't think for a minute you're going to get away with the things in *this* school that they put up with in Detroit. Do you understand?"

My heart sunk. He was referring to the incident with Miss

Salinsky and my expulsion. I should have known. I needed someone to help me explain how I had tried to make amends for that mistake.

The superintendent could not abide the idea of a kid from the Detroit suburbs, with my record, whose parents operated a bar in Maple City, mixing with his regimented and well-behaved children. The battle line had been drawn.

Even though his seagull story was a lie, the intimidation worked. It made my first week of school terrifying. Open hostility by Mr.Wall, the cold stares of Bernice Warner, the Principal, and the disdain of the teaching staff, made me doubt whether I would last the semester. No fresh start at this school.

I had enrolled the week of freshman initiation. As part of the hazing, freshman boys were required to wear shorts pants all day, which would have been okay, if it hadn't been for something that happened the day we arrived in Maple City.

After the deal was struck to rent the Davis house, Dad took Mom and me for a ride along Lake Michigan. I was excited about the wild and desolate miles of shoreline. I whined and complained so much about having to stay cramped up in the car all day, that Dad, in self defense, pulled onto the shoulder of M-22, along a stretch of beach called Bob's Park, and told me to go wear myself out.

I had no bathing suit so I kicked off my shoes, rolled the legs on my jeans up, and took off through the brush, the dune-grass, and the sand along the shore. After an hour of wading and running, I returned to the car in a much subdued mode. One variety of shrub through which I had been frolicking was known as poison oak.

At freshman initiation, my legs were covered with long, open sores from frenzied scratching. Several of the lesions oozed a foul smelling pus. The new kid from the streets of Detroit, with funny looking hands, had putrid sores on his legs similar to an advanced stage of leprosy. Great first impression.

There were twenty students in the Class of '49. At graduation, there would only be nineteen, but I had survived the embarrassment of initiation. The more important question was whether I could survive the hostility of the administration and faculty.

Mr. Dechow, the algebra teacher, never missed a formula when I showed up in class a month late. He acted like I wasn't even there. I had no clue what was going on, and was too embarrassed to ask for help. On a few occasions, I tried to formulate an intelligent question about the baffling alphabetic symbols and numbers everyone, except me, seemed to understand, but all I got was a cold and incoherent response. He soon broke me from taking part in class discussions. For the remainder of the year I sat there in a bewildered panic. The only thing that got me through the two semesters with Ds was the willingness, albeit reluctantly, of Steve Skipski and Jimmy Khars to let me copy their homework.

First semester freshmen were also required to take World History, and the man who hated me most, Mr. Wall, was the teacher. The class was taught in the basement next to the furnace room. I resolved to work hard. If I did well, maybe the shirt incident in Hazel Park would be, at least in part, forgiven. I read the chapters I had missed, and made up the home work. I had a natural penchant for the subject, so the course matter seemed easy, making it unnecessary to seek help from anyone. I was floundering helplessly in algebra, but I began to have hope that I could make up for an imminent bad grade by doing well in history. The first major test was scheduled for the week after I enrolled. I had to cover five weeks of material. It didn't matter. A good grade in the superintendent's class could go a long way toward proving that I was not the nemesis he suspected. Maybe I could have my fresh start at Leland High School after all.

The day the test paper was handed out, I read over the questions and was elated. I knew the answer to every one. I was the first to finish and in half the time allotted. What a surprise it would be when Mr.Wall discovered I had made a perfect score.

Papers were graded by exchanging tests with the student seated in front, which in my case, was Jim Novak. Mr. Wall read the correct answers. Jim handed the paper back. Two of my twenty correct answers had been marked incorrect. I would receive a grade of ninety instead of the one-hundred I knew I was entitled to. I leaned forward over my desk to explain the mistakes in grading.

When I pointed out what had happened, Novak said he he couldn't change my test score without double checking the answers with Mister Wall.

In the meantime, Mr.Wall had started calling for grades. Each student announced their grade as their name was called. "Ashe, JeanAnn; Buehrer, Carlton; Bufka, Jerome; Bufka, Joseph; Burda, Janet; Carlson, Carol; Kahrs, James; Houdek, Evelyn; Maleski, Anna Mae; Myers, Hiram."

I said, "There has been a mistake on my paper and I am trying to get . . ."

"Zero," he said.

The word struck me like a hammer blow. I had worked so hard, and without help, and he was going to give me a zero for a perfect test score. I had to do something. "But I made one hundred percent on the test . . . ."

He acted like he never heard me. In an instant I saw through his plan. The role call for grades was a ruse. He thought my test grade would be low, and wanted an oral response in front of the class to humiliate me. The meanness of the scheme, and the realization that he was going to get his way despite my hard work caused an explosion similar to the one in the shirt incident.

"You son-of-a-bitch!" I said. Every head in the class whip-swivelled. The room went dead silent.

For one wonderful moment, the superintendent was stunned dumb. His face turned fiery red, and he lifted out of his chair like a punctured balloon. "What did you say!"he roared.

It was too late to back off, so in a loud voice, I said, "You're a dirty son-of-a-bitch!"

"Get out of my class! Go to the office and go now!" He bellowed as he came around his desk, his chins quivering with rage.

He was pointing up the stairs to the first floor, so I picked up my materials, hurried to the back of the room, and started up. Two steps from the top, I stopped and turned to see where he was. He was coming at full throttle, taking stairs two at a time, one jump behind me. When I turned, he threw up both arms to ward off a blow from the kid who had struck a teacher in the eighth grade. It never came, but by ducking he nearly fell backwards down the steps.

There were snickers from some of the other students whose necks were locked in the backward position and saw Mr.Wall's reaction. It's hard to tell which enraged him the most, my identifying his ancestor, or the laughter of the class at his fear of a physical challenge from the one-hundred-fifteen-pound boy on the top step.

The office door slammed behind us. He leaned forward to within an inch of my face and said with a quaking voice, "You tramp. You're expelled. You'll never get back into this school, do you understand?"

I understood. And I wondered if "tramp" was the same as trash.

That night when I tried to explain, Mom and Dad took the same attitude as the superintendent: I had been a trouble maker in Hazel Park, and I was already causing trouble in this new school.

Mother wrung her hands. "You're going over there tomorrow and apologize," she said with finality.

"I'll burn in hell first!" I said. "What about my grade? Doesn't it make any difference that the asshole cheated me out of a perfect grade just because he doesn't like me? I'm not going back to that school."

"Oh really. And where will you go? There is no other school. And stop using that kind of language."

"Why can't I go back to Hazel Park. I could live with Sis."

Mother snorted, and said, "We've been over that a dozen times. You have no choice."

"What about my grade?"

"I'll talk to him about your grade, but you have to get back in that school."

The only other school within commuting distance was in Traverse City, sixteen miles away, in another county, and there were no buses that transported students there. On Saturday, Mother drove me to Leland.

We stood awkwardly in the living room of Mr. Wall's sparkling white Cape Cod home. His hands were folded across his massive mid-section. While he looked down at me from the top of his imposing, three-hundred pound pile of fat, I stammered an insincere apology. Mother, always cowed in the presence of male authority, meekly asked about the zero I'd received on the disputed test. He him-hawed around; said he would reconsider the matter depending on my conduct between then and the end of the semester. In other words, if I didn't kiss his rear, he'd flunk me. Mom had let him bully her like he did everyone else. When he said he'd reconsider my grade I knew he wouldn't.

Little changed. I was reprimanded daily for some infraction of a rule made specifically for me, or for one rarely enforced. Most concocted offenses were silly, all transparent. The results were always the same regardless of how hard I applied myself, so I quit trying. More often than not, I went to school without studying, and many times with little or no sleep.

Mr. Wall's alter ego was the Principal, Mrs. Warner. She was the archetypical reform school disciplinarian, with narrow pinched face, and dark beady eyes set in a face ravaged by acne and wrinkles. To the delight of some of the other students, I tabbed her, Old Prune Face.

The superintendent's office was above and adjacent to the library, which served as the study-hall. The observation wall over the library was glass, and from that vantage point Mr.Wall or Mrs. Warner stood watch over every limb and lip that moved in the room below. They thumped the glass constantly when I whispered, passed a note, or laughed. But I soon discovered a space in the room not subject to their snooping eyes. It was the row of chairs tight against the wall below the glass. It's a wonder that one or both didn't break their noses or push through the glass trying to see what I was doing directly under them.

My report card at the end of the semester showed "Ds" in every subject, including World History, the subject I loved. But somehow I had made it through the first half of the ninth grade at Leland High. And through it all, I made and kept friends. Maybe some of the other students were secretly on my side in the war against the dictatorial powers of Mr. Wall's administration.

Mr. Wall and certain members of his staff were insidious in their attack. Mr. Dechow, algebra and shop teacher, pulled Bob Stachnik, my best friend and the star basketball player at Leland, aside and told him it would be in Bob's best interest if he would not run around with the Myers kid. Bob was an easy going sort who would go out of his way to avoid trouble. He liked to hang out with me and raise hell on occasion, but never anything destructive, vicious, or against the law. He continued to be my friend, but his reluctance to demonstrate our closeness on the school premise was obvious.

They tried to persuade all of the students to treat me as a pariah, to isolate me, and make my life so miserable I would drop out. Me and my good friend, Steve Skipski, also from Maple City, bummed rides to the basketball games, sat in the balcony of the gymnasium, and screamed our hearts out for the Leland Comets. During half-time of a particularly intense game, we led the fans in a series of raucous and obnoxious cheers, our voices resembling a duo of horse whinnies. Mr. Wall suddenly appeared in the center of the court, threw us shrapnel sharp glares, tapped his foot, and made scribbling motions on a piece of paper, as if to say he was writing us up for future disciplinary action. Steve never again joined me in leading a cheer.

Isolate me, yes, but break my spirit—never.

CHAPTER 22

Bumps In The Night

The winter of 1945-46 was brutal. The wind howled out of the northwest like something gone berserk. Snow, driven horizontal, swept across Lake Michigan into Leelanau County where it piled unrelentingly. Days were dark gray on white and the nights as black as death with eerie shimmers of light on the northern horizon from the aurora borealis.

In those dismal months when the school bus disgorged its passengers across from Amidon's Grocery, nightfall was only minutes away. Great clouds of blowing snow swirling through dusky half light made it impossible to see our house, piled high to the eves with drifts, only one block from the bus stop.

The Maple Tavern opened for business at noon in winter, and closed only when the last customer was ready to leave. By the time I got home from school, the house had been empty for four or five hours, the banked fire long dead, and the house frigid. Instead of taking my coat off I grabbed the coal bucket and headed out the back door.

Snow banks along the path to the coal shed were higher than my head. I cleared the path again so that at night, I wouldn't have to wade drifts to my knees. By dark, a fire roared in the coal burner and the area in the vicinity of the stove warmed. I planned on staying home this night, so I built a fire in the kitchen stove as well. For supper I had two choices. I could heat a can of soup from our cupboard or go to the tavern for a hamburger. But when there were more than two or three cars at the tavern, it had to be soup at the house. Mom couldn't tend bar, wait tables, and cook at the same time. Dad was usually drinking with the customers.

I ate a can of beef noodle soup. I had homework, and wanted to study, but the house was cold and empty. A feeling of despair and loneliness had grown stronger day by day, making it impossible to think or concentrate. The north wind whistled freely through the clap boards while sleet and snow pelted and rattled the window frames. Curtains rustled and moved menacingly as drafts found their way through the large cracks in the casings. The floor creaked with every step and I became fearful of the dark corners. But these were private fears. I would be ridiculed if I told my parents, and lectured about how I had nothing to worry about. There was no one to whom I could confide my weaknesses. I would rather die than confess my fears.

It was only mid-November, and I shuddered at the thought of being trapped in this house in January and February. This storm seemed especially fierce. Hail clattered on the roof, the windows and doors rattled and shook. An hour after dark, the lights went out. Wind or ice frequently downed power lines, so I lit a kerosene lamp, set the card table up in the living area close to the pot-bellied stove, stacked my books, and with coat buttoned to the neck, opened my English Literature textbook. The assignment was to read the first ten pages of *Silas Marner* by George Eliot. A draft fluttered the curtains, made the flame in the lantern globe dance, and lifted the corner of my page. The sounds of the storm assailing the house were so frightful, I couldn't concentrate. If Elmer were here, I wouldn't be so nervous.

I put the last piece of coal on the fire. The coal bucket would have to be filled again, but I didn't want to go to the shed by myself. I would call Mom and Dad, and have one of them come and get me. I picked up the phone. The line was dead. As I replaced it in the cradle, the curtain blew aside. A face, its forehead pressed against the frosted glass, hands cupped around its eyes, peered at me. My heart stopped. The apparition disappeared as the curtain settled into place. The knob on the back door rattled. I grabbed the flashlight, ran upstairs, loaded the .22 caliber rifle, and half ran, half fell back down two steps at a time. Elmer would have scared whoever that was away. But he wasn't here so I had to do something on my own.

I pulled Dad's chair into the middle of the room. From there, I could watch the windows in the living area and the back door at the same time. I knelt on the floor, the rifle resting on the arm of the chair, and waited until the wind blew the curtain aside. When it did, I aimed at the spot of melted frost on the window, but the face was gone. The back door rattled again. I released the safety, and swung the gun toward the door. Was someone turning the knob or was it the wind? The kerosene lamp had been burning two hours. How long would the fuel last? There were candles, but I had no idea where Mom had stowed them, and I wasn't about to go looking. The wind stood the curtain straight out, and there in the swirling snow was the face. I shook so hard, I couldn't line the sights up, but pulled the trigger anyway. The report was deafening. I reloaded. The curtain settled into place obscuring the view. I was surprised there hadn't been the sound of breaking glass, but all I heard was the wind and the moans of the old house. Maybe someone was laying outside in the snow dead or wounded. Maybe the sound of the shot scared whoever it was away. I was afraid to look.

The phone rang. I jumped, pulled the trigger, and almost shot myself in the foot.

"Who is it?" I yelled into the mouthpiece. It was probably the sheriff, Bob White, telling me to come out with my hands up.

"Son?" my mother said. "What's the matter with you?"

"Uh. Nothing. I just thought the phone was out of service and it startled me."

There was a long pause. "Well I called to tell you the phone's working, and Dad and I will be home early. We can't keep this place open without power. It'll take about an hour. You sure everything's okay?"

"Yeah, sure. I'm fine."

"What're you using for light?" she asked.

"The kerosene lantern, but I don't know how much longer it will last. I was on my way out to get a bucket of coal. I'll see you, bye." My hand shook as I replaced the phone. Why did I tell her everything was fine? Now I had to go get a bucket of coal by myself. I put on a stocking cap and gloves, and with the flashlight, went to the front door and peeked out. Thank God, there was no one laying in the snow. There were no tracks, but that meant nothing. Snow flakes as large as half dollars were swirling in a howling wind and would cover tracks within minutes. Back inside I went to the window, and with the beam from the flashlight found the melted spot on the window. The bullet had hit the frame a foot and a half below and to the left of where the head had been pressed against the glass.

With rifle, flashlight, and coal bucket I ran to the coal shed. The path I had shoveled earlier was knee deep. I sat the bucket down, pushed the door open. With flashlight in one hand and the rifle in the other I edged close and peeked inside. Nothing.

Back in the house, I opened both doors to air out the smell of the gunshots, put the rifle away, and built up the fire. Then I took my coat off, spread books and papers across the card table and when my parents came in, I chewed on the end of a pencil like I thought a real student was supposed to do. I told them nothing about what had happened. If I had, Mom would say I was exaggerating or being over dramatic. Dad would have made fun of me for being a sissy. My sister and Dona were expected to visit soon. Maybe I would tell Sis, she'd know what to do.

The next day, at four-twenty in the afternoon, the school bus rumbled down Fire Tower Hill, past the ice and snow encrusted "Welcome To Maple City" sign, which looked more like a large white flyswatter stuck upright in a snow bank. Only those who had passed this way before would know that the sign contained the name of the village and the message, "Pop. 154."

At home, I pitched my school books on the kitchen table, and poked around in the belly of the stove for enough embers to sponsor a decent fire, threw in a handful of coal chips, and headed for the back door with the empty bucket. The smell of congealed grease in a cold skillet setting on the cook stove from this morning's breakfast sent my stomach into a half-gainer.

With my left arm flapping to the side like a one armed tight-rope walker, I lugged the load to the back porch, then went to the wood pile next to the outhouse. A mildewed tarp that smelled like asphalt didn't help my nausea. The frigid temperature and wind muted the smell of the outhouse and saved me from emptying my stomach.

Before the snows came, there had been several mice nests in the wood pile under the protection of the canvas. Now there was no sign of life. They were probably nesting in one of the many unpacked boxes stacked in the hall next to my bedroom. At night the sounds of gnawing and scurrying caused me to lay awake hoping it was mice and not another face at the window. I had stepped in mouse poop next to my bed twice the week before, proof that at least some of the nocturnal sounds were rodents. With a few swings of the axe, I filled the kindling bucket.

Most school nights were spent at home alone. The cabinet radio we had brought with us from Hazel Park was a life saver. My favorite station was a popular music broadcast out of Traverse City, sixteen miles away. I listened and memorized the tune and lyrics to the current favorites, and when the station went off the air at 10:00 p.m., I combed the airwaves for anything to keep me company. I blundered across a station out of Chicago transmitting a strong signal of classical music all night, and in the months to follow, listened to some of Miss Porter's favorites. I even learned to recognize and love some of the masters; she would have been proud.

Considering the episode of the previous evening, I decided I didn't want to spend another night alone in that house. I finished my chores, and walked the short distance to the tavern. Dad was drinking and chatting with the customers. Mom was nervous fearing a surprise visit from the inspector for the Alcohol Beverage Commission. The rule against owners and employees drinking on the job was strictly enforced, and would ultimately cause Dad to either sell or lose the license.

Because Mom had her hands full, I cut myself a slice of Limburger cheese off the block in the beer cooler. Cheese, crackers, onions, and a twelve ounce Pepsi was a tasty alternative to a can of soup. I'd tried every variety of the canned stuff. My favorite was Bean with Bacon over a bag of Fritos, which always gave me gas, but so did the Limburger.

I carried several cases of beer up from the basement and stocked the coolers. I was extra hungry so I cut myself another hunk of cheese, and helped myself to an orange-pineapple soda.

Mom, between one of her many trips to the bar, asked if I had homework.

"Finished it all in study hall." If she had paid the least bit of attention to my report card, the lie would have been apparent. I knew, even though I didn't want to admit it, that the Administration at the Leland Public Schools intended to force me out. If I made an effort, it was half-hearted, and the last book I opened each night was Algebra. Mr. Dechow, the Algebra teacher, hated me. He wouldn't look at me, answer my questions, or acknowledge my existence, and always ignored my raised hand until I became embarrassed and lowered it. I sat through his class stupefied at what was going on. On the rare nights when I bothered to open the text, the inability to solve the mysteries of the formulas made my stomach burn and caused guilt and resentment. The next day I'd have to copy someone else's homework, or pull another F.

To avoid anymore questions from Mom about school, I took a dollar's worth of change from the cash register, dropped a nickel in the juke box, and cranked the volume as high as it would go, which always drove Dad nuts. He gave me a dirty look. While I finished eating, I listened to the Mills Brothers sing, *I Guess I'll Get The Paper and Go Home.*

As I left the tavern Mom said, "Son, get in bed early, it's a school night." But she didn't understand. The problem was not going to bed, the problem was filling in the hours between now and then. The wind wasn't howling like last night, but it would still be hard to concentrate long enough to do homework. I wouldn't be able to keep my eyes off the living room window, and then there was the dread of going to bed alone.

Outside it was already dark, the nights becoming longer—not a happy prospect.

Vern Amidon was the nineteen year old son of the owner of Amidon's Grocery Store. He stood a fraction over three feet tall, had bowed arms and legs, and walked with a waddle like a penguin, an extreme exertion, which after a short distance required him to lean against the nearest support gasping. He was strikingly handsome, his voice deep and masculine. But his greatest asset was his intelligence, which I, in awe, regarded as near genius. During that first winter in Maple City, Vern taught me to play chess, the perfect pastime for long winter evenings. I loved the game, but no matter how hard I tried, during the three years we played, I didn't win a single match. But it was a challenge and a lot better than being alone.

Vern was perched atop a tall stool operating Amidon's Grocery Store cash register when I banged through the door stamping the snow off my boots. "Wanna play some chess tonight?" I asked and slid onto a stool at the tobacco counter where the punch boards were kept.

"Maybe after supper." He lowered his voice. "My old man's on a tear; got his ass in a frenzy; says he's the only one working around here. Maybe he'll quiet down after he counts the day's receipts."

I leaned forward and said, "Maybe that'll make him worse."

"My God, your breath smells like an outhouse," Vern said with a mock cringe.

"Must be the stale Limburger you sold my Dad. I just had a couple of slices for supper."

He held his nose. "Limburger is *always* stale. Go rinse your mouth out with gasoline."

Joy, Vern's oldest sister, came by smiling—soft, warm, and always smiling. She reached for a pouch of Peerless, the nastiest chewing tobacco ever concocted.

"You gonna chew that?" I asked her.

She took a playful swing at me and nodded toward the back of the store where Frank Weiss and Big Joe Shimek were propped back against the wall next to the stove.

I asked her to pass me the dime punchboard that offered the bolt-action, seven shot Marlin Rifle as a grand prize.

She smiled as she handed it to me and I pretended to count the remaining chances on the board while I watched her rear-end disappear around the counter.

Vern was shaking his head. "You'd better not fool with that."

"The punchboard or your sister?"

"Very funny," he said sarcastically. "My dad will accuse you of taking punches without paying."

"I wouldn't do that." I didn't want anyone thinking I was dishonest, especially in the Amidon family. I only stole stuff from my parents.

"Didn't say you would, but you can never tell what he's going to do or say in one of these moods."

I put the punchboard down and wandered over to the corner where the big coal burner was roaring, its sides bright orange from the prodigious amount of fuel in her belly. Frank and Joe, their heads against the wall, hats nearly over their eyes might have been talking to themselves. The cuffs of Frank's bib-overalls were steaming, giving off a fragrance reminiscent of my Uncle Vern's barnyard.

Big Joe Shimeck, so called because of the balloon like extension around his mid-section and for the way he swaggered when he walked, talked with a big black cigar in the corner of his mouth. He was telling Frank it had never snowed as early in Leelanau County as it had this year, and, if Frank thought it had, he was nuts.

Frank made a sound which might have been a whistle if he'd have had any teeth. Instead the noise was similar to that of wind blowing through a stove pipe—a rushing sound. "Don't be so sure about things that happened before you were born," said Frank. "In 1919, the year my boy came back from fighting, it started snowing before the apples were off the trees. My neighbor, Stan Pellovski had eighty acres of Jonathans. A week before the storm, a big shot buyer from Chicago told Stan he'd give him twenty cents a bushel for his crop. Stan turned it down 'cuz he'd heard the price was going to a quarter."

I could do math in my head faster than I could write it on

paper, so I did the figures. If what Frank said was true, Big Joe would be no more than twenty-five years old. Looked to me like he was at least fifty, but I was no judge of adult age. I thought Mom was ancient and she was only forty-one.

Frank paused, pursed his lips, and let loose a blast of air like he was trying to call a lost dog. "They started picking as fast as they could, but the storm was so bad most of the apples froze solid, and the snow was so deep they couldn't get wagons in the orchard to bring out the few they picked, so they froze too. That was in the middle of September. By Christmas that year, Lake Michigan was froze so thick they logged half of South Manitou Island. Mule teams dragged those logs ten miles across the ice. Didn't lose a single one."

Big Joe snorted sending a plumb of cigar smoke into my face.

The stove was almost hot enough to catch Frank's cuffs on fire, but I pitched in a piece of coal to make Frank and Joe think I had some purpose for hanging around other than to eavesdrop on their stories.

Frank opened the fresh package of Peerless tobacco Joy had given him, put a wad the size of a cue ball in his cheek, let his chair legs hit the floor, and said he was going to the tavern for a beer.

I smiled. Mom and Dad complained endlessly about old Frank sitting at the end of the bar making strange whistling noises every few minutes, and calling, "Mae." It drove them nuts, especially when they had a house full of paying customers.

The store closed at seven o'clock. Vern said I could come into their home, a large apartment behind the store, and wait while the family ate supper. I felt good when I was around the Amidon family, including Vern's dad, a dour, caustic individual who showed no affection for anyone. But he tolerated my smart mouth, and allowed me to be near Vern and the rest of the family. I loved them all, especially the wife, whom I affectionately called Missus A.

When I first started going into the Amidon home during supper, I stayed in the living area while the family sat at the table chatting about the days events. It was fun to hear the numerous complaints Mister Amidon had about the town, the people, his family, and the general state of affairs in the world. As I became more familiar, I started moving into the kitchen area where they gathered to eat the evening meal.

Tonight, I inched my way from the living area and leaned against the doorsill. The family was engaged in a lively round of banter when, without warning, Virginia, Vern's twenty year old sister, whom I idolized, turned in her chair, looked me square in the eye and said, "Don't you know it's not polite to stand around someone else's table while they're eating?"

It was like a kick in the groin, and took me completely by surprise. I muttered something about being sorry, as I backed red-faced out of the area. Actually, I *didn't* know that it wasn't polite to stand around someone else's dining table. My parents had never cautioned me against such conduct, and this family had never hinted I was doing anything annoying. If I hadn't been so eager to be with them, and had stopped to think about it, common sense would have told me I was wrong. The last thing I had wanted was to offend the Amidons. I stumbled dumbly from the house, and heard the door close and the lock click behind me.

In front of the darkened store windows, the wind swirled snow devils through the street. To my left, the outline of the two room house, now converted to a post office loomed bleak and empty. Through the blowing snow, gas pumps across the street appeared as specters, with round heads, floppy arms, and levers like jousting sticks. In the morning, this apparition would be the Standard Gas Station, where we huddled around the stove smoking and waiting for the school bus.

Across the street to my right was the black outline of the Odd Fellow's Hall. It stood like a large square box from which a dim light shone from the far corner. Wade Botze, who rode the school bus with me each day, lived there and was probably with his parents at the dinner table telling them of the days events.

On the left of the Standard Station, stood the long, low brick building where, in a small partitioned cubicle, the local telephone office was located. Mary Nash or Betty Fischer would be at the switchboard until it closed at 10:00 p.m. I had tried to persuade them to let me listen to the way they answered their calls, but they told me they'd get into trouble if I were allowed into the switchboard room. I suspected they didn't want me to know they listened in on juicy conversations.

The tavern was around the corner from the store, out of sight, but from the number of cars parked along the street I figured business was good. I shivered as I listened to the dull thump, thump of music and the occasional raucous laugh coming from that direction.

I felt empty, unwanted—I had blundered and alienated people for whose affection I hungered.

Headlights flashed around the curve leading to the store. A horn blasted and the car slid to a stop in front of me, its headlights blinding. The car rumbled like it had no tail pipe. I waited, expecting someone to cut the engine, exit, and head for the tavern. Instead, a voice called my name. I shielded my eyes from the lights, and as I did they were switched to low beam. I blinked, and there was Al Salzbury's head sticking out of the driver's window. The horn of the souped up '35 Ford Coupe blasted again and echoed off the wall of the grocery store. Al yelled over the roar of the engine for me to come to the car. I lit a Chesterfield and pushed away from the wall. The super-charged engine growled loudly, and Al revved it every few seconds to punctuate the power over which he presided. Steam raised off the hood into the falling snow.

Al's younger brother, Don, stuck his head and right shoulder out of the passenger's window and motioned for me to hurry up. Don was seventeen, and, like Al, had quit school to go to work.

"What you hanging around outside Amidon's for? Can't you see its closed?" Both brothers guffawed. I felt stupid. "You waiting on somebody?" This time it was Al speaking.

"No, why?"

"What you going to do, hold the wall of that building up all night?"

"No." I wished they'd go away and leave me alone. Maybe they wanted to pick a fight.

"Well, what you gonna do?"

"I don't know," I lied. "What business is it of yours?" I knew exactly what I would do—go home and spend the evening alone, there was no other option. The Amidon's house was locked from the inside, and the Stachnik brothers, my only friends besides Vern, lived two miles out in the country. The crowd at the tavern meant Mom and Dad would not get closed and cleaned up until 3:00 a.m., and then, if Dad was drunk, they'd fight until I left for school in the morning.

Don Salzbury reached between his knees, brought up a bottle, unscrewed the cap on the way to his lips, then handed it to Al. Don said, "Don't be so anti-social."

I sauntered to the car, put my elbows on the edge of the window, and lowered my head so I could see inside. Al was propped up in the corner behind the wheel. A lit cigarette dangled from his mouth which he removed, took a long noisy draft of the bottle, and said, "Want a pull?" He shoved the bottle toward me.

"What's in it?" I asked.

"What'd ya think? Wine."

"Naw, I don't want any." I muttered.

"Why not?"

"I don't drink." At fourteen, I had never tasted alcohol, and had promised my parents I never would. *The damned stuff will ruin you Son. It's no good. Promise me you'll never take a drink. Promise! Dad's right Son. You listen to your dad. Promise you'll never drink. Not even beer. Promise!* So I swore I'd never touch anything with alcoholic in it.

"What you mean you don't drink?" Al said laughing. "Everybody drinks, don't they Don? Hell, your old man sells the stuff."

"That doesn't matter," I replied weakly. But I believed them. Everybody did drink. At least everybody I knew—even my sister.

"Well make up your mind, Myers. We're going to the dance in Cedar and thought you might like to go along. Lots of girls at the Cedar dance."

"How much it cost?" I put my hand in my pocket and fingered the coins I had left from the dollar I took from our cash register.

"Fifty cents. You going or not?"

The Cedar Dance was held above the tavern, and any age could enter, all it took was the cost of admission. The palms of my hands were moist as I lit another cigarette. The promise—what about the promise? Were promises to be kept only by kids? How many times had Dad promised he'd quit drinking? How many times had both of them promised to stop fighting? Still I knew as I reached for that bottle they were right, it was something I should never do. "Sure, I'll have a drink." I took the bottle from Don and brought it to my lips, making a lot of noise so they'd think I had taken a lot. It was nasty. But that didn't matter. I squeezed into the narrow back seat. "That's pretty good stuff. Pass that bottle back here."

The car fish-tailed on the icy road, headed out of town, and sped toward a dance hall full of light, laughter, and people.

CHAPTER 23

More Grist For The Mill

The train that brought Sis and Dona from Detroit arrived in a blizzard. There was no one to meet them, so she called from the station and Mom told her to take a cab the sixteen miles to our house.

It was like a homecoming when Sis arrived in Maple City. I hadn't seen her in six months, except for a day or two after she got back from New York, and then we hardly spoke because I had spent my last days in Hazel Park looking for Elmer.

After she arrived, she went to the tavern every night. She sat at the bar fingering the rim of a wine glass with Mom telling her to be nice to the customers. The memory of the malaria stricken Marine made me wonder just how nice she would be, especially since Topper hadn't yet returned from the Pacific.

On Thanksgiving Day, Mom hung a Closed sign on the front door of the tavern, and we began preparations for a holiday dinner. Early that morning, Don Stachnik and I went hunting over at Bull Lake. The trees were bare and the hills heaped with snow drifts so deep that Elmer wouldn't have been able to get through them. The lake was frozen over except for a small circle of open water in the middle where dozens of water foul carried on a raucous variety of sounds. We couldn't get close enough for a good shot. Within seconds of stepping out of the woods the air was filled with birds spiraling upward as though in a funnel. We never got a shot off, but didn't have to. We found a dead Canadian Goose near the shore, and told everyone we had both shot at the same time so we couldn't tell which one actually killed it.

I cleaned and plucked it, and Mom put it in the oven with the turkey. That goose was so tough I figured it must have died of old age.

After dinner I took Sis aside and told her about the face in the window. I should have known better—she laughed, and told me how silly and stupid I was. The face was either my imagination, or an attempt to get attention.

I resolved to never confide in her, or in Mom or Dad again—about anything. None of them gave a damn. Every night after Sis left, I turned on all the lights in the house, loaded the rifle, tied the curtains closed, kept a flashlight and lantern handy, and built a roaring fire in the coal burner. I'd have to shoot the son-of-a-bitch to prove I wasn't lying or imagining things.

During my sister's visit, I took care of Dona while Sis went to the tavern. On this night, she was in the process of dressing in one of her New York frocks. "How come you're getting all dolled up?" I asked as she slipped into the black dress and a pair of spike heels. "The regulars at The Maple Tavern ain't never seen nothing like what you just put on. Frank Peplinski and the bib-overall gang will swallow their Peerless cuds if you walk through the door in that outfit."

She leaned into the mirror and applied more lipstick. "The older you get the more uncouth you talk—ain't and a double negative in the same sentence—you're hopeless."

"Pardon me, Miss Hoity-Toity, but I ain't been to New York. I may be hopelessly stupid, but I ain't babysitting till you answer my question."

She gave me a disgusted look. "It's because I may want to go somewhere besides Maple Tavern this evening."

"Where?"

She hummed as she put the finishing touches to her face in the dim kitchen light. "None of your business."

"Yeah. Well if it ain't none of my business, you can just get yourself another babysitter."

She glided across the floor to the doorsill where I was leaning and in her most syrupy voice sang, *Besame, Besame Mucho, kiss me my darling and tell me you'll always be mine.*

I put my fingers in my ears, and in a loud voice chanted the words to *Old MacDonald Had A Farm.*

"Come on Brudder," she said, "please babysit for your Sissy."

"Sweet talk won't help. Where're you going?"

She walked toward the door. "You know Paul Meuenburg?"

"Yeah. Isn't he the guy who delivers Polish sausages to Amidon's meat market?"

"Oh, aren't you hilarious? Paul and his older brother just bought the Cedar Tavern. He's real good-looking. He was in our tavern last night. Said he might be back tonight."

I started a slow burn. "When's Topper coming home?"

"Now don't be that way. There's nothing to it. I may just have a drink with him."

"Yeah, sure," I said. "When's Topper coming home?"

The question must have taken some of the fun out of her prospective evening. Her voice became subdued. "He's supposed to be discharged before Christmas. "You won't say anything to him, will you?"

"Naw. I wouldn't tell Topper." And I never did.

One cannot completely appreciate spring until they have lived through a winter in Maple City near the forty-fifth parallel, and gone through sixty consecutive days without seeing a ray of sunshine. The coming of spring in the North Country is truly a rebirth, an awaking, a joyous time—unless you're a fifteen year old misfit and enrolled at Leland High School, in which case, as in the spring of '47, it caused much dissatisfaction, and created a terrible itch in my britches.

Every tree had on its spring dress, each variety a different shade of green, from the lightest to verdant, the contrasts starkly delicious. And through the patches of green, emerald blue swathes of water beckoned. The bus had just picked up the Stachnik brothers. The next stop was the Richard Kreitz farm, four or five minutes away.

"You want to go to school today?" I asked the Stachniks.

Both shook their heads.

"Let's get off this bus at Kreitz's place, and go the lake or do something. I sure don't want to spend a day like this looking at old lady Warner. How 'bout it?"

Bob, the oldest of the two, whose basketball aspirations acted as a damper on normal instincts, said, "As much as I'd like to cut, I guess I'd better not." He would never do anything to jeopardize his standing with the coach.

Don said, "Hell yes, let's get off this rattletrap."

"What're you going to tell Mister Wickern?" Bob asked.

I was getting up out of my seat. "We don't need to tell him nothing—anything. When he stops for Richard, we just get off."

The bus squalled to a stop. Mister Wickern pressed the hydraulic lever and the door squeaked open. Don and I were out of our seats and down the steps before the driver knew what had happened. "Hey," he called, "you people can't get off here."

"Okay we won't," I said.

Don and I skipped off down the road, then cut across the field toward Bull Lake, a blue gem that lay hidden in the basin of a forest of maple and American beech trees. By 8:30 a.m., we were at the lake. On a grassy knoll beside the mirrored water we stretched out in the sun and watched patches of cotton-white clouds pass lazily overhead.

"Look there." I pointed to a billowing cloud. "See that mountain lion?"

"No. Where?"

"Right there. Look, there's its ears, and . . . ."

"Oh yeah. I see it. Neat."

"And there's the tail. It's breaking up; now the tail's gone." We lay still watching the sky. "Old man Wall's going to turn purple when Mister Wickern tells him what we did."

Don rolled to his side and propped his head on his hand. "You know something? I don't give a shit what old man Wall does. I'm quitting at the end of this year anyway."

"You're quitting? How come?"

"I don't like it, and I don't need it. I can get a job without going to high school."

I thought about what he said. Not having to face Wall and Prune Face everyday was appealing, but there was something in me that wouldn't let me quit. I had to finish. It had been stupid to get off the bus—more rope for Wall to hang me with. And Mom and Dad would take Wall's side, say I'm a trouble maker. "You hungry?"

"I'm starved," Don said. "Let's eat."

We opened our lunch sacks and devoured the contents. Mom had put a package of chocolate Hostess Cupcakes in my sack. I gave one to Don. "This is the life. No one yelling at you to do this or that."

We went to the lake for a drink of water. "Hey," I said. "This water's not all that cold."

Don stuck his hand in. "Hell you say. Feels freezing to me."

"Think I'll go for a swim." I unbuttoned my shirt.

"Not me." Don sat down on the bank. "Besides, I didn't think you were supposed to swim for at least an hour after eating."

"Adults tell you lots of stuff that's not true," I said, "I've been wanting to swim across old Bull for a long time."

"You can't swim that far."

"Oh yes I can. Hell, it's not much more than a quarter-mile." I dropped my pants.

Don got a worried look on his face. "It's too cold, Myers. You'll get a cramp or something. Stay along the shore."

"Naw. Don't worry, I'll be just fine." The hills across the lake rose up near vertical from the shoreline and cast back reflections of snow-birch in the silvery blue of the mirrored water.

Don put his hand on my shoulder. "There's no bottom in that damned lake. Ray Flaska said he put out two-hundred feet of anchor line in the middle and never did touch bottom."

"So? I'm not going to the bottom." I said.

"Well go ahead. But I sure ain't trying it."

"Start around with my clothes, I'll see you on the other side." I dove into the lake. The icy water was invigorating, my stroke strong. This wasn't the earliest I'd been swimming in the frigid waters of the north. Jim Novak and I had a dollar bet on who would be the first to swim in either Lake Michigan or Lake Leelanau each spring. I had jumped off the Leland bridge into the river, two weeks ago. But Novak wouldn't pay me; said he'd already been in Michigan. Ha!

I stopped swimming and treaded water. I could see Don walking the edge. He waved. I put my head down, cupped my hands and stroked. The water was crystal clear, and got darker blue the farther down it went—no bottom. That was scary so I closed my eyes and stroked harder. Maybe I had bit off a little more than I could chew. I looked up. Half way. No turning back, but I was breathing real hard. Had to be careful to not take a lung full of water. A coughing spell would mean disaster. The thought made me breath even faster. Whoa. I couldn't panic—the worst thing a swimmer in trouble could do. I wasn't exactly in trouble, but my breath came in hungry gulps. Why did I always have to show off? What was I trying to prove? Okay, no big deal. I turned over on my back and floated. The blood thickened in my arms and legs, causing them to tighten. It was best to swim steady, not hard, just an easy pace. Back on my stomach I swam a breast stroke—pull, kick, pull, kick. My legs weren't strong enough for the breast stroke. I laid my right shoulder in the water and side-stroked. I saw Don standing on the opposite bank waiting, holding my clothes. Jesus, I wanted to get there. What if I drowned? Would anyone care? I doubted it. They might pretend for a day or two, and shed a forced tear over my coffin, but in their hearts would proclaim my stupidity and be relieved that I was no longer a pain in their asses. *Hell, I'm not going to give them the satisfaction.* I stroked harder, turned on my stomach and did the crawl. Then I hit the wall, that place in exercise where the athletes body has nothing left to give, no calories left to burn, and the only thing left in the red blood cells is waste matter. I couldn't go another inch without resting, so I turned over again. The cold was savage, my teeth chattered.

I was alone, with only blackness waiting below. I thought about the water rescue course I'd had during my one year at Hazel Park High School. But there was no one to rescue me. Don was not a strong swimmer, and even if he could make it this far, he wouldn't know what to do. If I survived this most recent act of madness it would have to be on my own, as always. When I struck out again, I was so fatigued my head spun and my eyes blurred. How long had I been in the water?—fifteen, twenty minutes?

It hit like a striking copperhead in my right calf, and drew my foot and toes downward in a claw-shaped knot. The pain was like nothing I'd ever felt, knife-like, probing. I would die, but I'd rather die than call for help. The swimming coach at Hazel Park had said, "You can rub a cramp out." If only I could—I had to. I sucked my lungs full, turned on my stomach and pulled my legs to a fetal position, then slid my hands down my right leg, trying not to look down into the water. But I had to open my eyes. Were they playing tricks? No. There was the bottom! My god! I was going to drown in ten-feet of water. I kneaded the knot in my leg, took another gulp of air, repeated. My foot came out of the curl. I would swim with one leg. I turned on my stomach and pulled.

It was getting shallower with each stroke. I treaded water, put my good foot down, felt the blessed sand. Yes! I limped out of the lake.

"How was it?" Don asked.

"Nothing to it." I leaned over and casually rubbed the calf muscle until it loosened. "I'd swim back, if I wasn't so hungry. What time is it?"

Don looked at his watch. "Eleven-thirty. You looked like you were in trouble out there. How come you had your head under the water?"

"Soon as I get my clothes on, we've got to figure out a way to get something to eat. Lake's full of fish, they were swimming all around me. Th . . . that's wh . . . at I was looking at. Too bad we didn't th . . . ink to bring a line and a . . . hook." My clothes felt heavenly, but I was still purple with cold, my teeth rattled. "You ba . . . ba . . . build a fire. I'll be right back."

"What we need a fire for?"

I couldn't tell him it was to keep me from freezing to death. "To cook our lunch." I cut a six-foot maple sapling, trimmed the branches, and sharpened a point on the thick end. You can't throw a spear light-end first. I walked to a thicket of bull rushes. The sun on my back was like a warm blanket. Within half an hour, I had speared a mess of bull frogs. I walked back to the roaring fire with the frogs impaled on my spear, and in that instant understood exactly how the Neanderthals felt when they returned to the cave-fire after a hunt.

"What'cha gonna do with them?" Don asked looking at my trophies with his nose wrinkled.

"Eat 'em," I said with bravado, and started cutting off the legs.

"Jesus," Don said, "I don't know whether I can eat those things or not."

"Sure you can. In the big cities, they're a delicacy."

"Yeah. Well we ain't in no big city, and I ain't eating no damn toad."

I found a piece of shale, laid it across two stones and put the frog legs over the fire. They started jumping. One went in the fire.

Don laughed and said, "You should've killed the fuckers before you tried to cook 'em,"

"Ho, ho," I said. The skin turned brown, then crispy. I took one off the fire and peeled the skin back. The steaming white meat fell off the bones. I picked it up with the blade of my knife, washed it in the lake, and took a bite. "Hey, this isn't half bad. If we had salt and pepper this would be a feast fit for a king."

We ate the frog legs, laid around in the sun until time for the school bus to hit Maple City.

As expected, there was hell to pay the next day. I had to apologize to Mister Wickern and Mister Wall, and bring my parents to school to assure the administration that I would never get off the school bus other than at the school again. If I was going to play hooky, I'd have to figure out another way.

Don wasn't about to apologize. He said they could kiss his ass, and quit.

The tent had a wooden deck, an army cot, and an orange crate for miscellaneous necessities like a kerosene lantern, my Volume of *The Complete Works of Edgar Allan Poe,* and my toilet articles. The shelter was at the edge of a giant oak grove, twenty steps from the shore of Lake Michigan, and one-half mile from the dining hall of Camp Kohanna for Girls, where I worked.

It was the summer of '47. By some miracle, I had made it through my first two years at Leland High School. But my deportment in and out of school was so rebellious, so hostile, my parents decided I needed to be away from my friends who had been providing transportation to the dances and parties. Through some unknown connection, they got me the job of dishwasher at the girl's camp. The hours, work, and pay were miserable. But the job would serve to keep me out of trouble for the better part of three months.

The camp was located on a pristine tract of wooded hills overlooking Lake Michigan and the Manitou Islands, all sponsored and funded by the Church of Christ, Scientist. Students from various Leelanau County schools were employed. Cynthia Noonan was from the Empire schools. Four were from the Leland School: Bob Stachnik, my best friend, was the handyman's helper, Janet Burda and Eunice Boley were assistant cooks and servers, and I was the dishwasher.

We worked from 5:30 a.m. until 7:00 p.m., with an hour break in the morning, and two hours off between lunch and dinner. Pay was forty dollars a month plus meals, and use of the tent. The bonus was being able, albeit surreptitiously, to watch the stuck-up rich girls parade in their bathing suits, tennis shorts, and riding habits.

I finished the morning dishes early. Mister Graham told me to go help Bob who was carrying material to the beach in preparation for anchoring a swimming raft off shore. Our arms loaded, we strolled through the campus occasionally nudging one another to draw attention to some worthwhile sight. I gave him the elbow. We were approaching the queen of the campus. A green-eyed Eurasian, her father was a diplomat with the State Department. She walked with the presence and carriage of an aristocrat, and was by far the most striking of all the girls at Kohanna—and knew it. At the moment, she was sitting under a tree with an open book in her lap, her legs spread to the same extent as the book, an extremely unladylike posture. As we passed, out the corner of my mouth, I said, "Did you see that, or was I dreaming?"

Bob, always shy when girls were involved, was staring straight ahead, his cheeks puffed, face red, and his stomach jumping with a repressed laugh. "I saw."

"Did I see her you-know-what? Did she not have anything on under her shorts?"

"Yes and no," said Bob, a man of few words.

For years after, every time Bob and I would get together, we'd burst into a fit of laughter at the memory of the Eurasian Queen's compromising exhibit and speculate about whether it was intentional.

The kitchen was like a boiler room in the months of July and August. By two o'clock in the afternoon, everyone was dehydrated and exhausted. But when another noon meal was behind us, the galley spotless, and the evening meal planned, we left for the afternoon break.

At my tent, I hurried into my bathing suit and walked the short distance to the beach. After a few minutes, Janet Burda joined me and we dove into the chilly waters of Lake Michigan. In minutes we were refreshed, and fell upon a blanket to sip cool water from the thermos she brought from the kitchen.

By far the most beautiful girl in Leelanau County, Janet was without pretense or airs, and, as she confided to me, without confidence. When we were freshmen, she had talked of quitting school. Her father, from the area called Bohemia in Southern Europe, pressured her relentlessly to drop out of school and marry. He believed that only boys needed learning, and then only enough to enable them to support their families.

I had begged her not to do it. Everyone adored her unpretentious demeanor. She was intelligent, could easily make the cheerleader team, get scholarships to college, do anything she wanted. The world was hers for the asking. She smiled at the cheerleading suggestion. Maybe she was too shy to get out in front of a whole auditorium full of people and jump up and down. "You can, if you want to bad enough," I said. "Cheerleaders go with the team to every out-of-town game." She'd think about it.

In our sophomore year she tried out and was selected hands down. In later years, she would say I had been a major factor in her staying in school. The following spring, I urged her to enter the Grand Traverse Bay Cherry Festival Beauty Pageant—she would have been a cinch winner. But modesty would never allow her to parade in front of a crowd, in a bathing suit. It would be another two years before I would gain enough self-confidence to ask her for a date, afraid she'd say no because of my hands.

After swimming in the cool waters, we dozed in the sun rejuvenating in preparation for the hard work to come at dinnertime. I opened an eye and watched her for a minute before I asked, "What you gonna do after Leland? I mean, when we graduate?"

She raised her head from her forearm. Her eyes, the same shade of sparkling blue as the lake, were full of puzzlement. "We've still got this year and next to decide."

"Yeah. But it's getting more important all the time. I don't want to earn a living doing what we've been doing all summer."

"Me either, but my dad says I don't need high school, let alone college."

"Let's go to college together," I blurted. It was the closest I'd come to asking her for a date. The thought sent waves of goose bumps down my back. I couldn't hope it would ever happen.

"I don't have any money," she said laughing. My brother Jim had to give me enough last fall to buy the cheerleader's outfit."

"I don't either, but we could work part time and go to school."

"If you don't stop agitating Mister Wall, you're not going to finish high school."

She was right. Everyday there was another incident, another confrontation. I shook my head. "Honestly, I don't know what's the matter with me. I can't knuckle under to him and his stooges. Maybe if I could figure out how to control my temper, I'd make it.

But sometimes I think they don't want me to make it. You ever read Poe's, *The Raven?*"

"Huh uh."

"Well, there's this guy. And he's trying to figure out what's going on in his life, and is all worried about some lady called Lenore. A big black bird called a raven taps on his door at midnight. It makes him nervous and depressed. I read it over and over 'cause I feel just like that guy sometimes."

"Don't read that morbid stuff," she patted my arm.

The subtle attention made me swallow hard. "You don't know how much you and the kids in our class mean to me. You're more like family than my own." It seemed like the friends at school cared more about me than my parents. They encouraged me, helped me with my algebra. I longed to tell her how much *she* meant to me. But I couldn't.

She was quiet for a long moment. "There does seem to be something different about the way they treat you. The administration, I mean." She quieted, and I dozed again.

The week before the Kohanna job was to end, everyone except Cynthia Noonan was in a festive mood. I was up to my elbows scrubbing greasy pots and pans, and she was across the kitchen bent over putting silverware away.

"There," I said, in a loud voice, pointing a knife toward Cynthia's rear end, "is a broad expanse of potential pleasure."

The other girls giggled. Cynthia straightened and looked around, then it dawned on her that the remark had been aimed at her posterior. "You damned garbage mouth," she said, and hurled a handful of knives and forks.

I ducked and laughed as the missiles clattered off the wall and fell around my feet. I regarded the incident as a joke. Cynthia didn't, and filed a complaint.

Mrs. Baskcomb, the head cook, made inquiry into the matter. The next day I was fired. It was the first and only time in my life I would be fired from a job. I didn't mind the scolding I would get from Mom, or the ridicule from Dad. Rather, it was the prospect of starting my junior year having to face Mr. Wall. The incident would be the talk of the school, and another proof that I was a loser.

CHAPTER 24

On A Sunday Morning Sidewalk

January of 1948. An Arctic blizzard piled drifts of snow as high as the roof tops. Road crews, exhausted, couldn't keep up with the onslaught. Travel was at a stand still. Swirling clouds of snow limited visibility to a few feet, keeping all but the foolhardy from venturing out. The storm lasted two weeks. By Sunday afternoon of the first week, business at the Maple City Tavern was so sparse Mom hung a sign on the door, "Closed Until Roads Are Cleared."

Monday evening it was already dark as I hurried down the hill from the bus stop. Mom and Dad would be home, maybe we could have a meal together, and I would tell them about the adventure of the afternoon.

On the way home from school the bus had slid off the road into a ten-foot snow drift. The thermometer at school read fifteen below zero at 3:45 p.m. Within minutes after the engine died, the temperature inside the bus was as cold as the air outside. We stamped our feet to keep the circulation in our toes. Jim Novak and I were in our seats one row from the back where we lit a cigarette and tried to blow the smoke out a small hole in the floorboard, but the snow was packed so tight against the undercarriage there was no place for the smoke to go. It didn't matter. Mister Wickern, the driver, was outside digging a tunnel so he could get to the road and flag someone down to take him to a phone.

Everyone was complaining about their toes freezing when a monstrous, pre-historic-looking snow-blower arrived. In the numbing interior we shouted encouragement while Mister

Wickern connected a chain to the back bumper. A cheer went up when the powerful machine pulled us back on the road. While we were in the snow drift, darkness had settled.

Lights throughout the village were on as I waded in snow up to my hips toward the house. My thoughts were on the load of homework I had under my arm. The family car was buried under a pile of snow in the driveway. It was curious that our house was dark.

The instant I stepped through the door I knew Dad was drunk. I could smell it. Several hours of drinking made his breath and clothes reek. And it wasn't just Dad that smelled bad. There was alway beer bottles and whiskey glasses with stale residue, ashtrays filled to overflowing, and an un-emptied chamber pot. Those were odors I learned to recognize before I knew my ABCs. I stood silently just inside the door, the smells charging my senses. Tentatively, I said, "Where is everybody?" The only answer was the wind rattling the windows. The house was damp and cold. The remnant of a tired fire struggled against the winter storm. Above the howling wind came another sound—a muffled sob. The interior was black. I set my books on the dining room table, felt my way toward the living room, reached around the corner and flipped on the light.

Dad was slouched in his chair wearing a sleeveless undershirt, a beer bottle and empty whiskey glass beside him on the end table. Mother was across the room on the couch, bundled in a blanket, one corner of which she held against the side of her face. Dad growled, "Turn out the goddamned light."

"What's going on?" I asked, trying to sound upbeat.

"I said, turn out that fucking light!" Dad lurched out of the chair, careened across the room and fell against the light switch. The room went black.

Mother was crying harder, maybe because there was someone there. "He hit me," she said between sobs. "Hit me with his fist."

Dad stood in the middle of the room. I could see his outline against the frost covered windows. He said, "Ask her what she did to me. Go on, ask her!"

Mom and Dad's bedroom opened into the living area. Afraid

to challenge Dad over the living room light, I went into their room and fumbled in the dark until I found the string running from the light over the bed to the bedpost. I pulled it. The single bulb cast a feeble light into the adjoining area. I walked to the couch and pulled the blanket away from Mother's face. The right side was swollen, her eye almost completely shut. Something snapped inside my head, like a telephone line that becomes taunt and breaks in sub-zero temperatures. "You bastard!" There was a poison in my voice I hadn't heard before. "Look what you've done."

Dad sneered. "You always take up for her, don't you? Think she's so damned innocent. Well look at my face." He turned so the light shined on a trio of angry red scratches descending from eye to jaw oozing blood. He turned to her again and said, "Now, I want those keys, and by God if you know what's good for you, you'll give 'em to me now!"

I moved between them. He stood over me glaring at her with mean eyes. The muscles in his arms and shoulders bulged.

"Give him the keys, Mother," I said, "please."

She squared her shoulders and said, "I'm not about to give him those keys so he can go out and kill someone on these roads. We'd lose everything we've got." Then she changed her brave voice to the submissive. "Please don't go out, Honey. The roads are awful, aren't they Sonny?" She gave me a nod.

"That's right Dad, it's awful out there, the school bus ran off the road on the way home." I tried not to, but tears began to flow. He always made me cry. "Please stay home."

The muscle in his jaw bulged, his teeth made a grinding sound. He said, "I don't give a damn about the school bus. I'm going to have those keys."

There was no focus, no recognition in his eyes. It was like we were strangers, and there was danger in that. "Mother, let him go, for God's sake, let him go. It's not worth it." I ducked under his arm, ran back to their bedroom, and frantically dug through her purse. I jerked the dresser drawers open. "Where are they Mom? Please," I begged. "We have to give him the keys." I talked over my shoulder as I searched.

I heard movement. I ran into the living room in time to see him land a glancing blow off the side of her head. She screamed, "Don't touch me again you bastard! I know what you want to do. Well you're not going to her tonight." She came off the couch and went for his face with her fingernails.

I tried to separate them. He swept me aside, and I stumbled back by his chair. Muttering obscenities, he lunged, and pushed her. She fell backward and slammed into the opposite wall. Her head snapped. He stepped forward, and like a guy punting a football, kicked. The point of his shoe caught her just below the naval. She slid down, down the wall. My hand closed around the neck of the beer bottle on the end table. He turned toward me. It exploded in the center of his forehead. His knees buckled, then straightened, and he stood swaying in the center of the room. "Jesus Christ. Jesus Christ," He muttered, and shook his head like Billy Conn on the verge of going to the canvass. He staggered in a circle, blood ran from out of his hairline into his eyes. I backed into their bedroom, and looked frantically for another weapon in case he came after me. A heavy ashtray. I picked it up and stood in the doorway shaking, but ready.

He groped his way across the room to his chair. One hand held his head, the other found the arm to ease himself down. Blood oozed from around his fingers. He sat muttering.

Mother was on her knees holding her stomach. The ashtray clattered against the top of the night stand as I set it down. She struggled to her feet, came to the door of the room, and stood for a moment looking at me. "Son, you shouldn't have hit your father."

"I thought he was going to kill you."

She turned around, knelt in front of Dad, and said, "Let me see where he hit you."

My years at Leland High were a dichotomy of hell and happiness. The superintendent wanted me out of his school, but I was just as determined to stay. It was structured, and my friends were there every day, my enemies identified and predictable. As bad as it was, I had come to grips with the fact that there was no other place to go.

I improved my grades during the sophomore and junior years, but I was in hot water constantly. I was expelled or suspended for cutting classes, smoking on the school bus, for getting off the bus where I wasn't supposed to, for fighting, and on and on.

Outside of school, there was no home life, and I was allowed to roam the county every night completely unregulated. I came to school without completing assignments and many times with little or no sleep. Hostile and hot tempered, I needed counseling, but problem solving was not a part of Leland's curriculum. Mr.Wall and his staff operated on the premise that if a student caused problems he or she had no business in school. And my parents were too involved with their own problems to worry about my deplorable conduct and the resulting precarious tenure at Leland High School. Everyday, it seemed, there was a new incident, another crisis.

English Literature was one of my favorite subjects, as was Miss O'Brien, the young teacher who taught it. I sat one seat back from the front row in her class behind Jean Ann Ashe.

Miss O'Brien's backside wiggled in harmony with the motion of her arm as she moved in front of the blackboard writing the first line of *Stopping by Woods On A Snowy Evening*, by Robert Frost: "Whose woods these are I think I know, . . ."

I scribbled in my notebook: *Her ass* . . . then I drew a line through ass. The word was too vulgar to apply to a refined lady like Miss O. *Her caboose is fine I want you to know.*

The chalk continued to scratch across the board. Her skirt hiked up several inches when she reached up and wrote, "His house is in the village though."

I wrote: *I wonder if it belongs to some jerk named Joe?* Part of Jean Ann Ashe's rear was sticking out between the seat and back-slat of her desk presenting a tempting target. I edged forward until my knees were resting against her bulge. She didn't move. With a downward motion, I pinched the roll of fat against the seat of the chair. She whirled like a picador and stuck her pencil in the top of my shoulder. "Christ, Jeanne, what'd you do that for?" I tried to whisper, but it came out louder than I planned. I was truly amazed at the violent response. The sharp, lead point of her pencil had broken off and was embedded in my shoulder.

Most of the class snickered, but Carlton Buerhrer and Steve Skipski hee-hawed.

Miss O., following the eyes of the students, fixed a stern look in my direction. "Would you like to tell us what activity has been going on behind my back?"

I jerked my hand from under my shirt. My ears and shoulder burned with the same intensity. "Uh, . . . nothing," I said. The class tittered again. I cringed waiting for Jean Ann to report what would surely be grounds for my next expulsion. But she was turned in her seat staring at me with an amused look on her face—and said nothing.

In three steps, Miss O. was beside my desk. "Well," she said, "then you must have been working hard on the assignment I gave you." And with that she reached down and picked up the sheet of paper that contained my name in the upper right hand corner and the two lines paraphrased from Frost. *Oh, shit! Now I'm really in for it.*

As she walked slowly back to the front of the room, she read my paper, then turned and studied me for a long moment. "All right," she said, turning toward the class and dropping my poetry into the top drawer of her desk, "back to work, and leave your papers on my desk on your way out." Her cheeks were flushed, when she said quietly, "Mister Myers, I'd like a word with you after class."

I stayed in my seat until all the other papers were neatly stacked on the corner of her desk, then picked up my books, and in my most penitent posture, walked to where she was seated. She pulled my paper out and laid it on top of her desk. She retraced the lines with her pencil. I could count the thumps of my heart against my chest.

"I'm sorry Miss O'Brien, I didn't mean anything by what I wrote. I promise I didn't."

The tip of her pencil pointed to the place where I had crossed out the vulgar word. The hint of a smile played across her mouth. Then she looked straight at me as she tore the paper into tiny pieces, dropped them into the wastebasket, and said, "Drawing that line through your first description of my anatomy was what saved you."

"Thank you Ma'am," I stammered.

Her eyes were playful when she said, "His name's Tony. Now get to your next class!"

I couldn't believe what had happened. *She tore it up! It was the proof that Old Man Wall had been waiting for, and she tore it up! This must be my lucky day. Jean Ann didn't shoot me down, and then Miss O. tore up that stupid poem. That had to mean she was not part of the staff that intended to get rid of me. Hot dam! Bring on Saint Mary's!*

It was the night of the basketball game between Leland and the Saint Mary's Panthers. Saint Mary's, a parochial school, was in the village of Lake Leelanau. The teams always played like it was for the state championship. The small gym was packed to overflowing. It seemed the entire populations of both towns were there, Lake Leelanau on one side of the gym, Leland on the other. It was half-time, and I was looking for Miss O. I wanted to say something nice to let her know how I adored her for reasons other than her cute rear-end. And there she was, across the gym, sitting with the Lake Leelanau crowd. "What's Miss O'Brien doing over there?" I asked of no one in particular as I stood in the midst of several of my classmates.

"She graduated from Saint Mary's," someone offered.

There came a lull in the cheerleading activities. I cupped my mouth and hollered *real* loud across the gym, "Hey, Miss O'Brien, you sure do look purdy tonight." My classmates thought that was real funny.

The next day I was in Mr.Wall's office. His triple chin jumped like the back seat of Salzbury's coupe on Saturday night. "I will not tolerate that conduct from any student in this school." He was sitting at his desk with Mrs. Warner standing rigid against the back wall like an upright mummy. "And if I hear one more impertinent remark out of your mouth you will be out of this school. Understood?"

"Yes sir," I said, with just enough contempt in my voice to let him know I wasn't about to knuckle under.

"Well, you get out of here and apologize to Miss O'Brien. And you'd better hope she accepts it." With a wave of his hand he dismissed me.

I hated Mr. Wall and his stooge Mrs. Warner with a passion that matched their's. I wanted to continue in school, but had a growing sense that against these two, it was a losing battle.

With no insulation in the house, sounds traveled unobstructed through the spaces between the clapboard and into my upstair's room. On ordinary days, the crunch of gravel under every wheel entering our driveway could be heard clearly from my bed. A loud noise from somewhere outside demanded I wake up. The small effort to obey caused a sharp pain to pound down into my forehead. I laid still. Maybe this was part of another nightmare. I wanted to go back to sleep. I held my breath trying to figure out whether the sounds were real or from inside my head. For a moment, all I could hear was my heart beating. Then it came again. "Myers! Hey, Myers!" The voice would wake the whole village. I rolled over and looked at the clock on the chair next to the bed. 7:30 a.m. Jesus Christ! Who was screaming for me at this hour on Sunday morning? Or maybe it was some drunk from the tavern calling to my dad. I swung my legs over the side of the bed. A wave of nausea swept over me. It was a coin toss whether I would pass out or not. My head throbbed from too much alcohol and too little sleep.

The night before, I'd gone with the Salzburys to a dance at Rouche's on the other side of Traverse City. I wasn't sure what time it had been when I snuck up the stairs and fell into bed, but the dance always lasted until 2:00 a.m., and I could remember things that made me believe we had stopped for something greasy afterward.

I slipped into my jeans, picked up my shoes and shirt and

tiptoed down the stairs. The front door rattled. I glanced through the living room toward Dad and Mom's room feeling sure they would be coming out of their bed at any moment. I squinted. Someone was peering back at me through the glass of the front door. I turned the key and swung the door open. Pauley Shedek was standing on the porch. "Jesus, Pauley, your going to wake my folks up!" I said as I stepped out onto the porch and slipped into my shirt.

It was the fall of 1947. When we had arrived in Maple City two years past, the war had just ended and the Leelanau County men who had served overseas were coming home. They all had a pocket full of money and unquenchable thirsts. Business at the Maple Tavern boomed. Pauley was in his early twenties, and for some reason had not served in the war, but spent most nights in the tavern mixing with the veterans. He became Dad and Mom's party companion, and had gone out of his way to be considerate of me. But because of a seven year age difference we had never gone anywhere or done anything together, so what was he doing on my front porch shortly after sunrise on a Sunday morning?

He said, "That's what I want to talk to you about."

I sat down on the front step and began to put my socks on, not completely awake, nor alert enough to realize the implications of what he had just said. "Talk to me about what?" I asked.

"About your mom and dad not being in the house."

"Pauley, for God's sake, make sense?"

"Please don't get all upset," he said.

I walked back in the house, though the living room, and into my parents room. I was stunned, and felt like a fool. The bed had not been slept in. Last night I had crept into and locked myself in an empty house.

The implications began to penetrate. The possibility of catastrophe pushed its way past the haze. I ran back to the porch. "Where are they, Pauley?"

He looked at the step and told me maybe everything was okay. There had been no car wreck or anything like that. If I'd lock the house up and bring my shoes, he'd tell me all about it on the way to Lake Leelanau, which was twelve miles north and four east of Maple City. Two nights ago, I had been there watching a basketball game. While he drove, Pauley looked straight down the highway and talked.

He had been in the Maple Tavern most of last evening. The tavern filled up early in anticipation of a polka band that had been scheduled to play from nine o'clock, until midnight. At nine-thirty, Dad received a call from one of the band members. Their vehicle had broken down and they were marooned in a remote place between Manistee and Maple City. Saturday night in Leelanau County is dance night. By ten o'clock, the crowd had thinned, and by midnight Pauley was the only customer. A live band was playing at Danny's Powerhouse over in Lake Leelanau. Mom tried to talk Dad into closing early, and going home, but Dad had made up his mind he was going to Danny's, and nothing she said would change it. He told her to go home, that he and Pauley would go alone, but she refused. If Dad went, she was going. Pauley sensing tension, said he might have to leave early and would take his own vehicle.

When they arrived the party was in full swing. There were wall to wall people, most of whom had a snoot full. A small dance floor was too crowded and three fights erupted in the first thirty minutes of their arrival. Dad had been drinking all day. He proceeded to take over the party, and ordered several rounds for the house—compliments of Keith Myers, owner of The Maple Tavern. He was the biggest spender in Leelanau County, and was always surrounded by free loaders. I wondered if maybe Pauley was one of them. Dad danced with a young woman who had been in the Maple Tavern earlier in the evening. At forty-six years old, with a touch of silver at his temples, he was not only handsome, but distinguished looking, with a bank roll he spent like a drunken sailor. Half the women in the county had made a pass at him at one time or the other, and Mom suspected he was still carrying a torch for Eunice, the mistress he had left in Detroit.

At 2:00 a.m., Mom and the woman Dad had been dancing with started pushing each other around. That was all the detail I could get out of Pauley, except that Dad had left with our car, and no one knew what had become of Mom.

We arrived in Lake Leelanau at 8:30 a.m. The sidewalk in front of Danny's Powerhouse looked like the entrance to a garbage dump. Broken bottles and beer cans littered the street. Pauley parked, and we walked to the front entrance, where I peered through the glass, but the reflection of the early sun made it impossible to see the darkened interior.

This was a Catholic community. The parish, school, and gymnasium, where I had been two nights before, dominated the village. This morning, people on their way to Mass, drove slowly by Danny's, curious about a man and a boy pacing back and forth peering into the Tavern's windows. I asked Pauley why we were looking for my mother in front of Danny's Bar. He kept saying maybe she had gotten locked in when they closed, but that she had to be close by. She and Dad had gone outside together, then Dad had left alone. That was the last time Pauley had seen her.

I stood in front of the door without any idea what to do next. Maybe Pauley wasn't telling me the whole story. "How do you know she didn't leave in someone else's car?"

"The fight was before the party broke up. She and your dad had been gone thirty minutes before anyone else left."

"How come you didn't go out and see what was going on?"

"I stepped outside just as your dad was driving away. Your mother was no where to be seen. Besides, I didn't think it was any of my business."

"What do you think I ought to do? Should I call Bob White?"

Pauley shook his head. "Don't call the sheriff, not yet. You take one side of the street and I'll take the other. Circle the block and meet me back in front of Danny's."

I didn't want to get the law involved, yet. I walked down the street trying to appear inconspicuous. I casually checked the door front of each business. Cars slowed, and passengers stared suspiciously. I walked past a private residence looking over the fence and behind the shrubs.

Too tough and proud to cry in front of Pauley, as soon as I was alone, I was racked with sobs of fear. The village constable or a sheriff's deputy or, God forbid, the high sheriff himself, was going to come by and ask me what I was doing wandering around someone else's town crying, in an unwashed, disheveled state at this time of the morning. What would I say? That I was looking for my mother? How would I explain? How do you lose your mother? I was afraid I would find her dead, or with some other man.

At a used car lot a half-block past the tavern, I stopped. There weren't many vehicles in circulation this soon after the war; a few dilapidated old cars and trucks were scattered about with their windows covered with advertising. I peered into the front and back seats of the cars, and tried the doors, but they were locked. I climbed on the running-board of an old pickup truck—locked. I cupped my hands around my eyes, and peered into the cab. She was laying on the front seat with her head under the steering wheel. "Mother! Mother!" I cried. I banged on the glass and continued to call, but she didn't move. I needed help. Pauley would know what to do. I jumped off the running-board. The door lock clicked. I wheeled and ran back, grabbed the handle, and jerked the door open. She half fell out of the truck into my arms. I sat her back up in the seat and stood for a long moment holding her and crying. Both of her eyes were black. The left one had a deep gash under it. Her glasses were gone, her lips swollen and caked with dried blood. Blood had run down her face onto her stained blouse. Relief turned to rage. "Who did this to you, Mom? I'll kill the son-of-a-bitch, so help me God."

"No, no, Son," she muttered, "Don't say things like that, please don't say things like that."

"I don't care what you say, I will kill him." I cried.

Then she said, "Look at me." I turned and gazed into her mutilated eyes. "You'll do no such thing."

It had been Dad. I begged her to go to a doctor or the hospital. She just sat there shaking her head. Her breath reeked of alcohol. She was still half drunk. No hospital. No doctor. No police.

Pauley took us home. It was the second time Dad had almost

killed her. Next time, he might succeed. I knew I ought to kill him first. I'd think about it. The nightmares got worse.

At the end of the first semester of my junior year, I finished my exams before noon and had nothing to do until the bus left Leland. Russell Nash finished at the same time so we left the school grounds together. It was a raw winter day. The smoky warmth of the barber shop felt good when we slammed the door shut against the wind. The barber, a crusty old man who cut hair and chewed tobacco at the same time, loved to tell dirty jokes. When Russ and I entered the shop he teased us about skipping school again. We bragged about how smart we were to have finished our tests early so we could take the afternoon off. After the old man exhausted his repertoire of jokes, we wasted a quarter's worth of nickels in the pin-ball machine, then went into the back of the shop and turned the light on over the pool table. Under the glare, the rest of the shop faded to dark.

We racked the balls. This beat sitting in the study hall with Old Prune Face glaring down from her perch all afternoon. We were absorbed in the game when the barber said, "Hey, don't you yahoos know the superintendent has a rule against students playing pool during school hours."

"Fuck Old Man Wall and his rules," I said. Then both of us let out a loud whoop at the verbal bravado.

Mr. Wall stepped into the light of the pool table. He'd been standing inside the door watching when the old barber reminded us of the rule. The suggestion that he should have sex with himself almost caused him to stroke. "Get out of this place and up the hill this minute, you're both expelled."

The old barber was bent double with laughter as Russell and I ran out the front door with Wall in hot pursuit.

"Expelled again? What did you do now?" my mother said, wringing her hands. "You're in trouble all the time. What's the matter with you?"

I had no idea what was wrong with me. I thought it was Old

Man Wall who had a problem. I wanted to go to school, but could not abide constant harassment by the superintendent.

"Can I go to college?"

"That's ridiculous. My God, how can you go to college when you haven't even finished high school?"

I had no idea. All I knew was the situation at Leland was deteriorating fast. Chances of finishing looked dim even if I could get back into school after this incident.

"Topper didn't finish high school and he's going to college. Maybe he can get me in at Central." My brother-in-law, despite lack of a high school diploma, had enrolled at Central Michigan College after he was discharged from the Navy. I don't know why I thought I could cope with college when I was barely making it through high school, but something told me I could.

Mother scoffed at the idea, but finally agreed to call my sister. Later that week, Topper called back and said he had talked to the Dean of Men. They would enroll me on a probationary basis, if I completed my junior year at Leland. When Dad heard I wanted to go to college he laughed and said that was the best damned joke he'd heard in months.

Another humiliating apology and a promise to abide by the rules, got me back into school for the spring semester. In February, we ordered class rings out of a salesman's travel case. I studied a gleaming circle of gold with a black enameled top. Beautiful. One side of the school emblem was imprinted with the numerals "19." On the opposite side was the magic number, "49." In the coming fall I would be a senior! My optimism was reflected on my report card. I received a B, two Cs, and one D, the latter in the class taught by Mr. Wall.

The better I did the more hostile Mr. Wall became. He had made up his mind that I was not a proper person to be in his school, and he was going to do everything in his power to keep me from getting a diploma. And when he wasn't around, the Principal, Mrs. Warner, was a more than ample substitute. She watched me constantly and reported my every move. She was an ugly person, not just in character, but appearance. Skinny as a malnourished worm, she peered at the world through thick horn-rimmed glasses. Her nose, inordinately large for her pinched face, had at some time in her life been ravished by acne. She taught bookkeeping, typing, and shorthand, so I knew she could talk, but in the years that I spent at Leland, she never spoke a single word to me, *not one*. We communicated our mutual scorn in other ways. When classes changed, she stood at the spot where Mr. Wall and I had met on my first day at Leland. From there she had a clear view of the entire hall. As I passed on my way to the next class she fixed her furtive eyes on me and glared while tapping her pencil against a clip board to make sure I knew she was watching. Sometimes I would stare back, turning my head as I walked down the hall so as not to lose eye contact. When I felt real belligerent, which was most of the time, I would turn around and give her my most obnoxious grin.

The end of my junior year approached. Could I hang on for just one more? I wanted to so bad I ached, so why did I continually give Wall the ammunition he needed to get rid of me?

CHAPTER 25

Down And Out

There was cold, hard pressure against my back. I sat with my head in my hands cradling the worst headache I ever owned; and I felt nauseous, not hung-over, more like destroyed. I had no past, no name, and I could barely open my eyes. A pain dug into my right eyeball from inside, so I opened the left. Someone had been sick all over the street and on my shoes, and there was an overwhelming stench. Death was probably like this, and if there was a hell, I had arrived.

Something else touched my back, a light patting sensation. A voice close to my face asked, "Are you feeling better?" The sound was dream-like, but it pushed into my mind and demanded recognition. I was too tired to deal with it.

A car went by, close enough that I could feel the breeze. *Jesus! What's going on? Where am I and how did I get here?* I forced both eyes to a slit and parted my hands hoping to see something that might give me a clue. I was on the curb of some street, but recognized nothing. Maybe my name was Myers, and there was a hand on my back. I turned my head a degree and got a shock through my neck. "Mother, is that you?" *Jesus Christ, it even hurts to talk.* My tongue, lips and jaw felt like they had been hammered with a rock.

The voice said, "You're going to be all right. Don't move for awhile." The patting became a gentle rub. "Just stay quiet."

I sat stone still, until the nausea eased. Then through the haze and pain, memory came seeping. I knew who I was, and where I had been.

Saturday night at the Cedar Dance. It was a ritual I had adopted soon after the Salzbury brothers introduced me to wine and the night life. Patrons of the bi-weekly debauchery were teenagers and war veterans. The Meuenberg brothers, Clint and Paul, owned and operated the Cedar Tavern. They sponsored dances twice weekly to draw crowds into the village. Regulations of the Alcohol Beverage Commission prohibited minors from entering establishments serving liquor, unless accompanied by parent or guardian. And as Dad used to say, "You have to obey the A.B.C. or lose your A.S.S."

The Meuenbergs complied by holding their dances above the tavern, with a separate entrance from the street. The under-aged bought their tickets and entered the dance hall without stepping foot in the forbidden premises. Outside toilets accommodated the dance patrons.

The Statler Band played, and revelers came from miles around, many of which were old enough to buy beer and wine for the minors. I didn't need anyone to buy my drinks. I stole all the booze I wanted from the Maple City Tavern.

It was my chore to fill the tavern coolers with beer, wine, and ice. The last of which came from our ice-house five steps from the back door. In the winter, my dad hired a cutter to remove giant slabs from nearby lakes. Saw dust between the slabs kept the blocks from freezing together. One load lasted a year.

The Maple Tavern had been licensed to sell beer and wine only. Many of the veterans coming home preferred the stronger of the two, so Dad bought a truck load from a vineyard in Wisconsin. Customers loved it, so did Dad, not the wine—he wouldn't touch the stuff—the profit. It cost two dollars for a six-bottle case. The proceeds from the first glass and one-half, paid for the entire bottle. After that it was all profit—a whopping 657 percent! The Wisconsin wine was consumed by the truck load and the money rolled in. Robust sales kept me busy filling the coolers and my parents were too occupied with customers, and their fragile marital relationship, to bother doing an inventory. They never knew how much of anything they had in stock. When the stacks of wine cases started looking low, they'd order another truck load.

Earlier this night, after icing several cases of beer and wine in the reserve cooler, I took two bottles of my favorite vintage from a partially used case, opened a basement window, and laid the bottles in the window well. It was night, so there was no need to cover them. Upstairs in the bar, I helped myself to a five dollar bill from the cash register. The more money and wine I stole, the more my popularity grew.

The Cedar dance crowd had been wild. Newlyweds had made their appearance during intermission while I was outside drinking with the Salzbury brothers. As I staggered back up the stairs into the hall, the band struck up a polka. The couple whirled onto the dance floor laughing as friends formed a circle around them. Rowdy drunks clapped and cheered.

Spectators stacked three and four deep blocked my view. I elbowed my way through the crowd. A Polish fellow by the name of Schopieray stood between me and a clear view of the dancing bride and groom. I pushed him aside. "Who the hell do you think you're shoving?" he said.

He was big and ugly, and looking down at me in a hostile way. "Get fucked," I replied, and turned my back to watch the spectacle of the happy couple in their wedding attire.

The crowd yelled encouragement; there were lewd suggestions. *Wish I was your pecker tonight; hey darlin', how do I get on the waiting list? She looks pregnant again. Piepca stuey, pessa emma.*

"Why don't you come downstairs and say that again, you little piss ant?" It was the Polish fellow screaming at me over the bedlam.

I spun back toward him and said, "You want to fight? Let's go." My dad had taught me to fight like Joe Lewis, the Heavyweight Champion of the World. I pushed back through the ring of people, and headed for the stairs.

It would be a repeat of what had happened two weeks ago at a Cedar dance. I had provoked a guy into a fight by taking his date down to a friend's car during intermission. He was in a rage. It took three minutes to bloody him so bad he covered his face and quit fighting. The outcome had surprised the local toughs, and gave my ego a dangerous and undeserved boost. Then four nights ago, I had been with Yvonne Lyons at a dance in Glen Arbor. She was a willowy blonde from Traverse City, wearing a skin tight skirt and sweater that attracted a lot of attention. After several dances, she agreed to let me take her home.

A cocky looking character dressed in a broad shouldered sport coat, walked across the room, ignored me, and asked Yvonne to dance. I told him to take a hike. He pretended not to hear, and pulled her toward the dance floor. Enraged, I decked him. He jumped up and invited me outside to finish it. In the parking lot, I knocked him down again. By the time he went down the third time, I was a maniac. I wanted to hurt him, so I straddled his chest and pounded his face. Yvonne pulled me off, looked at me like I was crazy, and said she'd never go out with me again.

But the guy bounding down the stairs in front of me tonight was different. He was as wide as he was tall, and he was sober. *Well, what the hell. I'm a fighter ain't I? Not afraid of anyone. And besides, this son-of-a-bitch thought he was big enough to scare me. Well, I'll show him—big doesn't mean shit.*

A crowd followed us down the stairs, yelling, "Fight! Fight! There's going to be a fight!"

The wine in my gut, the hostility in my heart, and the need to be the center of attention, pumped adrenalin. I stripped my coat off, and felt power in my arms and shoulders—I would show this lumber-jack what street fighting was all about. We squared off in front of the Cedar Tavern. I'd been brawling in the streets for years, knew how to inflict pain, and I intended to put some on this asshole. I threw the first punch, a solid right, true as an arrow. It landed hard on his cheek. He blinked, charged, and telegraphed a round-house, which ordinarily I would have deflected. But the force of his swing was so powerful, it knocked my arm aside and tore the left shoulder out of my shirt. *Jesus, what have I got myself into? This guy isn't human. My best right hand didn't phase him and he swings like a goddamned gorilla. What had Dad said about power—it takes speed and power.* His next punch caught me on the left forearm and paralyzed it from the elbow down. Then the lights went out.

"Where's everybody," I was talking to my mother setting beside me on the step in front of the Cedar Tavern.

"You're going to be alright. Feeling a little better?" She asked.

"What time is it? Where is everybody?"

"Come on, let's try to walk to the car. She got up and tried to lift me by the left arm. Pain shot through like an electric current. I nearly fainted.

"Jesus, don't touch my arm. I can walk by myself." We made it to the car. "What time is it?"

"Two thirty."

"My God, you mean I've been out since . . . ." *How long was I out? Intermission had been at 11:30, and I stayed outside drinking until about midnight. Jesus, I'd been unconscious for two hours!* "Where was I when you found me?" I was looking at her face in the glow of the dash light as she headed the car across the Cedar Swamp Road toward Maple City.

"You were throwing up in the street in front of the Tavern," she said, and smirked.

She thinks it's funny because I got whipped, was knocked cold. "How did you know where I was?" I was still trying to clear my head.

They had closed the Maple Tavern at 2:00 a.m. Shortly after locking up, someone knocked on the front door. The man didn't want anything, other than to tell them I had been in a fight in Cedar, and there was a chance I was hurt bad because I had been laying on the street for a long time. She took Dad home and came looking for me.

The thing that bothered me most about that night, even more than having been pounded unconscious, was the smile on my mother's face as she drove me home.

The next day, I slept until three in the afternoon, then hung around the tavern to avoid facing my friends. I looked like raw hamburger. My eyebrow was split and my nose swollen. I had what looked like floor burns on my forehead, and my arm was too sore to lift a pencil. I'd have to figure some way to get out of going to school the next day. Every kid in Leelanau County would know about the fight in Cedar before the first bell sounded, and the Administration would be gloating.

I stocked the coolers, using my right arm to carry ice in from the ice house, then went upstairs and used part of the five dollars I had lifted the night before to play one of my favorite songs on the juke box. The Mills Brothers sang, *I'm Gonna Buy a Paper Dolly Just to Call My Own—*. I sat in an empty booth feeling sorry for myself.

At six o'clock, Mom came to the juke box with a worried expression on her face. "Run over to the house and find out what's taking Dad so long. He was supposed to be here two hours ago."

"Is he drunk?" I asked.

"When I fixed his breakfast at noon, he hadn't had a thing to drink."

"How come he didn't come to work when you came?"

"I don't know, but he was acting funny. Go check."

I walked the block to our house, and entered the back door. An empty quart bottle of Gilbey's Gin set on the kitchen table. If he had drank a full fifth he would be passed out. I went through the dining area. The living room curtains were drawn making the room dim. He was in his chair, chin on his chest, both arms hanging limply over the sides. "Hey Dad, starting a little early, aren't you?"

He raised his head slightly, and muttered, "Mind your own business. Leave me alone."

There was a pocket knife laying on the floor by his left hand, and beside the knife a pool of blood, and another pool by his right. I ran to him. "Dad! What have you done?" I picked up the knife, and looked at the cuts on his arms. They seemed shallow, but I couldn't really tell due to the lighting. I put my arms around his neck. "I love you Dad. We all love you. Please don't hurt yourself. Just stay where you are, I'll call an ambulance."

"No ambulance," he said.

"But you're hurt. I don't want you to die. Let me go get Mom."

He took hold of my arm with his left hand, and clamped down, not hard enough to hurt, but tight. His congealed blood smeared my shirt. The pain in my arm from last night seemed unimportant.

I tried to pulled back, but there was no breaking that grip. "Why? Why would you do this to yourself?"

"What have I got to live for?"

The question was bizarre, out of touch. He was having delirium tremors again. "You can't mean it. Mom worships you; Sis and I love you, and you have the best business in the county. What more do you want? What more is there? No man on earth has more than you."

"The only thing I ever wanted I left in Hazel Park . . . but you wouldn't understand. Nobody understands."

I thought maybe I did. "You don't love any of us."

He released the hold on my arm and pulled me onto his chest. "Sure I do, Son. Sure I love you. Give your dad a kiss and shake on it."

I kissed his cheek. "I need to get you to a doctor."

"No. I'm alright." He took my hand. "Shake on it. I hear you got your ass kicked last night."

"What's that got to do with anything?"

"Shit, you never could fight."

I looked at the pools of blood. There wasn't much. The cut above my eye had bled more. "I try Dad, that's all I can do." I put my hand in his. Maybe he wouldn't hurt me this time. His teeth ground, and he tightened the grip. Pressure built, my knuckles popped. "Dad, please don't do that. You're hurting me."

"You're not such a tough guy after all, eh?"

The tears started. He really didn't care about me or anyone except that woman in Detroit. We'd have been better off if his knife would have found its mark. He squeezed harder and harder, and I wanted him to die.

The month of May, 1948, had been a wonderful time. The weather warmed early, my classes at school seemed easy, there had been beach parties and cook-outs, and I hadn't been in a fight in a month. Today, the drive from Maple City to Leland was spectacular. Waters of the Lakes on both sides of the road displayed vast arrays of blues and greens as white clouds painted different shades across the vast liquid canvas. Trees were frocked with the subtle greens of spring and the flowers around Victorian houses lining the main street of Leland were in full dress.

I was loaded with good spirit, hormones, and unresolved conflicts, when I parked the car in the school parking lot. I had made a B on the physics exam the day before, reason alone to celebrate. I had two exams left, and knew I could pass them both. It looked like I was going to become a senior after all.

The car I parked in front of the school was one of the first new vehicles in Leelanau County since before the war. In the three years my parents had owned the Maple Tavern they had prospered beyond their wildest expectations, so when new cars began rolling off the Detroit assembly lines, Dad ordered one. It was a lime-green Dodge sedan, with a speedometer that turned different colors as your speed changed—green, yellow, and then red. What a car! And my parents had let me drive it to school on this last day of my junior year.

I twirled the keys on my finger as I entered the building.

"Just a minute Myers!" The voice was unmistakable. I stopped in my tracks. Mr. Wall was standing just inside the door.

"Good morning," I said, wondering what he was doing waiting for me before the first bell. My mind was racing trying to remember if I had done anything the previous day that would merit this ambush.

"Give me the keys," he said. His steely eyes malevolent.

"What do you mean?" I was confused. I knew he meant the car keys, but I couldn't think of why he would want to take them away from me. I had driven carefully the entire fourteen miles to Leland. The fact that my parents had trusted me with the car, especially considering my previous driving escapades, was reason enough for me to observe all the rules.

"I mean, give me the keys to that car."

Hatred and resentment boiled up from my belly. *What is this bastard trying to pull? I'll be damned if I'll give him the keys.* "Why? What have I done? I'm not giving you these keys!"

"You'll give me the keys or you won't take your tests."

"But why? I haven't done anything."

"No. And I'm going to see that you don't."

Classes were about to begin and students were coming in at an increased pace. Some hesitated momentarily as they passed, and then hurried on as they grasped the confrontation in progress.

"I'm not giving you these keys. Did you take the keys away from the others who drove to school?" There were several other student cars parked in front. I jammed the keys deep in my pocket.

The refusal infuriated him. He stepped to within a few inches of me. His face was flushed, his voice quivered. "Who do you think you are to question me? You'll either give me those keys or you'll get out of this school now!"

There was nothing to do but acquiesce. I could be free of him by refusing to surrender, but the desire to graduate with the class of '49 was greater. I pulled the keys out of my pocket and handed them over. I had such a mix of destructive emotions, I didn't know what to do. I couldn't think. How would I ever pass a test in this state?

Janet Burda caught my arm outside the Economics classroom. "What was that all about?"

"He took the keys to my car, and I swear to God, Janet, I didn't do one thing. You don't know how I hate him."

"Let it go. This is the last day. We'll have the whole summer to work it out." She put her hand behind my neck. "Please. Let it go."

"I don't know whether I can or not. I'll try."

The incident was the talk of the school. He had humiliated me in front of my friends. I couldn't concentrate on the tests. The fury was almost too much to bare.

By the last bell in the afternoon, the incident had smoldered in my gut like a lit cigarette in a pile of oily rags. I was so distraught I hadn't been able to formulate a rational approach for retrieving the confiscated keys. When the bell sounded, I was like a demented and beaten fighter coming out of the corner hoping that by some desperate act I could salvage a lost cause.

I bound up the stairs to his office. When he saw me at his door he rose and stood.

"Give me those keys," I said between clinched teeth. They were laying on his desk.

He smirked as he shoved the keys toward me and said, "Take your keys and don't ever step foot in this school again. Do you understand? Your through!"

"Take your school and stick it in your ass. You couldn't pay me enough to come back." I grabbed the keys, whirled around and ran down the steps. At the parking lot, three of my friends were waiting. Janet Burda got in next to me, Bob Stachnik and Steve Skipski got in the back. The minute I slammed my door, a chorus of questions went up.

I told them the details of the encounter, and that I had decided to never return to Leland High School. We drove around town while I spewed venom like an enraged rattlesnake. We passed the high school baseball field, I did a u-turn and wheeled the car into the parking lot behind the bleachers.

"What'd you pull in here for?" Janet asked.

"I'm going to leave that bastard something to complain about." I revved the motor and spun out onto the diamond. At the close of baseball season, they had re-sodded the infield. It was in perfect condition. The snow tires on the Dodge tore huge chunks of turf out of the wet ground and threw them into the catchers box, the bleachers, and the outfield. I did several figure eights and fish-tailed out of the park.

My passengers were white-faced. No one spoke for several miles as we headed toward Maple City. Finally Bob said, "Shit-O, we are in big trouble."

"No you're not," I said. I'm driving. You had no control over what I just did. If anyone asks, tell them you tried to stop me, but I wouldn't listen. You can also tell them, Hiram Keith Myers or "Lucky" said to kiss his ass." Everyone laughed and relaxed. Except me. It was the first time in my life I had ever maliciously destroyed anything.

"But what are you going to do?" Janet asked. "Mister Wall will never let you back in school."

I wasn't sure. But there was Mom's conversation with Topper. He had said if I would finish my junior year, the college would let me in on probation. I had taken all my tests. College was the answer.

CHAPTER 26

You Can't Go Home Again

Topper called. He relayed a message from Central Michigan College's Dean of Men. My application had been denied. My life was in shambles—expelled from high school, denied college admission, and all bridges burned.

When I had marched brazenly into Mr. Wall's office the last day of school and demanded he return my car keys, it was with the belief that I had an ace in the hole. College. The Dean had told Topper earlier that all I needed to do was complete my junior year. So what happened? Five years would pass before I was to learn that it was Wall and Warner, not I, who had played the last card. The letter had been addressed to the Office of the Dean of Men, Central Michigan College, Mt. Pleasant, Michigan. The words were burned into my brain:

> *Dear Dean Lauer:*
>
> *Thank you for your inquiry concerning one Hiram K. Myers, Jr., and whether he would be a proper candidate for early admission into Central Michigan College's September, 1948, freshman class.*
>
> *This student came to us out of the Detroit school system, and has been a constant source of trouble since his arrival three years ago. He is not a fit candidate for college, socially nor academically. His expulsions and suspensions from Leland High School are too numerous to detail in this letter. His last expulsion is not subject to review, and he will therefore never have sufficient credits to qualify for a diploma.*

We trust this information will be of use in determining whether to admit this individual into your institution.

Sincerely,

S/Bernice Warner, Principal

I had played right into their hands. I assumed that I would be admitted to college, not anticipating Wall and Warner's sabotage. I had outsmarted myself. Three years ago, I nearly shot myself in the foot. This time I had succeeded.

The weekend following my expulsion I got drunk and provoked two fights at the same dance. I was so full of hate and frustration that in one instance I walked up to some poor guy whose looks I didn't like and, for no other reason, busted him in the mouth. I had to do something about the hostility, or end up in jail just like Wall had predicted.

I was riding around with George Weiss, another unemployed high school drop-out, bitching about what a cruel blow fate had dealt, and bemoaning my dim future. George said, "Why don't we join the Navy?"

Now there was an idea. My dad had been in the Navy for a few months following World War I, and Topper had served in World War II, so why not? The biggest reason was that I was only 16 years old. "I can't. I don't turn seventeen for another three months." Then it hit me. Major, the perennial seventh grader at Lacy Junior High in Hazel Park; when he turned sixteen, he had lied about his age and was accepted in the Marines. If he could do it, so could I.

We approached Maple City in George's beat-up Model A Ford. At the bend in the highway where the town's tiny business section was clustered, I saw my mother walking across the street toward the telephone office.

"George, pull over in front of the phone office. Hurry, I want to talk to my mom." The old car rattled to a stop just as she was entering the building. "Hey Mom!" I yelled.

She stopped halfway in the door. "What?" Her tone was

defensive as though she expected me to ask for the car or money, which was what I usually wanted to talk to her about.

"I'm going to join the Navy."

She hesitated for an instant, then with the tips of her fingers she waved and said, "Bye-bye," before disappearing into the office.

Well! If she doesn't care, then I'm damn sure going to do it. She had embarrassed me in front of George. The least she could have done was suggest I wait until my birthday in September.

I wasted no time finding a place to enlist. The recruiter looked at my test results. "You passed with flying colors. But you still have to have your parents' permission."

I had filled out the application, taken the entrance exam, and lied about my age. I had said on the application that I was born in 1930. That would make me seventeen, but the recruiter said I would still need parental consent until September. I wanted to go now.

"I'll get it," I said to the Navy Recruiter who looked sharp with the medals pinned to the chest of his uniform. "Give me the papers and I'll get their signature, and be back in a couple of days."

That afternoon, I walked into the Maple Tavern, climbed onto a bar stool, and waited until both Mom and Dad were finished waiting on customers.

"I'm leaving for The Great Lakes Training Center, on the 14th," I announced matter-of-factly.

They came over to where I was sitting, and grinned like I had just told a joke. "What do you mean, you're leaving for boot camp? You're too young to join the Navy."

"No I'm not. All I need is your signature on these papers and I'll be gone."

I wanted them to protest, to try to talk me out of it. Maybe they would tell me that they didn't want me to be "gone." Surely they would think of some other alternative. Like going with me to make an appeal to Central Michigan College. Or by offering to send me to another college, a private school, or military academy. Money wouldn't be a problem.

They had been granted a full liquor license. Business at The Maple Tavern had doubled. A new addition was under construction, which would include a dance floor and triple seating capacity.

They studied the papers. "Is this what you want to do?"

"Yes," I lied. Without another word, they signed the papers and went back to tending bar.

On June 14, 1948, at the age of 16 years and nine months, I left Traverse City for the Great Lakes Training Center at Chicago, Illinois, to commence three years of active duty in the U.S. Navy. When the Korean War started, President Truman, would add another year.

For my father and my sister, my leaving home was a case of out of sight out of mind, and good riddance. I never heard from either of them in the four years I was gone.

Boston, Massachusetts, October, 1948, to February, 1949.

I was miserable. I had come out of a totally unsupervised environment, where for the past five years, I had made all of my own decisions, good or bad. Now everything was regimented. I wasn't allowed to make the simple choice of which color of socks I would put on in the morning.

A ray of sunshine was when the Company Commander at Great Lakes, told me I had made the highest score on my General Qualifications Test of any recruit in our company of sixty men, which qualified me for The Naval Academy at Annapolis, Maryland. The result startled me. Either the other fifty-nine men in Company 309, were extraordinarily stupid, or I had a lot more intelligence than I, or anyone else, had been giving me credit for. And if true, why had I made such miserable grades at Leland High School? I thought I knew the answer. As they say in the North Woods, I had been poll-axed. Actually there had been multiple stumbling blocks, but the one I understood perfectly was named "Wall."

The examining doctor was not very clear about why I had failed the physical requirements for the Academy. I had flat feet, but that hadn't stopped the Navy from accepting me as an enlisted man. I wondered if maybe it had something to do with my hands. As consolation for being rejected by The Naval Academy, I was given a choice of any Specialty School I wished to attend. I chose Radar in Boston. Not that I had an aptitude or interest in the vocation. I had none. But I had read about what a technological marvel it was, and how much it would have helped our ships during some of the famous World War II Naval battles. It had an adventurous sound to it.

The train ride from Chicago to Boston, had been one continuous party. A recruit by the name of Rogers got drunk and threw up between the seats. The stewards moved us all to another section of the train while they sanitized and air-freshened the party car, which we proceeded to trash for the second time.

After bunk and locker assignments were made, there remained two days before classes started. I wandered around the city gawking at the buildings, roamed in and out of The Commons, spent time playing ping-pong at the U.S.O. Club, and drank my first Orange Julius. I would have taken pictures of Boston and the Fargo Building, where the school was located, but my camera had been stolen out of my unlocked sea bag while I was waiting for travel orders.

School started October 4, 1948, and would continue eighteen weeks to February 4, 1949. Instruction on the operation of surface and air radars, was fun, and took one week. If the course would have ended then, I would have been in great shape and been top in the class. But the remainder of the course focused on the repair and maintenance of the radar units. I was not interested. Instead of studying, I spent free nights exploring the bars and tattoo shops of Scollay Square, downtown Boston.

James Jimerson, my upper bunk-mate from rural Pennsylvania, had graduated from high school the previous June. There were no personal problems in his family, such as alcoholism, but they were poor, and couldn't afford to have an unemployed son at home with four younger siblings to feed. Veterans returning from overseas had filled their former jobs, and were given preference over non-veterans in the labor market. Jamie couldn't find employment, had no interest in college, and as a last resort enlisted. The trait that we shared in common, and which bonded us like brothers, was our intense hatred of the regimentation. We spent entire nights huddled together drinking coffee, whispering our plans to go AWOL at the first opportunity. To avoid capture, we would go to Alaska, or the Hudson Bay area of Canada, run trap-lines, live off the land, and survive by our wit. Both of us had spent much of our youth in the wilderness. If a city slicker like Jack London could survive the wilds of Alaska, we could too.

"Jamie," I whispered. "I need to ask you something."

"Ask away," he said.

"You ever think about killing somebody?"

"Hell no! Unless it would be myself when I look in the mirror. Do you?"

"I can't make up my mind whether I love or hate my dad. I used to want to kill him, but I'm not so sure now. When you're away from someone you tend to forget the bad stuff. But there's someone else I'm sure about."

Jimerson came down off his bunk and sat on the edge of my mattress. "You gonna do it?"

"I might. I want to real bad. I think about it a lot. I know exactly how to do it and never get caught."

"Jesus. Who?"

"The fat pig that kept me from finishing high school."

He patted my arm. "A high school diploma's not that big a deal. I've got one, and I'm no better off than you."

"It's the idea he can do those things to people and answer to no one. You wouldn't believe the lies he made up to cheat me out of grades, and force me out of school. If he gets by with it then there's no justice."

"Forget that stuff. You don't need a diploma in the North Woods. Look at it this way. If he hadn't done all that stuff and forced you out, we'd of never met."

Jamie had a point.

Take home pay in radar school was seventy-one dollars per month. There was little to spend it on except booze and women, but those were expensive past times. Three days after payday, Jamison and I would be broke, but this was payday night.

Rogers, who had gotten sick on the train from Chicago, joined Jamison and me in a dive in Scollay Square called the Lost Goose. The Goose served boiler-makers to any and all comers, no questions asked. The only prerequisites were to be able to climb on a stool and lay your money on the bar. Which is what we did, and we were drunk, with our third beer and bump setting in front of us, our white hats perched on the back of our heads, our arms around each other's shoulder, singing, *Many's the night I spent with Minnie the Mermaid down at the bottom of the sea; down among the coral, Minnie lost her morals, gee but she was good to me . . .* We put our heads together like coyote pups, and wailed, *Many's the night, with the pale moon-a-shining down on her bungalow, ashes to ashes, dust to dust, two twin beds and only one of them mussed, . . .*

In those early days, it only took three boilers to paralyze me, and I'd already had two. I felt melancholy. These two guys were all the family I had, and we would stick together regardless of what the military dealt us. Jamison wanted to sing another song. I said, "Wait, wait a minute you guys. Are we blood brothers or not?"

"No son-of-a-bitch dare say we ain't," Jamie said.

"Yeah," I said, my speech sounding like I had a mouth full of modeling clay. "But we need something to prove it, something to remember this night by, like a tattoo. You guys know this one? It's a good harmonizer." With eyes half closed, I sang, *Sweet Adellette, your pants are wet; it isn't pee or sweat I bet; in all my dreams, your fair ass beams, you're the wrecker of my pecker, sweet Adellette, myyyyyyyy A . . . del . . . lette.*

Our trio sang the song two more times, dragging out the last Adellette, for at least half a minute. At the end of the bar, a civilian with an oily pompadour and wearing a zoot suit, said, "Jesus, you guys sound like you're constipated."

"Hey asshole," I said. "If you don't like it, get the fuck out of here." I slid off the stool and in two steps was within a foot of him.

Rogers said, "Come on Myers, let it pass, it's not worth it."

The zoot suit spun and started to put his feet on the floor. I hit him three times: a solid right to the gut, a left to the side of his face, and the sixth knuckle on my right hand just below his eye. He dropped to his hands and knees, forehead on the floor.

The bartender slammed a blackjack down on the bar.

Jamie was up. He grabbed my arm and pulled me away. Rogers joined him on the other side. Together the three of us went out the door and ran around the corner. A block away, we stopped in the doorway of a tattoo parlor.

"I left a beer and a bump setting on the bar," I said.

Rogers said, "Damn Myers, where'd you learn to do that?"

"Do what?" I asked.

"Fight. You don't look the type."

I guess he was referring to my baby face and weight of one-hundred thirty pounds.

"I guess my dad taught me. But listen, you guys. We need to be able to prove we're blood brothers. Look in there." I pointed to a buxom red-head motioning at us through the glass store front. We each paid the tattoo lady six dollars and fifty cents. She affixed to our left forearms an eagle perched on an anchor, balanced on top of a five pointed star. Blood brothers all. We staggered along the street, arms across one another's shoulders, singing ribald songs, and feeling too macho to admit the bloody tattoos were killing us.

* * *

Amanda Bradley wrote:

There's a place within
our hearts
Where we keep
our favorite memories,
The ones that never fail to
make us smile—
And when life becomes too hectic
it's such a special feeling
To close our eyes
and reminisce awhile—

And out of all the memories
Of family and friendships,
The ones that are most touching
to recall
Are joy-filled, love-filled moments
that we share
at Christmas time—
Those are the dearest memories of all.

December 23, 1948. I had scant money, but It didn't matter—I was going home. I had finagled ten days out of the Commanding Officer of the Radar School, even though I had already used up all my leave after boot camp. But ten days leave at Christmas! I was ecstatic; I would soon be with family and friends.

The announcement on the bulletin board in the study area had read: "Leaving December 23 for Meadville, Pennsylvania, will take three passengers and share expenses. Contact Pat Brown, ext. 391."

In the library, I pulled an atlas and found Meadville. The best route for Pat Brown would be through Erie, Pennsylvania, which was exactly the way I would go if hitch-hiking. Boston to Erie was four-hundred-fifty miles, almost half way home. I would do it. I sent a telegram.

The car wasn't bad, a '34, five-passenger Chevy, which appeared to be in fair condition. For one-third of the gas and oil, which turned out to be a little less than $3.00, I was going to go half way home in one ride. Pat Brown's front-seat passenger was a congenial fellow called Mickey. Riding in back with me was another sailor from Michigan, George Klinesorge. We had both been in Company No. 309 at Great Lakes, but had been on different floors of the barracks.

At 5:00 a.m., on December 23, we drove out of Boston under a sky as dark as the dress uniforms we wore. Everyone agreed to forego restaurant stops, and eat only snacks, in order to make the best time and conserve cash.

At 6:00 a.m., the radiator boiled over. The old Chevy wheezed into a service station. Pat assured us he could handle it and would have us back on the road in a jiffy. Despite the winter chill, he removed his jumper and dived under the hood. Mickey, Klinesorge, and myself went to a grocery across the street for something to eat.

A gray, sunless daylight lit the sky behind us as the Chevy pulled out of the station and headed west. The weather had been unseasonably mild and we figured with any luck we would make Erie by 5:00 p.m. We broke out the junk food and had breakfast. Klinesorge had two paper sacks tucked between his knees. From one he fished Twinkies, cream-filled Hostess cupcakes, and two Baby Ruth candy bars, all of which he wolfed down with gusto. From the other sack he extracted a bottle of Nehigh Orange-Pineapple soda, called for an opener, and with a single tip of the bottle drank it dry.

We rolled down the highway leaving the shoulder littered with donut boxes, cellophane wrappers, candy bar papers, and empty pop bottles.

Mid-morning Klinesorge reached into his paper sack and retrieved a bottle of Mogan David Grape Wine. He took a long pull on the bottle, wiped his mouth on the back of his hand, and smacked his lips. "Would anyone like to partake of a little grape?" he asked.

Pat shook his head. Mickey reached back for the bottle. He'd have just a touch, as a way of compensating for the lack of a workable heater in the car. I decided alcohol would hurt my chances of getting rides later in the day so I declined. Mickey took one swig, grimaced, and told Klinesorge he had punished himself enough for one day. Klinesorge would just have to drink by himself.

At 11:30 a.m., Klinesorge passed out. He snored like a ban saw while the empty wine bottle rattled around on the floor board. At about that time, we entered the Catskills in central New York, and there was an ominous change in the weather. Purple clouds rolled over the mountains from the west. The temperature dropped, and the wind whipped the car from side to side. Pat slowed down.

It rained in torrents, then when we reached the higher elevation on the eastern slope, the rain changed to sleet, then produced snow so heavy that even with headlights, Pat had to slow to a snail's pace to stay on the road. The outline of the highway became so uncertain that several times the car thumped off the road perilously close to ditches and gorges. The wet snow stuck like glue, so we stopped every two or three miles to clear the windshield. Traffic disappeared.

The ferocity of the wind and the disappearing roadway caused the mood in the car to tense. It was drafty and cold, the heater made almost as much racket as Klinesorge, and put out the same amount of heat. It was obvious to all, except the peaceful Klinesorge, that if the car broke down in this storm we were in serious trouble.

Pat bent over the wheel, his nose inches from the windshield. Mickey and I were bundled in our pea coats with the collars turned up against the freezing draft. Klinesorge suddenly set up in his seat and launched a spray of half-digested Twinkies, cup-cakes, and chocolate candy onto the back of Pat's head, the dashboard, and the windshield.

"Jesus Fucking Christ!" Pat screamed, and slammed on the brakes. The car went into a three-hundred-sixty degree turn in the middle of the road.

The smell of Klinesorge's vomit elicited a series of heaves from me. Chances were fifty-fifty the junk food in my stomach would join Klinesorge's which was running down Pat's collar and the dashboard into the odometer. Before the car had time to come to a complete halt, Micky jumped out, ran around to the driver's side, and jerked Klinesorge out into the storm. He no sooner grabbed the front of Klinesorge's blouse, when he pulled his hand away and started wiping it in the snow. "You gross bastard, I ought to beat you to a pulp and leave you in a snow drift." He was bellowing like a mad bull as he scrubbed at the splatters of undigested food across his left shoulder. Klinesorge, a blank look on his face, acted as though the whole thing had happened to someone else.

I was feeling pretty good about escaping unscathed when I felt something warm on my upper legs. Before my hand hit my butt, I knew what I was going to find. "Kill that asshole!" I yelled, "He peed his pants, the back seat's soaked."

Klinesorge set on the running board of the car with his head in his hands while the rest of us ranted and raved about what a sorry specimen of humanity he was, and how we ought to leave him in the blizzard to freeze. He looked at us with an innocent stare.

After a heated discussion, we decided we had to take him along, otherwise he'd die in the storm, which would be too painless. We wanted Klinesorge to suffer. We had no idea how far we were from a town and there was no traffic. So back in the car he came.

I huddled in the corner of the seat as far away from him as possible. We rolled all windows down an inch to dilute the air, but there was no way to escape the stench, or the urine-soaked seat. Pat cleaned himself and the dashboard with a handkerchief wetted from the snow. Mickey glared over his shoulder at Klinesorge. And Klinesorge? He promptly went back to sleep and lay with his head against the seat, snoring.

At 1:00 a.m. on December 24, 1948, we reached Erie, Pennsylvania, seven hours behind schedule. Klinesorge and I were dumped on the outskirts of town at the Meadville junction. Thankful to be rid of Klinesorge, Pat and Micky sped away without so much as a goodbye.

Klinesorge and I shivered in the frigid air, discussing our options. Snow flakes, which at first had been large and wet, were now icy, driven across Lake Erie with such fury they stung the bare skin. We crossed the highway, in knee-deep drifts, to an all night truck stop. Most drivers had given up and parked their rigs. Klinesorge rented a trucker's shower and a bunk.

I sipped coffee in the restaurant wondering what I should do next. At 2:00 a.m., a gorilla sized man entered shaking snow and ice from his back like an Alaskan Husky. He twisted the top off a gallon thermos. "Hey Gloria, you got enough joe to fill this thing?"

The waitress, crushed a cigarette into a counter ashtray. "Sure, we could fill three of 'em. Sold only one cup in two hours," she said nodding in my direction. "It's rough as hell north of here, Mack, you'd better set this one out."

"Naw. Roads won't be any better in the morning. This load's supposed to be at the dock by seven."

"Snow flakes flying in your face will put you to sleep," she said.

"Not after I have a couple of jolts of your battery acid." He slapped his thigh and laughed loud enough to rattle my cup.

"Excuse me," I said. "What dock you trying to get to?"

"Toledo," he replied.

"Any chance I could ride along?"

"Hell yes, buddy. You can help keep me out of snow drifts. Let's go."

The eighteen wheeler's lights shot double beams into a solid white wall. Mack, his eyes squinting as he strained to find the road, nudged the accelerator, and handed me his empty cup for a refill. Best I could tell, we were making between thirty-five and forty miles an hour. "How far is it to Toledo?"

"From Erie, around two thirty-five."

"You might have trouble making that seven o'clock deadline."

"Ain't exactly a deadline. I knew I couldn't make it, but I won't be more'n an hour or two late. Hell, I'll be a hero. Where you headed?"

"Little town on the west coast of Michigan, called Maple City."

"It's durned sure little. Ain't too many towns in Michigan I ain't heard of, but that's one of 'em. Guess you're trying to get home fer Christmas?"

"Yes, sir."

"Tell you what little buddy, we git into Toledo, I'll try to hook you up with somebody pulling a load that direction."

Noon, Christmas Eve day. I climbed stiffly out of a warm vehicle on the outskirts of Manson, Michigan. I pulled the rim of my sailor's hat down to my eyes, lowered my head, and trudged into the snow for the walk across the deserted business district. My feet were wet within minutes of exiting the car. Signs in the shops said, "Closed until the 26th." Traffic, sparse on a good day, was now practically nonexistent. On the outskirts, at a place that seemed best for catching a ride, I turned and looked back to where I had just been. The town had disappeared in a cloud of swirling, dancing snow. No cars were in sight, and the footprints I had just made were fast vanishing.

I rummaged around in my duffle bag, found my stocking cap, and pulled it down over my ears. My pea coat and woolen gloves would enable me to withstand a fairly severe spell of intense cold. Everything was warm except my feet, which felt like they were burning—an ominous sign.

Through the wail of the wind and the rasp of my own breath, came the belch and cough of an engine, which, if sounds have any reliability, was on the verge of dying. A rattle trap of a truck chugged out of the maelstrom looking like a prehistoric beast on its way to the burial ground. I waved frantically fearing it would either not see me or pass me by. The ancient machine rattled to a stop.

The needle on the speedometer hiccupped and flapped back and forth between zero and eighty, making it impossible to tell our speed, but twenty-miles an hour in this weather would have been too fast. The wind-scored old man behind the wheel, drove with his head outside the truck searching for signs of the vanished roadway. Every mile or two he'd reach around the window frame and shake the wiper until it resumed scratching feebly across the frozen windshield. With the driver's side window open and holes in the floorboard large enough to spit through, the heat filtering through the rattling heater was lost. But it was a ride. In the moments before the relic had appeared out of the wall of white, I had decided to walk back to Manson and find a church willing to give me shelter until the storm passed. But the truck had gathered me in.

The old man at the wheel explained he was on his way to his daughter's home for the holiday, and she lived in a little place called, Glen Arbor. I let out a whoop. What a stroke of luck! The road to Glen Arbor passed through Maple City. If the old engine kept chugging, I would not have to spend Christmas Eve alone in a strange church after all.

We coasted down the long hill outside of my hometown, the old man down-shifted, and pumped the breaks gently. I struggled into my wet shoes. It had taken the truck three hours to make the sixty-five miles from Manson to Maple City.

The Winter Solstice had celebrated by burying Maple City

under three feet of snow. Drifts next to the houses were as high as the roof line. One could only presume that the humps under the snow were the townspeople's cars. It was the most beautiful sight I had ever seen.

I thanked the old man profusely, wished him a Merry Christmas, pulled my duffle bag from behind the seat and walked the block to my home. It seemed like a miracle, one made possible by Gorilla Mack. The ride he had arranged from Toledo to Manson saved the day. Thirty-six hours before, I had been in a big unfriendly East-Coast city, but was now walking up the road in front of my own house on Christmas Eve. Through the early dusk of evening and the swirling snow, lights from the frosty windows in my hometown twinkled like happy stars. In my heart I imagined that the hundred and fifty people who lived here were warmly and busily engaged in the pleasant tasks of Holiday.

The back door was unlocked, as usual. I quietly turned the knob and stuck my head in the door. "Merry Christmas", I shouted. There was no answer. In the dim light I saw the outline of a body lying on the hall floor. I stood still, my heart suddenly pounding. The body lifted its head, then tried to push into a setting position, but failed and fell back on the floor. Dad.

"The dirty son-of-a-bitch!" he said. The utterance was a cross between a strangle and a gurgle. "I can whip him with one hand tied behind my back."

I threw my bag to the floor and ran to him, fell to my knees. "Dad, Dad, what happened to you?" I tried to pick him up, but two-hundred pounds of dead weight was too much. I wanted to lift his head onto my lap, but he pushed me away and mumbled, "I can whip any son-of-a-bitch in the world." He clinched his fists so hard the skin squeaked in the palms. My eyes adjusted to the dim light. There was blood on his face, one eye swollen shut. I closed my eyes. "What in God's name is going on here? Where is everyone?" I asked. A sound behind caused me to turn. My sister was outlined in the door leading to the living room. "Sis, what's going on?"

She looked at me as if I were a stranger. "He's been drunk for two days, kept threatening Topper, so he knocked him down." Her voice was a dull monotone as she continued, "Mother slipped Dad a pair of scissors and he tried to kill Topper with them, so Topper hit him again and took the scissors away."

"Jesus Christ!" I said to no one. Didn't they know I was coming? I staggered into the living room and fell against the wall. "Dad!" I screamed, "Didn't you know I was coming?"

From the hall he mumbled, "I'll cut his heart out."

Sobs racked me; I was dying. Hat, coat and gloves still on, my head cradled in the bend of my arm, I prayed it was a bad dream. Something touched my back. Mother stood next to me with her hand on my shoulder. Through the crook in my arm I could see her shoes. She continued patting my shoulder so I lifted my head and looked into her eyes. She was drunk! I jerked away. "Didn't you know I was coming, Ma? Didn't anyone know I was coming home for Christmas?"

It was there, laying on the table by the couch, my telegram that read: "DECEMBER 22, 1948. GREAT NEWS stop I'LL BE HOME FOR XMAS stop LOVE, SON."

I know what I really want for Christmas.
I want my childhood back.
Nobody is going to give me that . . . I know it
doesn't make sense, but since when is Christmas
about sense, anyway? It is about a child
of long ago and far away, and it is about the
child of now.
In you and me. Waiting behind the door
of our hearts for something
wonderful to happen.

Robert Fulghum

CHAPTER 27

The Nineteenth Chair

I lay in my bunk and watched Calvin Medlock move his gear from his locker to his sea bag. "Hey Cal, what'cha doing that for?"

"My friend," he said, "I am gone like the wild goose—headed south."

"Get kicked out of Radar School?"

"God no, Myers. You are gazing upon a future ensign in the United States Coast Guard."

"What makes you think so?"

"I mean, last fall I made application to the Coast Guard Academy. I've been accepted. I got my travel orders today; train leaves tonight for New London. Classes start January 15."

I told him about passing the Annapolis exam in boot camp, and then flunking the physical.

He said, "I didn't have to take a written test. They accepted me on my high school transcript."

"That leaves me out. Those people see my transcript, they'd have a heart attack."

Cal stopped packing. "I thought you had to have a pretty good transcript to get into Radar."

"I doubt anyone in the Navy has seen mine. If they had, I probably wouldn't be here. They let me come to Radar 'cause of the Annapolis thing."

Cal stuffed his rolled whites into the bottom of the sea bag. "It might be a good idea for you to talk to Mister Carter, the Education Officer—neat guy. You wouldn't believe some of the opportunities available."

The next day I was sitting at the desk of P. T. Carter, Lt Cmdr, U.S.N. My hands sweated as he thumbed through my service record. He closed the folder and leaned back in his chair. "Pretty impressive scores," he said. "The veteran's test for high school diploma should be a snap for you. Why don't we arrange for you to take it?"

"What if I flunk it, Sir?"

He laughed. "I doubt seriously you'll do that. If you did, you could sit for it again after a year. But in case you don't want to take chances, go down to the library on the third floor. They've got a whole shelf of high school text books you can use for a brush up. They might even have a high school refresher manual. Whenever you think you're ready, let me know, and I'll arrange for you to take the test."

"Sir. What if the high school I went to doesn't accept the results?"

"They have to. Congress made it the law, so more Vets would have an opportunity to go to college."

"Thanks Mister Carter. I'll be back."

We were going into the last five weeks of Radar School. My grades were atrocious. I didn't care, I spent every free minute in the library reviewing high school courses. History, Physics, English, Algebra, Civics, and Biology. The only one I needed help with was algebra. Jimerson said he was good at math, so I asked him to explain the basics.

The third week of January, 1949, I walked into Mister Carter's office. I was ready. The following day I took the exam.

For the next two weeks, I was a nervous wreck. In the Navy, depending whether on shore or at sea, for an enlisted man, sweeping, swabbing, or buffing, are basic to every assignment. At the Fargo Building, all students pulled duty on the broom, mop and buffer, which was what I was doing when the intercom squawked my name. I was to report to Chief Bentley's office on the double.

The Chief was so short it was hard to see him over a stack of papers weighted with a coffee cup. His head bobbed up from behind the pile, and he motioned for me to take a seat. "Okay, Myers," he said, "What's the story? I thought you were one of the brightest kids in my unit, but your last test, the one covering trouble shooting, makes you look like an idiot."

I couldn't tell him I wasn't interested in Radar School. "To tell the truth, Sir, I've been involved in studying for another exam."

He scooted forward in his chair, peeked around the coffee cup. "Really? And what, pray tell, would that be?"

"I took the Veteran's High School Exam last week, Sir."

He stood up. "You did, eh?"

I figured he was no more than a foot and half taller than Vern Amidon. "Everyone says a high school diploma's important, that you can't do anything without it."

"It's your timing, Myers. You could have taken the Vet's test anytime during your enlistment. Instead, you spend time studying for that damned thing at the risk of getting kicked out of Radar, and that makes me look bad. Well, let me tell you something dumb-ass, you've got two and a half years to go in this man's Navy, and you're about as near to flunking out of Radar as is possible. You know what that would mean?"

I shook my head.

"The Navy has spent a lot of money trying to teach you something, and if you fuck up, we'll ship your butt out of here to some scow where you can spend the rest of your time swabbing decks, chipping paint, washing pots and pans, and cleaning latrines. You ready for that?"

"I'll try to do better, Sir." I said, half meaning it.

"Then get on out of here and get with the program."

As I headed for the door, he cleared his throat. "And by the way Myers, Mister Carter asked me to tell you—you passed the Veteran's Exam."

I spun around. "You mean it? I passed? You wouldn't bull me about that, would you, Sir?"

He smiled. "Nope. In fact, he said you got better than ninety percent on everything except algebra. You pulled seventy-eight percent on that one."

I jumped up and down. "Hot damn! I can graduate." I went back and stood behind the chair. "Is there anything else I need to do, Sir?"

"Nope, it's all taken care of. We'll send a copy of the test results to your school board, and the superintendent of your high school. It's a done deal. In fact, the public relations officer might want to run a story in your hometown paper. Now back to Radar. If you can do that well on the high school test you can damn well do better than you've been doing in Radar. Best you do some serious studying the rest of this session. You got that?" "Yes Sir! Thanks Chief, thanks a million. Tell Commander Carter I said . . . . no, I'll tell him myself. And Chief, don't worry, I'll study for the Radar finals." I floated back to the buffing machine, laughing out loud. I turned the power on, and skipped down the hall like a fool. It had been a long time since I felt this good. I had finished high school, and I had done it four months ahead of my class!

Guantanamo Bay, Cuba, February, 1949.
Carribean War Games.

The Battleship Missouri, her big guns belching fire, dropped twenty-inch shells on the Island of Vieques, from a distance of fifteen miles. The USS Towhee, AM-388, all hands at battle stations, was picketed ten miles south and seaward of the Big Mo's exposed flank as a radar station. Mister Hammersjold, the Executive Officer was on the flying bridge, Mister Wiley, "O" Division Officer at the charting table in Central Intelligence Communications, and I was operating the surface to surface radar. The Towhee's surface to air unit had been out of order for a year, and the requisition for a replacement had not been filled.

I didn't know the insides of a surface radar from a yo-yo, but I knew how to fine tune one, which is what I had done when they sounded battle stations. The scope's field came in sharp as a razor, and I was getting a range of fifty miles. The sweep showed the Mo and her support group, bright as the Morning Star.

Seaward of the Towhee, and at fifteen miles out, I picked up a pin-prick of light. It disappeared on the second sweep but showed again on the third. Each concentric circle on the screen represented five nautical miles or ten-thousand yards. Whatever it was, that little prick was moving at about one-hundred-eighty knots. There was only one thing it could be. I turned to Mister Wiley and said, "Low-flying aircraft approaching at zero-six-zero, range fifteen thousand yards, speed one-hundred-eighty knots, Sir."

"God damn Myers, you don't have surface to air radar. What's the matter with you? Jesus, you keep that up we'll be the laughing stock of the games. Now, give me the range on the Missouri again."

"Mister Wiley, I'm telling you, I have an aircraft approaching at zero six zero, and he's closing fast."

Wiley jerked the speaker lever to the flying bridge. "Ah, Sir, this new radar operator in C.I.C., ah, he says there's ah, ah low-flying aircraft approaching."

In thirty seconds, Mister Hammersjold banged through the radar shack door. "What's this about a low-flying aircraft?"

"It's right here, Sir," I said and nodded to the screen where I had the sweep locked on the target. "See, it's closing at over one-hundred-eighty knots." I pointed to the pin prick of light.

Hammersjold put his nose to the screen and squinted. "I don't see nothing . . . you mean that little thing right there? You'd better be right, boy, or I'll have you're ass. You understand?"

"It's a low-flying aircraft, Sir; that's all it could be, and if we don't do something quick, it's going to nail us *and* the Mo."

Hammersjold grabbed the loudspeaker. "Attention all hands. Enemy aircraft approaching at zero six zero. All batteries be prepared to open fire."

Wiley and the Exec stood silently staring at the radar. I put the tip of a pencil on the speck moving closer and closer. Hammersjold ran out the hatch. Back on the flying bridge, he yelled into the intercom, "I don't see a goddamned thing!"

"You will," I said to myself.

Mister Wiley looked at me with a sneer.

Then the sound of an engine. Hammersjold, his finger still on the intercom, screamed into the loudspeaker, "Here he comes, here he comes—out of the sunrise. Fire, fire, fire!" A fighter plane, with its undercarriage skimming the waves, swooped upward and over the Towhee. Every gun aboard was pointed right at its belly.

The loudspeaker: "We got the son-of-a-bitch, we got him!"

The crew cheered.

On our way back to port, Hammersjold came into the radar shack, put his hand on my shoulder and said, "Myers, for someone who finished Radar School second from the bottom of the class, you've got the goddamndest pair of radar eyes I've ever seen. I'm going to see you get a meritorious mass for that piece of work. Welcome aboard." Then he turned to Wiley. "Mister, from now on, when Myers says he has a target on this radar, best you listen."

The observers from the War College analyzed the War Games. Our Captain was notified that we had achieved the highest possible score. Even some of the ships with surface to air radar had missed the wily fighter plane. The officers of the Towhee were ecstatic. The crew was allowed to sew an "E" on the shoulder of each uniform, the badge of "Excellence."

Charleston, South Carolina, May 15, 1949.

Mister Wiley, fresh out of Annapolis, and still smarting from the reprimand during the War Games, acted like a snit. He looked at me like I'd asked for the moon and wore a superior little grin that said, *You're too stupid to understand the simplest and foremost principle. You don't embarrass your Division Officer in front of the Exec.* To my face, he said, "Myers, you used fifteen days of your leave after boot camp and ten days at Christmas, which leaves only five days. That's not enough time to travel to some place in the north woods and back in five days. Got that?"

"Excuse me, Sir, but I have to go. It's a long story, but there's this superintendent . . ." Wiley looked at me like I was crazy, so I tried again. "I mean, I finished high school four months ahead of my class. I have to be there when the diplomas are handed out."

"No, you don't. They can send you your diploma. You don't have enough leave time to make that trip. End of discussion."

"Mister Wiley, you don't understand. I have to receive my diploma in person. Guys get advances on their leave all of the time. In fact, I was granted an advance when I finished boots. Why can't you let me take a few extra days against next years leave? What would it hurt?"

"Myers," he said, with a long sigh, "I'm not setting that kind of precedent. I'd have every enlisted in "O" Division pestering me about advances. No way." He waved his hand to dismiss me.

In the passageway of the Officer's Quarters, I fumed. Mister Hammersjold's stateroom was the next door down. I knocked. He was in a bathrobe, his hair tussled like he had just got out of the shower. It took two minutes to explain the problem I'd just had with my Division Officer.

"I'm not going to tell Mister Wiley how to handle his men," he said. "There would be no end to the discipline problems on board this ship if every man thought he could run to me and override his Division Officer's decisions."

"Mister Hammersjold, I won't ever, under any circumstance, ask you to do it again, and I won't tell a soul. That's a promise. But, I have to be home for that graduation."

"I don't understand the compulsion, Myers, but I guess you have your reasons. I'll see if I can find a way to mention it to Mister Wiley without seeming to interfere. That's the best I can do. Now leave me alone so I can get dressed."

I secretly packed my bag. If leave was not granted, I would go AWOL. A letter from Mom, said Baccalaureate was Sunday, May 29; Graduation, Wednesday, June 1. I could catch a train in Charleston, Saturday, the 28th, travel that night and all day Sunday, and arrive in Traverse City Monday afternoon. Perfect. Eleven-hundred-eighty-six miles in forty-eight hours. I would miss Baccalaureate, but it didn't matter.

Friday, May 27, 1949. The intercom blared, "Myers, report to the wardroom on the double."

Mister Wiley sat at the wardroom mess table drumming his

fingers on the green felt table cloth. I saluted and stood at attention. "Myers reporting, Sir."

"Okay, Myers, you've got my ass in another crack. Mister Hammersjold mentioned that it might me a good idea to give you some leave time. Now, how you pulled that, I don't know and don't care. But, you listen up, Mister, I'm going to give you every day to which you're entitled, which according to Navy Regs is five days, but not one minute more. You got that? You and I both know you can't make that trip, spend two days at home and make it back in time. So you're going to be absent over leave, and I'm going to throw the goddamned book at you. Now go down to the yeoman's shack, have him cut you papers for five days of leave and get the hell out of here."

I knew he was right. It was a physical impossibility to get back in time. I'd worry about that later. The important thing was to be at graduation.

Leland, Michigan, June 1, 1949

Mister Wall didn't think I'd show up, but there I was in my dress blues with the "E" sewn on the left shoulder. His face was the color of old asphalt as he added a chair to accommodate the nineteenth member of The Class of '49 who would graduate.

I looked around the semi-circle of classmates dressed in their purple robes, and thought about how these friends, former children of simplicity, were pressured to ostracize and isolate me, never surrendered, but in their silent and unobtrusive way, rallied to my side, and listened to my pleas when no one, not a parent, sibling, or teacher—except Miss O'Brien—would help.

Beyond the glare of the stage lights were the faces of the families, friends, and loved ones of the graduates. My family was not there, but it was okay. I had known for a long time they didn't care.

There in the semicircle was my friend Steve Skipski, whose family lived in poverty on a farm outside Maple City. He had listened to my complaints when his own life was severely troubled, had shared his homework in times of my desperation and told me of his dreams of becoming a sports writer. He had remained loyal even after Mister Wall had threatened him for sitting with me at the basketball games.

The Bufka twins, Jerome and Joseph, so shy and backward that they would hardly speak to anyone under any circumstance, but who blushed, smiled, and spoke to me everyday, and sometimes even laughed at my zany conduct.

Jimmy Kahrs, from East Leland, who often did a day's work before coming to school, whose parents were kind enough to let a miscreant spend an occasional evening at their house before a ball game. Ethical reservations and guilt notwithstanding, he and Steve had allowed me to copy enough homework to get through Dechow's algebra, the toughest academic hurdle I had to overcome; without them it would never have happened.

Carlton Buerher, whose fiery temper should have exploded at some of my outrageous conduct, but who never treated me with anything but kindness, who laughed uproariously at my vulgar jokes, and who mesmerized me with his skills in shop as he finessed a piece of hardwood like a musical instrument. Tonight, his face wore a mischievous grin as he watched me take a seat.

Eunice Boley, so close to her mother, always the friend, whose intellect sparkled, and secretly shared my contempt for the ignorance of Mister Steer, son-in-law of the superintendent, hired on the pretense of teaching us English; she was always the listener, and my fan, who thought my clownish and risqué antics at Camp Kohanna during the summer of '47 were hilarious.

Nora Lou Waterman, the female daredevil, proud of her sexuality, the girl with the brass, not cowed by authority like so many—full of laughter, song and confidence.

Deloris Neadow, so shy, so responsible, so soft-spoken, and so in love, who married her heart's desire in our junior year.

Leona Houdek, my buddy, gentle and tolerant, a mother to us all, and Valedictorian of the class, who cared not a twit that I had strange hands, and who posed with me that very afternoon in a hugging picture on the front steps of Leland High School.

Charlie Stander, a '49er from affluence, but who never made

anyone aware of his privilege, and while shying away from involvement, offered smiles of understanding.

Violet Shaub, who, on so many mornings had shivered in the cold on the side of the road waiting for the bus, dressed inadequately for the weather, skin purple from exposure, left out of class activities, but who felt an affinity with me—the misfit.

Lois Weiss, the gentle, shy one; her eyes averted, hiding her secrets within herself, but warm and caring, and so gentle of voice one had to strain to hear her speak.

Robert Saledek, the ultimate student, always attentive, easy to laugh, yet so businesslike, and eager to lend a hand whenever needed.

Carole Jean Carlson, the class cut-up, quick witted, sharp tongued, but ready with a word of encouragement, a smile, candid commentary and a joke, and always positive.

Janet Burda, reserved, unsure, the girl of my dreams, whose beauty and modesty made me feel so inadequate that for three years I was unable to muster the courage to ask her for a date, only to learn she had been waiting for me to do so; and who, through it all remained my confidant, shared my secrets and fears, and became a lasting friend.

Anna Mae Maleski, Pat Knox, and Evelyn Houdek, were the shyest, most reserved, of the rural students; they isolated themselves, but were never petty or resentful. Perhaps, they had been afraid or unsure.

The only one who had started with the '49ers, but failed to finish, was Jean Ann Ashe—she would have filled the twentieth chair.

Nineteen students in a half circle, Mister Wall and Missus Warner in the middle. After the Valedictory, the Salutatory, and the Commencement Address, Mister Wall called our names in alphabetical order to approach and receive diplomas.

He came to Myers, the trouble maker from the streets of Detroit, who he and Missus Warner had vowed in writing to Central Michigan College would never receive a diploma, was next in line to graduate. He cleared his throat. "This student," he said, "felt he could accomplish more by spending his last year of school in the military. Please come forward, H. Keith Myers."

I wondered how long it had taken him to compose that lie. He had no idea what I would do when I walked out of the school one year ago and could have cared less. Whatever he had hoped, it was not for my success, nor for my presence on this stage to remind him of his failure as a teacher.

I wanted to protest. Then Leona, Janet, and Jerome Bufka smiled at me and nodded. Carlton's face was red from suppressing laughter. Out the corner of my eye, I saw Steve wink. My classmates knew. They were pulling for me, as they had all along. I felt like whooping and hollering for joy. I couldn't ruin it.

Mrs. Warner, a sour expression on her face, handed me the diploma. Mister Wall stood at the end of the stage. As I approached, he extended a quavering hand. Maybe in his heart he feared that I would refuse to shake and embarrass him in front of an auditorium full of parents. But, the joy of accomplishment and the warmth of my classmates overwhelmed me. The hatred and resentment disappeared, not forever, but for the moment. I reached out and shook his hand.

Relief washed me with new confidence. I had prevailed without support from family, and in the face of Wall's hatred. I was ready for whatever obstacles life might put in my path. Perhaps my old friend, Henry, had been right when he said, " . . . you ain't no white trash, never will be."

—End—

AFTERWARD

The elation I felt the night of my graduation from Leland High School was short lived. I arrived at the Minecraft Base, Charleston, South Carolina, three days Absent Over Leave. I trudged along anxious about the punishment I was sure to receive. The real shock hit me when I approached the wharf where my ship normally birthed. It was gone. When I inquired at the Duty Officer's Station as to its whereabouts, I was placed under arrest, and transported the next day by train, complete with leg irons and cuffs to the Naval Ship Yard, Norfolk, Virginia. True to his word, Mister Wiley had filed charges of AOL, and added "Missing Ship," the latter being one of the most egregious charges in the Navy's Code of Military Justice. But again, Mister Hammersjold, came to my rescue and negotiated a plea bargain. I would plead guilty to both charges and be fined a months pay and confined to ship for fifteen days. The agreement was more than fair.

While AOL, I had my first and only date with Janet Burda. That night the car we were in was rear-ended. Janet and I suffered what we believed were only minor injuries, but within a week of my return to duty, I had an onset of severe headaches, sore neck, and general malaise. Unable to move my head, the Chief Pharmacist Mate, our only medical personnel, ordered me admitted to the Orthopedic Unit of The Naval Hospital, Charleston, South Carolina. There, the diagnosis was confirmed: severe whiplash injury.

At the end of the second week, I no longer needed a brace, normal function of my neck had returned, and the headaches had subsided. It was only a matter of days before I would be transferred back to duty. While in my room the young doctor who had been treating me tapped on the door and asked if I had time to chat.

The doctor, in the last year of an orthopedic residency, had noticed the unusual boney protrusions on the sides of my hands. Correcting the deformity would be good for his resume. Would I like for him to do it? Having normal appearing hand was something I had dreamed of since attending kindergarten at Custer Elementary in Detroit.

They would do one hand at a time to avoid my being completely disabled during the healing process. The operations required the removal of the extra knuckle, cartilage, ligament and bone on the outside edge of each hand. The first surgery was performed on my left hand, the one with the least prominent growth, in July, 1949. When the bandages came off, my knees buckled. My hand was swollen to the size of a catcher's mitt and taped to a board, with fifteen ugly stitches decorating the outside. But when the swelling subsided, and the stitches were removed, I could see a dramatic improvement and agreed to go ahead with the right hand. Including the whiplash injury and the two surgeries, I was hospitalized for a total of four months. During that period, no member of my family visited.

The summer of 1952, when I was discharged, Congress passed a bill extending the G.I. Bill to Korean Veterans. Dean Laurer, at Central Michigan University admitted me to the freshman class on probation, which I mistakenly believed had something to do with the abominable grades I had made in high school. My grade point average for my first year at CMU was 3.5, based on a 4.0 scale. In the fall of 1953, I was sitting at my advisor's desk in the Administration Building. She had opened my file to review the courses I had taken. We were discussing what areas to concentrate on to round out my pre-law curriculum. Someone called her away from the desk. I turned my file so I could look at the transcript. On the inside of the file cover, was the vilifying letter written by Leland High School's Principal, on behalf of Mister Wall, dated June, 1948. Its content is recited almost verbatim at pages 335 & 336.

Rage and joy do not seem like compatible emotions, but they surged side by side when I read how determined the administration had been for me to fail. I was enraged that two adult educators whose jobs were to teach and counsel young people, could focus such hatred toward one youth. Their attack had been vindictive and malicious. At the same time, I felt joy in the knowledge that despite their concerted effort, I had gained admission and had been on the Dean's and the President's Honor Roll for two consecutive semesters.

In 1959, while employed at the First National Bank of Tulsa, Oklahoma, I entered the Night Division of the University of Tulsa's School of Law on a partial academic scholarship. For five years I worked and went to school at night. In 1964, I graduated with a class standing of eighth in a class of forty-three. At the time, I had four children.

Shirley Jean Scott's husband, Topper, graduated from Central Michigan University in 1949. He and my sister, lived in Hazel Park, Michigan, one block from the house on Browning Street, where they raised two wonderful daughters, Dona Mae, and Claudia Jean. When our cousin Weldon died unexpectedly in a car accident, and his wife, Fern, passed away less than two months later from acute alcohol poisoning, they left a seven year old orphan, David. My sister and Topper obtained legal custody and raised him as their own through high school.

My mother and father, Keith and Mae Myers, owned and operated the Maple Tavern until 1951. That year, an inspector for the Michigan Alcohol Beverage Commission caught my father for the third time drinking alcoholic beverages while operating the business, and gave him the option of selling or losing the liquor license. They sold. Dad continued to drink and carouse. In 1964, four months after I graduated from Law School, he died of a massive heart attack while sitting at the table in the kitchen of their home in Traverse City. He scorned the idea of my attending college and did not attend the awarding of my Juris Doctorate.

Mom, unable to adjust to a life without the constant tension and harassment of her alcoholic husband, lived unhappily and died of a cerebral hemorrhage on New Year's Day, 1975.

In 1982, I returned to Utica, Missouri, the place of my birth. My Grandmother Carpenter's house and the house next door that had served as both Dr. Carpenter's office and our home during the depression were still standing and in the same condition they had been fifty years before. I walked down the sidewalk where I had riden my wagon to the railroad station. The depot was gone, as was my Grandfather Sherman's old house, and Romeister's barn. I turned into the field where old Henry's house once stood. There was no path, no foundation, and no debris. I walked to where I remembered the cistern's location. Again there was nothing.

The woman who had bought the house where I was born said she didn't know what had happened to old Henry's house. But she remembered that years before, a fire had swept through the grove of trees where the house had been situated. During efforts to keep the blaze from spreading, someone discovered a dry cistern covered with a round stone, a death trap for an unsuspecting child. They filled the hole with gravel and dirt.

My wife, Nancy, and I located Charles Crain, Henry's nephew, living in Chillicothe. He and his wife Betty were very gracious and invited us in for a long discussion about Utica in the old days. I was pleased to learn that he had been a friend of my Dad's. Charles dug around in a pile of photographs and to my delight found a picture of him with his arm around my father taken on Dad's last trip to Utica.

I told Charles I had gone to the Utica Cemetery in search of Henry's grave, and had been told by the Head Groundskeeper that he would have been buried in the "colored" section, and that no records of those sites were kept. Nancy and I searched the area of the grounds where the black residents of Utica had been laid to rest, but most graves were not marked, and those markers in place were wooden, the lettering long since faded and illegible. I told the attendant I wanted to purchase a headstone for my friend's grave and would appreciate any help he might give in locating it. I never heard from him.

At night I fret about my gentle old friend lying in an unmarked grave.

Hiram K. Myers
December, 2003